AMERICAN COMPOSERS AND THEIR PUBLIC

A Critical Look

by
NICHOLAS TAWA

ML
3795
.T25
1995
West

The Scarecrow Press, Inc.
Metuchen, N.J., & London
1995

British Library Cataloguing-in-Publication data available
Library of Congress Cataloging-in-Publication Data
Tawa, Nicholas E.
  American composers and their public : a critical look / by
Nicholas Tawa.
      p. Cm.
  Includes bibliographical references (p.) and index.
  ISBN 0-8108-2954-1 (acid-free paper)
  1. Music and society. 2. Music--United States--20th century--History and criticism. 3. Composers--United States. I. Title.
ML3795.T25 1995
780' .973' 0904--dc20   94-34217

Copyright ©1995 by Nicholas E. Tawa
Manufactured in the United States of America
Printed on acid-free paper

Table of Contents

Preface	vii
Chapter 1. The Advent of Modernism	1
The Twentieth Century Begins	2
Musical Modernism and the Public	6
Music and the Democratic American Society	11
The Music Public	13
Notes to Chapter 1	15
Chapter 2. Modernists and the Public:	
The First Contact	17
The Composer's Values and Perceived Role in Music	19
The Composer as Superior Being	31
What Modernism Reveals	35
The Disdain for the General Audience	38
Notes to Chapter 2	43
Chapter 3. Music from a Lost Generation	50
Five Radicals	52
Neoclassicists	58
The Contributions of Jazz	65
A Miscellany of Composers	71
Supporters of the Vanguard	74
The General Public for Music	81
Notes to Chapter 3	85
Chapter 4. Modernists and the Public:	
The Second Contact	91
Revised Values and Perceptions	92
Musical Centralism	98
A Changed Valuation of the General Audience	101

Redefining the Vanguard Audience	104
Linking the Twenties to the Fifties	106
Notes to Chapter 4	110

Chapter 5. Music for a Burdened Homeland — 116
The Compatriotic Composers	119
The Nonaligned Composers	128
A Second Look at the General Audience	137
Notes to Chapter 5	141

Chapter 6. The Resurgence of the Avant-Garde — 144
The Transformed Musical Environment	145
Postwar Conundrums	154
The Shifting Public Scene	157
The Trials of the Traditional Mainstream	163
Notes to Chapter 6	168

Chapter 7. Insular Modernism — 172
Serialism and Atonality	174
The Move to Isolation	177
The Resurrection of the Autonomous Artist	185
The Public Response	189
Notes to Chapter 7	198

Chapter 8. Iconoclastic Modernism — 204
Adventuring Into the Unthinkable	206
John Cage: Music from a Singular Perspective	213
Radically Different Musical Approaches	219
The Audience Gives Its Answer	227
Notes to Chapter 8	231

Chapter 9. The Second Wave of Conciliatory Composers — 235
Changing Viewpoints and Approaches to Composition	236
Trying to Find an Appropriate Music	245
Reading the Listener's Mind	257
Notes to Chapter 9	259

Contents

Chapter 10. Denouement   263
    The Condition of Musical Culture   267
    The More Immediate Residue of Modernism   276
    The Music Public: Its State of Mind   282
    Afterword   286
    Notes to Chapter 10   290

Bibliography   293

Index   310

About the Author   317

Preface

The whole idea and practice of modernism in music has had important and unfortunate consequences in the relation of native composers to the American music public and ultimately to the soundness and vitality of art music as a whole. For most of the twentieth century we have seen the incessant advancement of uncharted forms of artistic expression in the United States. The close of the century has witnessed what appears to be the demise of these forms. Two of modernism's regrettable bequests, with which this study is concerned, are the widespread alienation of the American music public from all art music that exhibits a severe posttriadic style and, just as sad, the reluctance of audiences to listen to most American works written from the 1920s onward. It has become urgent for us to learn how and when the aversion to contemporary American music took place and make a start at understanding what its consequences have been, since the survival of art music, at least as we now know it, may soon be at stake. This is the purpose of the detailed investigations and analyses that follow.

I do not advocate a return to any style of the past, nor do I presume to know what future styles will emerge and prove viable. I do insist, however, that a clear perception of what has taken place in the music world over the last century is needed. Only then can we know how to nurture American art music and help it to thrive.

The modernism with which we are concerned was, in general, the intellectual and artistic reaction to the vast changes in every aspect of life that plagued the nation during the course of the twentieth century. To be sure, large cultural shifts and the influences that gave direction to them were already in operation during the last quarter of the previous century. Cities grew ceaselessly. Rapid industrialization and the exploitation of America's natural resources affected every walk of life. While these changes were taking place, concerned citizens with an interest in the arts witnessed the loosening of communal solidarity, the weakening of cultural consensus, and the rapid succession of new technologies which forced people to see themselves, each other, and their culture in a new and uncertain light. There was also the growing dependence of art music, still in its youthful stage, on urban middle-class sponsorship even as a rootless lower class moved swiftly into the cities. Our first composers, left more and more to their own devices, inclined toward greater dissonance and chromaticism as the years passed by.

These several elements came together in the second and third decade of the twentieth century to produce a drastic revision in what was considered to be serious contemporary music. At the same time, an even more extensive metamorphosis in the existence of every American took place.

When twentieth-century modernism reared its head, it found itself in utter opposition to every aspect of traditional culture. Whether in the person of Ezra Pound, Gertrude Stein, Man Ray, Leo Ornstein, Edgard Varèse, or George Antheil, it hammered away at the old notions of sentiment, beauty, and spiritual transcendence through literature and the arts and raised the banners of emancipation for the composer and ceaseless innovation in all of the arts, including music. Its attitude was anti-provincial and seemingly in favor of savage or grotesque expression. It appeared bent on smashing into fragments anything that stood in its way—or so critics said.

Nevertheless, although conscious of, even glorying in, the scattering of older values and the confusion that ensued, the early music extremists had not yet distanced themselves completely from the thinking and systems of the past. Whatever the novel shapes their art forms took, they could not help but reverberate with hints of past practices. These are conclusions, however, that hindsight has reached, not ones harbored by the post-World War I advocates of artistic reform nor ones detected by contemporary listeners who rejected the results of this reform. All of these men and women still brooded over the horrible images of wartime and its wiping out of past certainties. The victory of machines over human feeling seemed imminent. It impelled artists to take drastic action.

To cut oneself away from the oppressive present and progress toward the future was an obligation that advanced composers saw as necessary. They, therefore, set themselves up as pathfinders, avant-gardists adventuring into an undiscovered region that they were determined to inhabit. Nevertheless, as the years went by, the artistic vanguard would encounter a paradox once voiced by Ellen Glasgow in *The Sheltered Sky*: "People who have tradition are oppressed by tradition, and people who are without it are oppressed by the lack of it—or by whatever else they have put in its place."*

It resembles an act of faith for the musician or listener to believe music has a meaning beyond its mere sound. One must respect the composer, avant-garde or otherwise, who puts his creative life on the line in demonstration of that faith. We must have sympathy for him when the listener does not accept his particular definition of meaning, because meaning has been found elsewhere. We must also accept the fact that many a serious listener has his own particular faith regarding sound and has sincere perceptions not necessarily coinciding with those of the composer, however much the latter may wish it otherwise. Nor is it proper for the composer to revile the contrary listener, nor the listener the contrary composer, because faiths and meanings differ.

The saddest realization in the artistic world is the moment when a composer, who has labored tirelessly and over a lifetime to produce significant compositions, discovers that hardly anybody cares about his devotion or accepts the importance of what he has created. It is appalling to note that, in the twentieth century, rejection of contemporary American composers and their works reached epidemic proportions in the three decades after World War II. How did this state of affairs come about? Will it always be so? Is it so at the end of the century? The answer to the first question is what this book tries to offer; unequivocally, the answer to the second is no; as for the third, the reply is maybe.

There must and will continue to be a music beyond mere entertainment, in which both composer and a more than minuscule audience have faith and find meaning. This book can only suggest, never define, what shape that music may take, based on the evidence of the past century and the lessons it teaches. There is a universal, if not instinctive, need and desire for music of some

---

*Ellen Glasgow, *The Sheltered Sky* (New York: Doubleday, Doran, 1932), 295.

sort in people's lives, that will never go away. How to meet that need and satisfy that desire is the paramount problem facing serious composers at the end of the century. If the composer wishes to satisfy himself and only incidentally others, then he must face the consequences for better or worse. If he chooses not to listen to others and insists that others listen to him, music lovers will lend their ears neither to his words nor his music. This is the reality that the modern artist has not wanted to accept, whatever he has said about needing nobody. Does he mean nobody to afford him a living, a performance, a hearing, a publication, a recording? Applicable here is Immanuel Kant's categorical imperative that admonishes the artist to deal with men and women on every occasion as "ends" and not ever as "means," that asks what would come to pass if everyone behaved as does the artist?

Part of the problem, too, is the way the United States, in social, economic, political, and cultural ways, has managed to defeat its native art composers by imposing conditions on them that are impossible to meet. Among these conditions are the equating of artistic value with a huge audience, large monetary profits, and only amusement rather than also the enlightenment of listeners. The nation has bequeathed to contemporary composers a music public that includes too many Americans immersed in the European musical past, which is for them the one and only changeless verity. These listeners do nothing on their own account, not willing to think independently about what new sounds they may hear nor to show any openness to styles other than the tried and true ones of the previous centuries.

Yet, to find the public or the composer completely wrong would amount to an oversimplification. A discussion in some detail is required to understand the underlying causes for the dilemma with which the art-music community must learn to cope today. The chapters that follow try to clarify the changes in America's cultural situation as the century progressed, and try to uncover the actions that led to music's present-day predicament.

Throughout the volume the reader will find a constant reference to democratic principles and the necessity for a system of cultural checks and balances. The United States Constitution makes a considerable effort to avoid a "tyranny of the majority." In the spirit of the Constitution, what our nation must unequivocally commit itself to is a state of musical culture distinguished by

Preface

fair treatment for every viewpoint, whether of the majority or a minority. We must grant freedom for composers to express themselves honestly and concurrently have a regard for the inherent dignity and claim to respect of every music lover. As far as we are able, we must afford humans the same opportunity to achieve their maximum potential as composers, performers, and listeners, all three a part of a united community.

Finally, in the pages that follow, I hope to examine how we have failed and, just as important, how we have succeeded in advancing the cause of cultural democracy—for this is the road to our musical salvation.

Chapter 1

The Advent of Modernism

This study deals with the relationship between American composers of concert and operatic music and the American music public in twentieth-century America. It examines the pivotal issues that have involved and often separated art composers and the music public over the past century. A critical inquiry into these issues, long overdue, will be pursued in the chapters that follow.

Troubled commentators find most composers of serious purpose becoming superfluous in American society. In fact, they have never been truly essential to it. These composers' devotees keep declining in number. Only a few specialized musicians perform the newest music and usually in ghettoized situations. Recordings of most of the recent American works hardly sell at all. Private and government subsidies are ordinarily necessary for the publication, performance, and recording of modern music. Probing this problem as the year 2000 approaches, one or two writers predict the death of all artistic music, old and new.

After three decades of examining the link between American composers and their public, I cannot say that I share this complete pessimism. However, there is a great deal to worry about, plenty that demands airing. Therefore, my object is not to write the history of musical styles. I want, instead, to study twentieth-century American composers' and the music public's views of, and reactions to, each other as they evolved through the give-and-take of twentieth-century musical experience.

Over the past 100 years, a great deal of writing has appeared on past and present-day art music, its composers, styles, techniques, and performers. Yet, thorough studies of the various audiences for this music are meager. As a result, we do not know enough about why the musical public attends or avoids concerts. Nor do we know why most people reject art music altogether.[1]

In addition, partisans of the newest music still lament the naiveté of music lovers. They refer to the public's duty toward composers, but not vice versa. Deliberately, or perhaps through ignorance, they distort the relationship between composers of the past and their listeners in order to bolster their own claims. Aficionados of one or another advanced style, for example, regard Johann Sebastian Bach as the creator of the purest music. They rarely concede that he was also concerned over how society would employ and enjoy his compositions. Bach has received the crown of "Artist." To see him as also a craftsman wishing to offer comprehensible music for use by his community distresses them.[2]

Some members of the general music public, on the other hand, write to newspapers and magazines about their dislike of most compositions written after 1920. The remainder complain to each other about or carefully avoid contact with modernism. Listeners claim an inability to cotton to the sound. One or another wonders about the modern composer's responsibility toward his society. At the same time, they neglect his just claims on that society. Moreover, they are disinclined to make any effort to hear him out and instead flee his music. The contemporary public is not always right about music, but neither are modern composers and their partisans.

The Twentieth Century Begins

The history of this schism goes back at least to the opening of the twentieth century. Several cultural historians have related its beginning to the International Exhibition of Modern Art, which started in February 1913 at the 69th Regimental Armory in New York. The exhibit traveled later to Boston and Chicago. The show symbolized a turning point in the artistic annals of the United States. More than a thousand works, mostly by French artists, challenged American viewers. Forward-looking creations by Cézanne, Gauguin, Duchamp, and the Fauvists held prominent places in the exhibition. Modernism had come to the fore; simultaneously, the debate over new ways of thinking in literature, poetry, painting, sculpture, and dance reached a singular intensity. Henry May describes what happened around 1912-1913 as an insurrection exemplified by the "disturbing new paintings in such exhibitions as the famous Armory Show for 1913," the writing of poetry "in exciting new forms," the birth of "a series of lively little magazines," and the appearance of newfangled plays in "new little theaters."³ Amy Lowell's poetry, the provocative articles in the *Dial* and the *Seven Arts*, Isadora Duncan's dance innovations, and the repertoire of the Provincetown Players were important components of this insurrection.

Young artists and writers began to perceive themselves as having unique capabilities that American society, now defined as bourgeois, and prosaic education were trying to destroy. They were suspicious of democracy; to them, it bred mediocrity. For the most part, they were the children of the middle class, many coming to the city, and New York City in particular, from smaller municipalities; others were the offspring of immigrants. Almost all endured rootlessness of some sort. Alienation ran rife among them. They feared the complacency, materialism, and narrowness of vision that they claimed allowed no room for creativity in the United States.

Some resorted to living in urban bohemias with others of like spirit, Greenwich Village being the most famous of these. Others escaped to Europe and to what they thought was transatlantic freedom.⁴ What began as a trickle of transoceanic travelers reached flood stage after World War I. Woodrow Wilson's willingness to compromise his principles, in the Versailles Treaty, caused his stature to shrink from giant to pygmy in intellectual eyes. President Harding and a Republican regime brought with it labor strikes, race riots, attacks on foreigners, and the relentless search for "Reds" in American society. The native atmosphere seemed stifling.

To cross the Atlantic, to sojourn in a foreign land, became almost a mandatory rite of passage for creative people. Influential books, like *Civilization in America* (1922), "an inquiry by thirty Americans," stressed in article after article that American artists were homeless and their destiny lay across the Atlantic.⁵ Few Americans wished to expatriate themselves to Germany. Germans had been the enemy. German culture and ideals, so admired in nineteenth-century America, were now suspect, if only because they smacked of the stale thinking of the past. A fresher breeze seemed to blow from France. Living in Paris was the chief goal of men and women with artistic pretensions, said Van Wyck

Brooks, right through the 1920s. Parisian residence eventually gave rise "to the religion of art." With trust in humanity gone, "art, form, color, craftsmanship was something to cling to, something solid and real in a world of ruin."[6]

It took longer for the spirit of revolt and the valuation of novelty to affect American art music. For one thing, artistic musical creativity had a much briefer history than painting, literature, and poetry in the United States. Only after the Civil War did American composers of stature first come to public notice: John Knowles Paine, George Chadwick, Horatio Parker, and Edward MacDowell. German pedagogues of conservative outlook had educated them. Regrettably, these American musicians found scarcely any professional performing groups to give them a hearing. In addition, an American public for artistic music compositions was still in the formative stage. Support for any musical undertaking, conservative or radical, was weak. It was not until after World War I that American composers in strength embraced modernity.

A group of progressive composers had succeeded the older musical generation in the first two decades of the twentieth century and had been active just before the advent of the music modernists. For the most part, they were comfortable with themselves and subscribed to an idealistic view of their mission to society. They felt an urge to freshen musical sensation and to integrate concepts, emotion, and style in unconventional ways. This meant that the ties to German music gradually came undone as did the adherence to the standards of their Victorian heritage. Henry Gilbert explored a rawer sound with large admixtures of American-minstrel and African-American tunes and rhythms. Arthur Farwell wavered between capturing the spiritual essence of Amerindian life and that of a more visionary world. John Alden Carpenter, whose general style was more French than German, mixed Spanish sounds with music inspired by jazz and popular American dance. Charles Griffes abandoned Germanisms altogether in favor of a sensitively expressed impressionism and, toward the end of his short life, with a novel music beholden to China and Japan. Still, none of them was really a rebel against his society and none completely repudiated the musical practices of the past.

In contrast, when America's music students flocked to Paris in the post-war years, they transported with them remembrance of indifferent federal, state, and local governments, chosen by an unprogressive electorate whose allegiance to art music was apathetic at best. Although an influential teacher-composer like Edward Burlingame Hill of Harvard might urge the young musicians to take note of the achievements of Claude Debussy and Maurice Ravel when they got to Paris,[7] the eager musical neophytes found Arnold Schoenberg and Igor Stravinsky to be the leading lights in Europe. Of the two, it was Stravinsky who would dominate. Adolph Weissman, critic for the *Börsen Zeitung*, felt impelled to write to the recently founded League of Composers that, by the 1920s, Debussy and Ravel had become modern classics; Schoenberg was a revolutionary but with a small following. On the other hand, Stravinsky fascinated the young: "Through continued contact with Paris, and collaboration with the Russian ballet, Stravinsky paved the way for that music which we recognize as a synthesis of barbaric folk-feeling and the highest refinement, which finds its supreme expression in the *Sacre du Printemps*."[8]

Awaiting the youthful Americans in Paris was the charismatic teacher Nadia Boulanger, an admirer of Stravinsky. Her numerous American students sensed a sufficient bond between them to name themselves the "Boulangerie." To Paris and Boulanger flocked Aaron Copland, Virgil Thomson, Walter Piston, Roy Harris, Marc Blitzstein, David Diamond, Elliott Carter, Irving Fine, and Harold Shapero, among others. Most of them, though not all, would return with a French-Stravinsky veneer layered over whatever was American in their expression. Copland, in 1967, said to Edward Cone that when he was 18 or 19 years of age, to be "finished" as a composer meant going to Europe. Since Germany was very unpopular, the inclination was toward France. As for himself, the discovery of Nadia Boulanger was fortuitous. He had read about a new Fontainebleau music school in 1921, in *Musical America*: "The idea that a school was being started in the summer, just for Americans, made me think that in that way I might have the chance to get to meet more people. . . . I was the very first student to sign up." Besides, Copland said: "Schoenberg . . . Berg and Webern were under something of a cloud for the reason that they were still writing German music, and German music was the thing we were trying to get out from under."⁹

Only an occasional voice was raised in warning, and even then only at the end of the twenties. Paul Rosenfeld, the cheerleader for advanced musical ideas, waited until the beginning of 1931 to give his reprimand. Composers, he said, had derived many benefits from growing up in America. It was unfair to hold their country responsible for the frustration of genius and to believe their native climate was unfavorable, "forbidding as it may periodically appear." There was much that was unstimulating and empty in Europe. Furthermore, "the young artist is deprived of the opportunity of learning to draw stimulation from his native environment and thereby enriching it as well as himself."

Expatriation, Rosenfeld insisted, denied the composer those necessary American relationships so vital to his future. Besides, Europe had its own list of frustrated, scorned, and laughed at artists. "In surrendering his native environment," the American composer relinquishes "all hope of harmonizing his own impulses through that which, as the product of impulses related to his own, is best fitted to accommodate them and respond to them." The expatriate lives among "exiles like himself," many of whom are "equally disabled." He also finds people who will not respond to him "because of the complete dissimilarity of their backgrounds and early experiences." Consequently, he is apt to undergo "desolation in the midst of crowding culture, art, historical atmosphere, duchesses, bull-fights, [etc.]."¹⁰

Musical Modernism and the Public

Skilled American musicians normally created the "art music" that I have mentioned, whether a symphony embedded in tradition or an experimental work drawing on everyday street sounds. Audiences having at least some education and cultivation listened to it. Popular acclaim and financial reward were not the composers' immediate aims, although they might wistfully yearn for fame and fortune. One post-World War I pathway that this music took was a German-oriented, highly dissonant and chromatic atonality. In Europe, Arnold Schoenberg pioneered this route. Nothing in such music sounded melodious or harmonious to ordinary listeners. Only high tension and complexity came across to them. Some practitioners were Carl Ruggles, Wallingford Riegger, Roger Sessions, Milton Babbitt, Elliott Carter, and Charles Wuorinen.

Another track was a "neoclassicism" derived from Igor Stravinsky and the French, particularly the teachings of Nadia Boulanger. The sound was more rhythmic and tonal, and less dissonant than the above. Dispassionate discourse, sometimes to the point of desiccation, was prominent. More than a few people complained of the obnoxiously mechanical, machine-like, nonhuman impression the style produced, as in the works that George Antheil composed in the first half of the 1920s. Often, overtones of musical Americana eased the dry effect of this music, as in mid-1920s works indebted to the jazz of Aaron Copland.

Iconoclastic and experimental are the primary labels for the contributions made by Henry Cowell, Edgard Varèse, Harry Partch, and John Cage. These musicians sought out highly percussive or unearthly sounds. They wrote for traditional instruments whose tone-production was deliberately distorted or wrote for newly invented instruments. The boldest composers called for noisemaking devices like anvils, sirens, water glasses, blocks of wood, and blunt needles scratching disc recordings. Tape machines and electronic sound synthesizers later came into use. They amplified the sound of brain waves, the chatter of people, and the clatter of pneumatic drills. How seriously, listeners wondered, should they take this assault on their ears and apparent insult to their intelligence?

Idiosyncrasy like that of Erik Satie best describes the approach of Virgil Thomson. His incongruous juxtaposition of unblendable tunes and idioms and featuring of cliché and vulgarity bewildered listeners. Finally, exotic or mystic offerings have come from Colin McPhee, Lou Harrison, and George Crumb.

The five creative directions mentioned above were commonly designated as "modern." The term "modernism" itself implies a musical ideology and creativity that is quite self-conscious and consists of a premeditated split from tradition and an investigation of undepleted modes of expression. As a further distinction, those modern works that most repudiated tradition received the sobriquet "avant-garde." What their creators mostly had in common was an intense hostility to the customary and primarily restrained American tastes in music. In short, their role was oppositional, a fight against the musical status quo, which, modernists said, favored innocuously sweet to emotionally overheated works, particularly from the nineteenth century.

To the ears of average listeners, however, the avant-garde compositions sounded too aggressively harsh, intricate, and difficult to understand. The music repudiated beauty as they understood it. Nothing pleased the senses. The lyricism and sonority expected by the general music public were totally absent.

During a visit to Europe in 1927, the American composer Henry Gilbert was confronted by the new atonality, polytonality, nontriadic chord structures, and other accouterments of modernity. His own roots were in the nineteenth century. Not surprisingly he voiced a common complaint of the time. He said that "the salient characteristic of the new music" was "its discordance. The proportions of discord and concord have been entirely upset." Discord has become "an end in itself" and not "a means of expression." Quite a few new works sounded "positively disagreeable" to him.[11]

In contrast, when Paul Rosenfeld, music commentator and early defender of modern American composers, first heard Schoenberg's *5 Orchester-Stücke* (1909) and *Pierrot Lunaire* (1912), he detected "the breath of a new force" and the "tempo of the modern world." However, he found the moods this music projected were "tortured and bizarre." Stravinsky, he said, was not as flagrant in his boldness, although his *Le Sacre du Printemps* (1913) seemed "more completely alive and vibrant" than any of Schoenberg's works.[12] Aaron Copland, one of our finest twentieth-century composers, said that for "more wide-awake" music lovers, modern music was "a new departure" signaled by "the uncompromising [a favorite word with modernists] atonality of *Pierrot Lunaire* and the intense dynamism of *Le Sacre du printemps*."[13]

Other more traditional movements existed concurrently with the above. Composers, thus inclined, believed in gradualism —change brought on in small, subtle, or indiscernible stages. This was the view of older musical progressives like Henry Gilbert and Arthur Farwell. Especially in the first two decades of the century, they worked for a distinctive American music, but one that could reach the contemporary public. The congenially tonal-

Americanist works of the younger Douglas Moore, George Gershwin, Randall Thompson, and Morton Gould, and of Copland beginning with the mid-thirties had a large following. Warmly lyrical romanticism prevailed in the well-received works of Howard Hanson and Samuel Barber. These musical leanings were considered "conservative." Interestingly, Americans listened to such music with some pleasure. Recordings of it sold well.

However much listeners favored their music, the conservatives lost influence in the musical world as the century wore on. Spokespeople for modernism mounted relentless attacks against all works indebted to the immediate past. Position papers of every description advanced the more radical views. Influential writers, artists, and academics converted to modernism and backed these ideas. Modernists gained power by winning dominant positions in conservatories and college music departments. A host of young music-composition students received their instruction from them. They soon held seats on committees that doled out awards, prizes, and commissions. Because their music offered novelty and had a certain attention-grabbing shock value, the modernists won the attention of newspapers and magazines more successfully than did the conservatives. Douglas Moore, therefore, had to admit that "the modern period" was "an age of experiment and unrest." However indifferent the public was to "the modern idiom," music was seen as "a changing art . . . never standing still."[14]

Throughout history a select group of innovators has claimed it foresaw what had to be. Alongside it has also existed a more restrained crowd responsive to the standards and values of the past, worried about reaching an audience, or both. Novelty, as might be expected, does not betoken worthiness. Nor is conservatism inevitably a defect, as disdainful advocates of modernity presume. Much of the innovation has fallen by the wayside. Nevertheless, some lasting and meaningful advances by the experimenters have eventually attracted the rest of the composers and been accepted by some though not all of the music public.[15]

The various practitioners of musical modernism defy description as a group. Yet, generally, their stance was adversarial—not only to earlier musical practices but also to most accepted ways of behaving and thinking. Nor did any of them show much love for the public at large. What helped bring this rejection on was the industrial, profit-minded, materialistic America that existed after World War I, which repeatedly projected an ugly image to sensitive minds. Dedicated artists wished to escape its corrupting influence and demand for conformity. Conform they would not. Instead, the composers insisted upon complete liberty in order to seek fresh, honest modes of expression. Flight to Europe, and particularly to Paris, was the assured way of achieving this liberty during the twenties.

Modernists were soon trying to deny contemporary conservative composers any serious consideration in America's cultural history. Conservative music struck them as clichéd, belonging to the past rather than the present or future. Roger Sessions, who equated "contemporary" with "modern," stated in 1947: "When we speak of 'contemporary music' we are generally referring to the work of contemporary composers and more specifically to the part of it that differentiates itself most sharply from the work of previous generations and in particular of the generation immediately preceding."[16]

An unfortunate result of modernism was music's separation from its previous audiences without finding new followers in any significant numbers. The "I" factor replaced the "we," in terms of aesthetic fulfillment and concerns. Art became more a private rather than a shared experience. Criteria like "integrity," "meaningfulness" and "reflecting the contemporary spirit" replaced "beauty" and "enjoyableness." The idea of some balance between euphony and disruption, whether acoustical or expressive, was upset in favor of the latter. Stylistic specialization began. Various backers promoted twelve-tonalism, percussive "machine" sounds, primitivism, dadaistic simplicity, indeterminacy, and Far-Eastern music systems. The faceless financial support of uninvolved patrons (government bodies, foundations, corporations, universities) insured the absence of a necessary human coefficient in the evaluation of this music. It also insured the continued sustenance of an art not amenable to reactions from listeners, since the sponsors relied on the advice of the composers themselves.

In the name of artistic freedom, established musical precepts gave way to the privatization of standards, which wreaked cultural havoc in the community. Shared guidelines for interpretation and understanding disappeared.

How could one explain the lack of intelligibility and immediacy in the listening experience that put off audiences? Modernists explained that a time-lag existed. Their music was not for the present-day mass society but for the enlightened few or for a future generation.

Whatever American modernists may have said, they did produce several outstanding works that deserve to be taken seriously by more sophisticated listeners. Among these are Ruggles's *Sun-Treader* (1932), Copland's *Short Symphony* (1933), Sessions' Symphony No. 2 (1947), Cage's *Sonatas and Interludes* for Prepared Piano, and Carter's String Quartet No. 2 (1959). It is lamentable that they seldom appear on concert programs and that more of the finely experienced and enlightened listeners have not accepted them.

Music and the Democratic American Society

We understand as citizens that our democracy, under the Constitution of the United States, features a system of checks and balances. The object is to curb power, inhibit excess, counterbalance contrary forces, and achieve accord and equilibrium. This philosophy as applied to musical culture involves a check and balance between composer and audience. It equilibrates modernism and traditionalism, serious art and entertainment, ambiguity and accessibility. It allows room for private vision and communicability, profundity of utterance and appeal on a visceral level. Originality matters but so also does building on the past. The same holds true for a composer's academic sheltering versus his coping with the real world, also for creative autonomy versus accountability to others. After persistent endeavors at reconciliation of opposing forces, our democracy hopes to achieve a healthy artistic tension. By this, one means a reconciliation of contrary elements and a stable yet dynamic setting for cultural expression. The rapprochement aims to keep the production of new music viable, vital, worth seeking out, and contributing to the good of society.

Regrettably, most exponents of musical modernism would brook no checks and spurned the idea of balances. The relationship with the past and the bond of rapport it promised was neglected. They pushed American musical culture toward internal conflict, hoping to force American music to rethink its aims. The price paid was the surrender of peace and any pretense at oneness. To paraphrase Irving Howe, at one extreme Americans in the first two decades of the century witnessed the laying of violent hands on culture (Edgard Varèse, John Cage) and at the other, a quasi-religion of culture (Carl Ruggles, Roger Sessions).[17]

A civilization will make a major effort to cherish only those cultural products that it finds important. My thesis is that art music must have social worth and a social role to fulfill. Otherwise, it may ultimately face devaluation and extinction. I agree with Lucy Lippard's statement that cogent art "offers a vehicle for perceiving and understanding any aspect of life," from "metaphors for emotion and interaction, to the most abstract conceptions." Effective art is not just created. It is also "communicated within carefully considered contexts. The social element of response, of exchange, is crucial even to the most formalized objects or performances."[18]

The egocentricity, intolerance, and exclusive dogmas of some composers have no place in a democracy; also having no place is the reactionary's insistence that only the tried-and-true must prevail and that placating the multitudes of America, however unprepared to accept art music, is of the utmost importance. Authoritarian pronouncements have come from several modern artists and from diehard politicians. They are equally reprehensible. About ten years ago, a retired longshoreman, who was enrolled at the University of Massachusetts to earn a Bachelor of Arts degree, was talking to me about statements made by Milton Babbitt and Charles Wuorinen that he had read. He said: "The smugness of the avant-garde staggers me. These guys say the listener has to accept their theories and viewpoints. If he doesn't, he can't share in any debate about music. This isn't my belief. I get angry at the gall of anybody saying he's got a handle on the truth, with no real proof offered. He hints that what he says *ought* to be, *must* be universally held." On the other hand, a well regarded composer living in the Boston area has complained to me of a prominent music director who wouldn't play his music. The manager objected; the board objected. The conductor himself was convinced they were right in negatively assessing the music's style and its acceptance by the audience. Money had ruled, not artistic considerations.

In a noted Supreme Court decision, Justice Oliver Wendell Holmes said that those convinced of their own rightness regard mistreatment of others as natural. When we grow aware "of the number of passionately held notions which have been undermined and exploded in the course of time, one's conclusions change. It is quite clear that the highest good we desire is most readily attained through the freedom to exchange ideas"[19]—an excellent precept applicable to the American left and right, to cultural minorities and majorities.

The Music Public

We should keep in mind that in the same way as different contemporary musical styles vary from the most reactionary to the most bizarre, different musical publics exist for art music. The largest public, the men and women attending symphony concerts and opera productions, belong to the middle class. These Americans make up the backbone of our art-music world. The working class contributes a smaller public. There is also a small affluent public, from which come most members of boards of trustees for various musical establishments. In all three publics, taste tends toward the conservative. In addition, the contemporary composer has other, more inconsiderable publics: himself as auditor, his family and friends, his students, a few other composers, one or two music teachers, artists from other fields, writers, and intellectuals. Whatever support he gets comes chiefly from them.

Over the last thirty years, I have repeatedly interviewed music lovers from the first two publics about their attitudes toward music. A demotic cultural humanism has emerged from their answers to my questions.[20] I learned that they did want diversion and did prize likable melody. But this was not all. These men and women treasured most those works highlighting human dignity and evoking significant human feelings. Music cited included Beethoven's Ninth Symphony, Tchaikovsky's Fourth Symphony, and Verdi's Requiem. When American music entered the conversation, pieces like Barber's *Knoxville: Summer of 1915* and *Adagio for Strings*, and Copland's *Fanfare for Common Man* and ballet suite *Appalachian Spring* came to the fore. Nobody mentioned any militantly modern work. Yet more than a few people said they were willing to give new works a chance, provided the music didn't sound absurd or too strident.

Such valuations are doubly consequential in a century where people may otherwise feel beset by uncertainty about what they can believe to be true in their lives. Americans have learned to distrust their subjective experiences. Men, women, and children have endured a constant manipulation of their emotions. Newspapers, popular magazines, radio, and television have offered advertisements, sentimental "human interest" items, slanted articles, and mendacious shows that corrupt life itself. In this atmosphere, the public's longing to maintain a genuine human-oriented culture has experienced a rebuff from contentious avant-gardists. They have ridiculed ordinary people's preferences, arguing that most listeners have false cultural values, avoid listening challenges, and favor the easy way out.

The avant-garde's appraisal of the general music public has a basis in fact. Yet, the case against the feasibility of a great deal of modernism, as the larger public perceives it, deserves to be outlined. Critics of conservative inclination have voiced an assortment of rationales for their position that have a foundation in reality. It is unfair to discard the complaints of thoughtful listeners who dislike the new forms of expression, especially atonality and noise-centered experimentation. For one, they find too much influence from European artistic movements and a tendency to meet European rather than American criteria of excellence. They detect in the newness an avoidance of the surrounding world, a resistance to addressing the public's perception of life. Men and women of goodwill are put off by music centered entirely on the composer alone. He exploits esoteric artifices to which the average listener cannot relate. Commonly held standards are scrapped and music becomes anything the composer says it is. Consequently, the gate has opened for gimmickry, the production of shoddy musical goods, and the entrenchment of musical incompetence.

The first two questions that I will try to answer next are how did this predicament happen and what forms did it take?

Notes to Chapter 1

[1] Philip Hart, *Orpheus in the New World* (New York: Norton, 1973), 401-02, 422; Christopher Ballantine, *Music and Its Social Meanings* (New York: Gordon & Breach Science Publishers, 1984), 4.

[2] Alfred Einstein, "Art and Technology," *Modern Music* 12 (1-2, 1935): 57.

[3] Henry May, ed., *The Discontent of the Intellectual: A Problem of the Twenties* (Chicago: Rand McNally, 1963), 3.

[4] William E. Leuchtenberg, *The Perils of Prosperity, 1914-32* (Chicago: University of Chicago, 1958), 140-42; Malcolm Cowley, *Exile's Return* (New York: Viking, 1951), 59-61.

[5] Harold E. Stearns, ed., *Civilization in the United States* (New York: Harcourt, Brace, 1922).

[6] Van Wyck Brooks, *An Autobiography* (New York: Dutton, 1965), 411-12.

[7] See Virgil Thomson, *Virgil Thomson* (New York: Knopf, 1966), 51; Edward T. Cone, "Conversations with Roger Sessions," in *Perspectives on American Composers*, eds. Benjamin Boretz and Edward T. Cone (New York: Norton, 1971), 91-92.

[8] Adolph Weissman, "Race and Modernity," *The League of Composers' Review* 1 (February 1924): 4, 6.

[9] Edward T. Cone, "Conversations . . . Copland," in *Perspectives on American Composers*, eds. Benjamin Boretz and Edward T. Cone (New York: Norton, 1971), 133-34, 140-41.

[10] Paul Rosenfeld, "The Destiny of Exile," *Modern Music* 8 (January-February, 1931): 5-8.

[11] Henry Gilbert, "Notes on a Trip to Frankfurt in the Summer of 1927," *Musical Quarterly* 16 (1930): 28-29.

[12] Paul Rosenfeld, *Musical Chronicles (1917-1923)* (New York: Harcourt, Brace, 1923), 300, 306, and 312.

[13] Aaron Copland, "Music Since 1920," *Modern Music* 5 (March-April, 1928): 16-17.

[14] Douglas Moore, *From Madrigal to Modern Music* (New York: Norton, 1942), 257.

[15] See Erwin Rosenthal, *Contemporary Art in the Light of History* (New York: Wittenborn, 1971), 16.

[16] Roger Sessions, *Roger Sessions on Music: Collected Essays*, ed. Edward T. Cone (Princeton: Princeton University Press, 1979), 147.

[17] Irving Howe, *Decline of the New* (New York: Harcourt, Brace & World, 1970), 6-7.

[18] Lucy R. Lippard, *Overlay* (New York: Pantheon, 1983), 5.

[19] Herbert Tingsten, *The Problem of Democracy*, transl. arranged by the Swedish Institute (Totowa, NJ: Bedminster Press, 1965), 69.

[20] Three of my previous books—*A Sound of Strangers* (1982), *Serenading the Reluctant Eagle* (1984), and *Art Music in the American Society* (1987)—discuss my approach to obtaining this information.

Chapter 2

Modernists and the Public: The First Contact

The twenties and early thirties were crucial years for American music. For the first time in American history, more than a handful of fully trained American composers arrived on the native scene. These were starkly different creative individuals from those of previous generations. They labored to achieve fundamental change in the way American music lovers thought of art music. None heeded the warning that most of what public there was for art music had just begun to listen and was still busy digesting Beethoven and Brahms. Several of the composers set out to upend a métier that still contained musicians normally mindful of their audiences, appreciative of what little help they got from others, and not obstreperously determined to stand on their artistic rights. Committed and contentious American returnees from overseas and some foreigners resident in America launched persistent efforts to advance the latest musical trends from Europe. In 1921 Carlos Salzedo and Edgard Varèse, both born in France, founded the International Composers' Guild in New York. In 1923 the League of Composers came into existence. Five years later, Aaron Copland and Roger Sessions began a cycle of performances consigned to contemporary music. These three composers' alliances sought out the daring compositions of the current European and the developing American avant garde and engaged in spirited attempts to present them to whoever would listen, especially in New York. Holding to no one persuasion, American composers began to explore unknown musical territory. They expected that organizations like the three named above would help expose their wares to the public.

Just before the 1920s, the frenzied rhythms and reckless stridencies of Leo Ornstein's "futuristic" music had unnerved listeners. They discovered their long held precepts for judging excellence in sound and the generally-held principles of musical fabrication ignored in his music. In 1916, the novelist and outspoken music critic Carl Van Vechten was already saying: "Is anything true? I hope not. At dinner the other evening a lady attempted to prove to me that there were standards by which beauty could be judged and rules by which it could be constructed. She was unsuccessful."[1]

Next, in the course of the twenties, Americans, especially New Yorkers, heard just as iconoclastic but more orderly endeavors to update musical idioms—by Varèse, Cowell, Antheil, Ruggles, and others. A statement that Copland made late in his life will help to focus this chapter: "I have often thought that all our preoccupations in music since [the 1920s] may be traced back to that period. Nothing really new, with the possible exception of electronic and computer music, has happened since. That is to say, nothing that did not have its origins during the twenties."[2] Note that Copland talked about technical concerns pertinent to the composer, not expressive ones relevant to the listener. Innovation commanded his attention.

Summing up the activities in the ten or so years before 1932, in *Modern Music*, Randall Thompson mentioned first the "nationalists," comprising composers like George Gershwin, Aaron Copland, Douglas Moore, John Powell, Louis Gruenberg, and Virgil Thomson. He himself was also a part of this group. However varied their general styles, all of them revealed some kind of national awareness and drew upon one or more native musical sources. Two older composers, Daniel Gregory Mason and Edward Burlingame Hill, were "eclectics," that is to say they employed whatever appeared useful from diverse sources. (Yet, Mason drew mainly from nineteenth-century German romanticism, and Hill subscribed to the emotionally reticent and rational French tendencies in place at the turn-of-the-century.) Edgard Varèse, Leo Ornstein, Charles Ives, Carl Ruggles, and Henry Cowell were "esoterics." They wrote abstruse music for, and that was understood by, listeners specifically versed in their particular styles. Therefore, they had only small, restricted followings. Virgil Thomson was an "eccentric," because he veered away from established prototypes, recent or old, and spurned approved usages, radical or conservative. Henry Cowell was an "innovator" who originated unorthodox sounds that had previously not existed.[3] Thompson should have included George Antheil as an "esoteric," and Howard Hanson and Deems Taylor as romantic "eclectics."

The Copland and Thompson attributes above differ from mine in Chapter 1. The musical features they seize upon are intrinsic to the professional's craft and approach to writing music. My previous categorization of styles in Chapter 1, which took into consideration most of the twentieth century, ponder on attributes intrinsic to the music itself and its effect on listeners. The former is obviously a composer's view; mine more an audience's view. What follows is an examination of the composer's view of his values and what he sees as his role in music. Musicians who regarded themselves as "modern," and had a major influence on the art music to come in the United States, will receive emphasis.

The Composer's Values and Perceived Role in Music

From the twenties on, reasonable discussions about music could not take place when a composer and the touchy apologists for him declared that his music possessed a self-validating authenticity. At the same time, they accused every adverse critic as irreparably flawed and capricious in his judgment. Information from direct study and experience might be collected and appraised by one critical party or another, but the composer and his critics were essentially entangled in a contest over values.

"We have no heritages or traditions to which to cling except those that have already withered in our hands and turned to dust. . . . There must be an entirely new deal of the cards in one sense; we must change our hearts," wrote Harold Stearns, in the preface to *Civilization in the United States* (1922). He was summing up the conclusions of intellectuals and artists who accounted themselves abreast of their times. Carl Ruggles would later reach an almost identical conclusion.[4] Nobody heeded the public, which usually concluded otherwise.

The "entirely new deal" involved not only a renunciation of the immediate past but also a reinterpretation of history. "Pioneers" and "ultra-modernists" have been around since the fifteenth century, claimed Henry Cowell around 1925-26. Then, he was a bellwether of musical modernism. Ultra-modernists, he said, are invariably reviled by critics and rejected by a conservative majority. During the twenties a "powerfully organized" establishment made up of "the Big Orchestras" and "the Big Publishers" has frustrated them at every turn. A conservative music world refuses them "the means of livelihood and also expression." Reactionaries must understand that the very few great masters of yesterday used their material superbly but exhausted it, so why emulate them "and be only second rate?" Indeed, it is the unenlightened "composer who clings to the old, rather than the innovator, [who] should make explanations and apologies, if any are to be made." Trailblazers always remain in the minority. Nevertheless, it is their music that has survived and "come down through the ages." As has always been true, what changes today's innovators cause must ultimately prevail, no matter what critics and the public might say.[5]

A few years earlier, Van Vechten had heard Ornstein play his *Seven Sketches* and *Two Shadow Pieces* for piano. He writes of the experience:

> Mr. Ornstein's compositions have no truck with majors and minors, thirds and fifths, pentatonic and diatonic scales. His descending figures strike masses of keys; some auditors seem to think there is no plan in these assaults on the board. Personally, I am willing to wager that the last piano sonatas of the deaf Beethoven meant just as little to their first hearers. We have become accustomed to the sweet and unsubtle way of the tonic and dominant. Arnold Schoenberg and Igor Stravinsky are yet discordant to our melody-soaked and harmony-demanding ears.[6]

Cowell's and Van Vechten's logic cannot withstand scrutiny. For example, to whom should Cowell's "composer who clings to the old" make his apologies and why should he? Why is the "ultra-modernist" excused? Cowell did not prove his case. As for Van Vechten, equating the reaction of listeners to the last sonatas of Beethoven with that to the piano music of Ornstein makes no sense. Beethoven had not repudiated the musical language linking him with his audience; Ornstein had. Both Cowell and Van Vechten reinvent the past to suit their purposes. Their comments, early in the century, signaled the beginning of the "false notions" which eventually were "made into folk myths" by the American modernists.⁷

Even the present was subject to reinvention and "false notions." Copland sounded as if he were indulging in wishful thinking when he said in 1933:

> It has been a comparatively short time since so-called radical music began making its way. Yet, at the end of a decade, music which was greeted with snickers and sarcasm on the one hand and enthusiasm on the other had concededly won its place in the sun. . . . For the most part, even those who were reluctant to allow that composers had broadened the language of music in a manner not to their liking now seek formulas with which to accommodate themselves to the inevitable.⁸

He was then in the midst of an obdurately atonal and highly dissonant period. If his glasses had been a little less rose colored, he would have seen that the enthusiasts were few and falling away rapidly. Two years later Copland lost his special audience and was accommodating to a different inevitability: the need to revert to tonality and greater consonance in order to reach a general public. Such a reconstitution of events as that of Copland, to suit what the composer wished were true, has gone on repeatedly in the twentieth century.

Twenty years after Copland made his statement, Arthur Berger explained that at that time forward-looking people were busy defending the difficulties contained in modern works. They wanted composers not to modify their extreme styles because the public refused to accept them. He said further: "It was to this tendency that Copland responded around 1930 and he produced, under its influence, some masterpieces that will undoubtedly endure."⁹

Berger's comment brings up another tendency of the contemporary music world—the tendency to find considerable merit in any work outside the conventional. "False notions" invested the assertions, year after year, that modern masterpieces were continuously being created. As early as 1925, an exasperated Oscar Sonneck was complaining that one musical "ism" was rapidly succeeding another and that with each new "ism" at least a half dozen to a dozen composers were hailed as "immortal." He continued by saying: "With a growing population [of composers] the crop of new geniuses assumes alarming proportions."[10] In 1933, Arthur Mendel protested that "Cowell and his companions are too ready to place absurdly high estimates upon one another's work, or upon the work of other innovators. Of Henry Brant, 'nothing is too great to expect in the future.' Ives 'is independent and is truly great.' Of Charles Seeger, 'few modern composers, either in America or abroad, are entirely uninfluenced by him'." The claims were preposterous.[11]

Thomson showed more probity when he said, in 1925, that he was uncomfortable living in America and preferred Paris: "I'm a misfit [in America]. I'm not a vegetable, a salesman, or a joiner [read Mencken's "boob," "huckster," and "Babbitt"]. He said he was writing the "maxims of a modernist," prompted by the Darrow-Jennings Monkey Trial: "I am consequently engaged in producing a statement of radical antagonism—to include work, sex, pleasure, art, war, theory of the state, ethics, and so forth."[12] What is important to note is that Thomson recognized, as other composers did, an inability to fit into American society, of which the general music public was a part. He perceived the public as having nothing in common with him.

Later, Sessions displayed even greater sense when he told Copland not to exaggerate the advantages of Europe over America. Nonetheless, he admitted to one difference, that America had no mature and organized music life, so that the American modernists were "looked upon . . . as 'interesting' abnormalities [Thomson's misfit]." The composers therefore tended "to assume that character" and to concentrate in small groups "apart from the main current of life, musical and otherwise."[13]

Concentrating together did not mean close bonding. Everybody felt free to attack others whose ideologies and modern styles did not fit with theirs. Henry Cowell considered hearing the compositions of most Americans who had studied with Nadia Boulanger a waste of time during the twenties. He gave lectures that tore apart Russian composers whether resident in Russia or America (Stravinsky, Prokofiev, Shostakovich). They had no genius and showed no inspiration. Stravinsky was "sugar-water," his neo-classicism ineffective imitation.[14]

Edgard Varèse would tolerate no opposition to his views and the way he ran the International Composers' Guild, which he cofounded in 1921. As a result, differing composers, led by Louis Gruenberg, Lazare Saminsky, and Claire Reis, split away to form the League of Composers in 1921. Copland joined the League a little after its founding.[15] Apparently, these musicians were misfits not only in American society as a whole but also in modernist circles with opposing views.

Even within their group, they sometimes failed to adjust and took refuge in combativeness. To cite one instance, Copland, in 1932, helped found the Young Composers' Group (Arthur Berger, Israel Citkowitz, Lehman Engel, Vivian Fine, Irwin Heilner, Bernard Hermann, Jerome Moross, Elie Siegmeister), whose members spent most of their time arguing and fighting. They tore each other's music apart and showed no affection for anyone except themselves. Nor were they friendly toward expatriates like Virgil Thomson and Paul Bowles. At the end of 1932, Siegmeister told Copland that the Group planned a concert for January 1933. Sarcastically, he added that no member would touch anybody else's music "with a ten foot pole. . . . The best thing for the success of the concert is to have the group meet as rarely as possible. It always ends up in a fight or in somebody singing songs they heard in a Harlem speakeasy."[16]

During the 1920s and 1930s, most modernists were split between the more revolutionary avant-garde and the Boulangerie. The former, guided by Varèse and Cowell, included the composers Carl Ruggles, John Becker, and Wallingford Riegger, and four associations: the International Composers' Guild, Pro Musica, the New Music Society, and the Pan-American Association of Composers. The latter, soon headed by Copland, included the composers Roger Sessions, Walter Piston, Roy Harris, and Virgil Thomson, and had exposure through the League of Composers, the Copland-Sessions Concerts, and the Yaddo Festivals.[17]

It is a short step from speaking about misfits to describing composers as preoccupied with understanding their mental and behavioral needs and strivings in psychoanalytic terms. Sigmund Freud and Carl Jung's analyses of the human psyche were in fashion among writers, artists, and composers during the early part of the century. For some composers, psychoanalytic theory offered an explanation for their excesses and their inability to adapt to American society.

Mabel Dodge Luhan, a strong advocate for and patron of the modern arts, says that in the winter of 1915-16 her circle was taken with psychoanalytic theories. She arranged sessions for herself with a Jungian psychoanalyst, Dr. Jelliffe. Soon he drew her into a new world. Matters that troubled her now fit together in ways she had never dreamed were possible. She found her problems simplified: "There was the Electra complex, and the Oedipus complex and there was the Libido with its manifold activities, seeking every chance for outlet, and then all that thing about Power and Money!" She thought she had learned who she was, inhibitions and all, and should shed her repressions in order to express her true self.[18]

Young Virgil Thomson, like many of his musical colleagues, shows through his reading his interest in Freudian ideas. He enjoyed Petronius's *Satyricon* (first century, AD), which is almost pornographic in its low-life descriptions of characters without the Puritanical inhibitions prevalent in America. (Puritanical, after the turn of the century, became the American equivalent of Victorian in England—signifying false gentility, repression, sexual prudery, and hypocritical morality.) James Joyce's *Portrait of the Artist as a Young Man* (1915), another admired book, involves a Stephen Dedalus who sheds off the stultifying mores of his community, discovers his own inner artistic nature, and ultimately departs his country [as did Thomson] to confront the actuality of his own experience. Samuel Butler's *The Way of All Flesh* (1903), according to Thomson, is "a book to be reckoned with" and is undergoing "a terrible vogue." In it, Earnest Pontifax goes through a process of freeing himself from his narrow surroundings so as to realize his inborn instinctive nature. Henry Fielding's *Tom Jones* (1749) allows the protagonist to fulfill his natural sexual urges without hampering feelings of guilt. James Branch Cabell's lusty depictions in *Chivalry* (1909) and *Beyond Life* (1919) show that the old ideals run counter to one's primitive psychic energies, which demand gratification.[19]

According to Freudian precepts, composers needed, like Mabel Dodge Luhan, to cast off their inhibitions and learn to express their true selves. Expressing one's self sometimes resembled a confessional session on a psychoanalyst's couch. A close friend of Thomson, Gertrude Stein said: "After all everybody, that is everybody who writes, is interested in living inside themselves [sic] in order to tell what is inside themselves."[20] When the *Seven Arts* magazine was founded by James Oppenheim, Waldo Frank, and Van Wyck Brooks, in November 1916, the editors claimed to have no tradition or style to build upon. They asked contributors to give regard to "self-expression without regard to current magazine standards."[21]

Deems Taylor, in 1922 (not yet the musical conservative of later years), admonished the composer not to try "to express America," but to be "true to himself." Self-expression was a duty for creative people. To think otherwise was unreal and irrational, and denied the self its expressive rights. The current attempt to use Amerindian and African-American tunes communicated no "common racial emotions of a nation." He praised the composer Charles Griffes for his inclination to ignore, "the land of chewing gum and victrolas," in his music in order to enter a personal expressive world. Just before 1929, Paul Rosenfeld was inveighing against the use of any American folk music in artistic compositions. These folk songs and dances were derived from Europe, but were coarse and degenerate versions of the originals, according to him. In November 1933, Lehman Engel, a member of the Young Composers' Group, met Schoenberg when he arrived in New York from Europe and announced to him: "In America there is no musical past."[22]

When, in 1951-52, Copland looked back at his youth, he said:

> We in the twenties were little influenced by the effects of [the nationalist composer] Henry Gilbert, for the truth is that we were after bigger game. Our concern was not with the quotable hymn or spiritual: we wanted to find a music that would speak of universal things in a vernacular of American speech rhythms. We wanted to write music on a level that left popular music far behind—music with a largeness of utterance wholly representative of the country that Whitman had envisaged.[23]

An accusation that has afflicted American art music for decades received renewed emphasis: older American composers, whether nationalist or not, now appeared uninspired, sterile, tasteless, and, said Taylor, writers of "square-toed Kapellmeistermusik." Second-rate Europeans wrote better music than Paine, Chadwick, Parker, Foote, Hadley, and Converse. At least the Europeans were less repressed, less timid, and had a better command of their craft.[24] The most nonconforming composers uttered the most extreme condemnations. Ruggles's vituperation of traditional American composers, in 1922, was unconscionable. Cowell reported that he heard Ruggles speaking at a Whitney Club Concert: "He determinedly and painstakingly read out sizzling criticisms which called composers names and by name. The presence of Mrs. Hadley in the audience did not deter him from opening his lecture with this remark: 'I thought that music had reached the lowest possible point when I heard the works of John Alden Carpenter. Now, however, I have been examining the scores of Mr. Henry Hadley'."[25]

Although not pursued with the same intense vituperation as the older Americans, most nineteenth-century European composers whose music was given a warmly lyric and emotional content received strong criticism. Those Americans who studied with Nadia Boulanger learned that Brahms was tedious, Bruckner and Mahler trivial, and Sibelius hopeless.[26] Piston said that while studying with her in Paris, he heard a great deal of music not played in Boston: "We were hearing concerts of modern music. Of course, in those days we wouldn't have gone to a Beethoven symphony if you had paid us."[27] Romantic eloquence was pompous, neurotic, and revealed an exaggerated estimate of the composer's own importance—not honest expression but a sick distortion of human feeling, said Sessions in 1933. It "has, in fact, practically disappeared and is only to be found in a few provincial survivals [Howard Hanson, Samuel Barber?]."[28] It had, in fact, not disappeared and was not relegated only to the provinces. Here is another example of asserting as true what the modernist wished were true.

The drive for self-expression fused the teaching of Freud with the individualism inherited from the American pioneering experience and the egocentricity from Europe's nineteenth-century romanticism. Earlier, Cowell was quoted as speaking up for musical "pioneers." John Vinton mentions that "the American tradition of reckless individualism, expressed most strikingly in the lives of many industrialists, frontiersmen, and outlaws," set a precedent for composers.[29]

Music as recreation was inimical to self-expression. We find Arnold Schoenberg, the internationally influential German atonalist, repudiating a prime function of music with his denunciation of composers who entertained an audience. Entertainment signified mendacity to modern composers. Entertainers were not real artists, that is to say musicians who felt pressed to say something vital, not caring if everybody disliked it. Sincere creators "must open the valves in order to relieve the interior pressure of a creation ready to be born," Schoenberg said.[30] Eric Salzman, in his *Twentieth-Century Music*, underlines the "notion of the artist as an individualist" that formed "the modern impulse toward originality and uniqueness."[31]

We find Wallingford Riegger, an American atonalist educated in Germany, delighted that Philadelphia and New York audiences hissed his *Study in Sonority* (1927). He declared that his musical modernity "is the manifestation of an instinct which asserted itself in some of my childhood efforts, but which has been dormant through the years of inhibition." This obstacle to inner expression was now swept away.[32]

One of our first radical composers, Leo Ornstein, criticized Schoenberg for being all brain and no spirit. He believed that the composer should let himself go completely, disregarding all rules in order to write as spontaneously as possible: "Suddenly the new thing came to me. . . . I realized that I had become myself at last, although at first, to be frank, it horrified me as much as it has since horrified others."[33] He allotted to himself the title of genius, an artist who owed his individual gift to inspiration. This inspiration defied rational analysis and owed nothing to constant effort, careful planning, and mastery of technique.[34]

Whether Ornstein, Cowell, Riegger, Thomson, or Copland, all these composers practiced, in varying degrees, the recklessness that Vinton mentions. Freedom from restraint meant the right to pursue only one's own ideas. It did not mean what it once had signified, the freedom to write mainly within the limits prescribed by a collective style tied to shared standards and obligations between composers, performers, and audiences.[35]

The latter meaning had presumed a uniform artistic culture, one that no longer existed in the twentieth century. A common belief, which composers held to at least in part, was that within each person hid an individuality fertile with possibility. It hunted a means for fulfillment. Because the restrictions, dogmas, and functions decreed by society impeded its realization, then shared standards and obligations had to disappear. Being true to oneself meant liberation from the encumbrance of accumulated knowledge, norms, and ideals handed down by previous generations.[36]

To subscribe to a previous style was to imitate and imitation was not creative, said the composer John Becker, an ally of Cowell, at the opening of the thirties: "To follow the paths of any previous composer is but to be imitative. The modern and ultra-modern composers of America today have recognized this very definitely. They are developing a distinctively individual, new, and beautiful music. They rebel violently against any sort of imitation." He named Charles Ives, Henry Cowell, Wallingford Riegger, Adolph Weiss, Carl Ruggles, and Ruth Crawford, and concluded with: "Laws are made for imitators. Creators make laws."[37]

Copland, whose circle was less belligerently ultra-modern than the above group, admitted nevertheless that in the twenties the word "modern" was electrifying: "The air was charged with talk of new tendencies, and the password was originality—anything was possible. Every young artist wanted to do something unheard of, something nobody had done before. Tradition was nothing; innovation, everything. . . . We were left with no anxiety complex. . . . Money and art patrons were plentiful, and there was the conviction that nothing but prosperity and good times lay ahead."[38]

A major problem arose with the declaration of the new individualism—its connection with artistic originality. Copland's statement paints a thin line between believable artistry and clever artifice. Anybody with a modicum of intelligence can be singular (and thus "original") by stressing technical traits that nobody else has featured. Assuredly this thought is on an audience's mind when it listens to extreme compositions. For example, in the winter of 1940-41, I was part of an invited audience that listened to a three-movement *Kitchen Sonata* for pots, pans, cutlery, and garbage cans, written by a student at Harvard. On that occasion the listeners understood that the resultant cacophony made, if anything, an outlandish political rather than an artistic statement. To cobble sounds together is neither a brave nor daring act, as some avant-gardists would have you believe. This feat, witness the *Kitchen Sonata*, may be an example of a childish, immature, or self-indulgent action. A conscious effort to discover immoderately individualistic sounds is not the primary purpose of artistry. Originality should be a conclusion reached after interpreting what a composer has done, subject always to who does the interpreting.

The problem of "imitation" versus "originality," which John Becker brought up, has produced uneasiness in music. Composers know that the works of the eighteenth and nineteenth centuries provided a large and highly prized repertoire for the public. What could a contemporary composer do after Bach, Mozart, Beethoven, and Wagner? This feeling of rivalry with the past helped lead not only to a twentieth-century rebellion but also to a self-consciousness inseparable from original self-expression. The dilemma is an old one. W. Jackson Bate quotes the Egyptian scribe Khakheperresenb who, as long ago as 2000 BC, could lament: "Would I had phrases that are not known, utterances that are strange, in new language that has not been used, free from repetition, not an utterance which has grown stale, which men of old have spoken."[39] Bate also warned that originality was a Trojan Horse. Men and women of slight talent railed on about it and doomed writers and artists to worry about it. They made originality "as much a tyranny to the human spirit as what they themselves had earlier reacted against." He voices a warning similar to the one I have just given: "'Originality' in the arts need not imply vigor, range, or even openness of mind—or power of language or anything else of a qualitative nature."[40]

Beginning with the piano music written in the second decade by Leo Ornstein, the aberrant sounds of the most insurgent composers have joined originality to charlatanism in the minds of most listeners. Charles Buchanan, in 1918, found Ornstein to have "protuberant and irritating characteristics." Perhaps he was a charlatan, piling up his half-tone spaced chords without an expressive imperative. At the least, he was someone one might admire or hate but never ignore. Like other up-to-date artists, Ornstein had "constituted himself so domineeringly a law unto himself that we are totally deprived of whatever standards we have ever had to guide us." Buchanan wondered whether Ornstein's "masses of crackling, screaming [chordal] sounds follow one another because they are impelled to do so by some occult inner dictation, or whether they are a mere idiosyncrasy expressing itself." He said he did not know.[41]

An obvious corollary to Buchanan's confusion is the issue of musical meaning. What is the real expressive significance of a highly individualistic work, say Ornstein's *Wild Men's Dance* (1915), as opposed to what appears to be its significance but is not? Does it have value? Since meaning and value in music tend to be intangible matters, they do not emerge after pragmatic inquiry. This leads to the suspicion that the significance composers attach to their works actually may not exist. Until the modernist movement, meaning and value had not been real problems, since composers, performers, and audiences agreed about the yardsticks that measured them. In the twentieth century the yardstick was gone. More often than not, what the modern composer valued, listeners devalued.

The one action left for the composer was to make a unilateral assertion of value. A self-referential axiom was formulated: the composer decides his own standards; he writes according to the standards he sets up, which few others or nobody else can adopt or cares to adopt; then according to his standards, his music is outstanding. Whatever anybody says to the contrary is a lie arising from ignorance, laziness, or a willful refusal to understand him. This is the curious reasoning behind Carl Ruggles's imperious claim that his own music is better than anybody else's because nobody writes according to his standards and nobody else's music reveals the positive values he discovers in his own works.[42]

"Musical value, and the expression and communication of it, is primarily the function of the composer," writes Charles Seeger, leaving nothing to the performer or listener. As convoluted a logic as appeared earlier in the statement by Cowell, and above by Ruggles, invests Seeger's next comment: "So every composition embodies, among other things, a critique of the art of its day, a revision of its criteria, a revaluation of its values." He goes on to say: "Ruggles has not informed himself historico-critically of the past, nor has he bothered much with the question of the social usefulness of his aims or his deeds. . . . What is lacking in balance is there in conviction—sheer arrogant assertion—of value."[43]

Seeger would not allow that listeners can follow the same logic as Ruggles. After all, they, too, are entitled to set up their own standards and make assertions of listening value, which is their function. Audiences have no obligation to try to understand the artist's standards and divine his meaning if he in turn feels no obligation to make that meaning clear to the public. A composer like Ruggles, therefore, has no license to criticize them as Philistines.

With greater reasonableness than Ruggles, Copland admitted that his austere *Piano Variations* (1930) had won over hardly any performers and listeners. Yet, he said, practicality could have no part in the creative experience. He alone, as a composer, had to be convinced of the value of what he was doing, that the work had meaning for him. People might not understand and appreciate the *Piano Variations* for years, but eventually they would come around.[44] Copland is right about the artist's need for a personal conviction of value. However, if the public does not subscribe to his view, it may not eventually come around.

The Composer as Superior Being

The romantic notion of the "artist" theoretically aloof from, and neglected or misunderstood by his society persisted into the twentieth century. The balancing nineteenth-century reality of the composer having to live in and write in some measure to please his society did not survive, at least among modernists. To them, the artist now stood detached from ordinary beings, with no feeling of belonging, which every culture before had taken for granted. He reflected the decline of a perception of community that had once affected every area and every class. He adamantly refused to amuse or to please others. As Robert Phelps put it, he became an observer of himself, a bringer of revelation, a self-ordained priest. "The artist offered us not only his work, but the gospel according to his own committed living." One result was aloneness, isolation from the musical community.[45]

The conditions outlined above did encourage a degree of selfishness. The "artist's" first duty was to himself. Roger Sessions, in 1926, scolded Copland for wasting his time on the music of young Americans: "Any two pages of your symphony are worth all the collected works of the 'jeune Americains'." He advised Copland to "push your own fortunes, without wasting precious energy on those of other people or on anything so vague and dubious as the 'future of American music'."[46]

Estrangement from his community also encouraged the composer or his backers to consider the "artist" a second God, the divine creator "divorced from the rank and file of 'normal' people," states Rudolf Wittkower. In the twenties, the influential Paul Rosenfeld described art as pure and composers like Carl Ruggles and Roger Sessions as sacrosanct. Anybody challenging these claims committed treason. "The artist meant for him [Rosenfeld] a being unique and godlike, and . . . he would not admit for a minute that a philosopher or a scientist or a statesman could achieve an equal creative importance," writes Edmund Wilson.[47]

Cultural authoritarianism, the demand for blind submission to artistic authority, with a downgrading of the public's freedom to think and act, also permeated musical and other artistic circles, European and American. These coteries denigrated democratic canons and concern for ordinary people, without any reflection about the price that would be paid, including the contemporary inhumanity they might help cause.[48] Writers like William Butler Yeats, T. S. Eliot, Ezra Pound, and D. H. Lawrence all had fascistic leanings.[49] One American composer or another was friendly with one or more of these men. Ezra Pound, a supporter of Antheil, insisted the artist was not dependent on a "mutton-headed" public. Humanity was a "rich effluvium, it is the waste and the manure and the soil, and from it grows the tree of the arts." Only "a few intelligent spirits" and not "this rabble" is a fitting audience for the artist.[50]

The curmudgeonly H. L. Mencken, an admirer of Friedrich Nietzsche, hated the whole progressive movement in the United States, which struck him as the triumph of people of little worth over the superior individual. Many young intellectuals admired him, and acquired his contempt for the majority, "a position they had not really thought through."[51] Mencken's only hope for improving the climate in the United States lay in the development of a native aristocracy that would stand between the public and the artist and writer, supporting and appreciating the arts and forming a "cordon sanitaire between the individual and the mob."[52] Mencken was dreaming of the never-never country that could exist only as illusion.

Edgard Varèse enjoyed Mencken's company and was of one mind with him, especially about the "cancer" of democracy, states Louise Varèse, Edgard's wife. Varèse, too, was an autocrat in all matters: "I remember that Mencken particularly liked Varèse's quotation of Clemenceau's definition of democracy: le nivellement par en bas; that is, the equalization of everyone on the lowest intellectual, artistic, and spiritual level."[53] Carl Ruggles was also an "absolutist" with a sharp antagonism toward works of art and people he judged not worthy of his approval.[54]

Roger Sessions gives a couple of compelling reasons for his questioning of American democracy. After he learned of the Sacco-Vanzetti execution in 1927, he wrote to Nicolas Slonimsky about "this wretched business" and how he could understand Slonimsky's "hesitation in becoming an American citizen." He viewed the event as evidence of what he has long known: "that America is no longer an Anglo-Saxon country, and that in fact these elements are simply in the way of her development." He agreed with Slonimsky about "the charming institution known as Democracy [which] seeks to make us all responsible for its vagaries." Needed were "a few intelligent people like yourself," otherwise he could "see no hope that those institutions will ever change."[55]

An anti-democratic and authoritarian attitude in artistic circles persisted throughout the twenties and early thirties. Indeed, it would linger throughout much of the century. It legitimated one-sided pronouncements like Rosenfeld's on Sessions' First Symphony (1927), which he found had "more warmth and necessity in it than the Octuor or the Concerto or any other" work of Stravinsky. To Rosenfeld, this was an accomplished work—stark, serious, unyieldingly complex, though "dry in spirit."[56] His enthusiasm is admirable, but he is carried away by it. Whether Sessions' symphony or the works of Copland in his early-thirties style are supreme artistic achievements is not the issue here. What is the issue is the modernist assumption: because I say it is so, it must be so.

Ruggles maintained that for music to be great, it had to be "sublime," and his music reached for the "sublime," wrote Seeger in the *Musical Quarterly* of 1932. Fourteen years later, Lou Harrison explained: "Sublimity . . . is the sense of an elevated, individuated, new, explorative, serious adventure on the edge of faith; sublimity in this sense Ruggles aims towards and to a great measure sets forth." The *Musical Quarterly* of 1932 also had Farwell stating that Roy Harris aimed for "a new vision of music's potentialities, a fresh-breath-taking of Truth in his . . . art."[57]

The music of Ruggles and Harris contained sublimity and truth: the promoter of contemporary music was constantly making inflexible statements of this nature, as if they were entitled to unquestioning acceptance. Irving Howe, in his study of Ralph Waldo Emerson and Henry Thoreau, makes an insightful observation that helps to put such statements into proper context. Thoreau's idea of freedom and sublimity, Howe says, was personal and disavowed communal experience, while Emerson knew better and considered the sublime "a gift of moments." Thoreau [like Ruggles] fell "into the rigidity of the fanatic, perhaps the crank. Emerson never did." Rules, limits, obligations toward society were not for Thoreau [or Ruggles]. Thoreau had said, "A man more right than his neighbors constitutes a majority of one already," without adding "how that rightness is to be established or how competing claims to rightness, all of them, let us say, forceful and sincere, are to be adjudicated." Nor have the devotees who admire "this sentence troubled to explain." Thoreau pushes, as far as he can, an excessive interpretation of individualism "that in later decades would lend itself to conservative bullying and radical posturing, both of which can undercut the fraternal basis of a democratic polity."[58]

Two terms that are more frequently employed than sublimity to assay contemporary works are sincerity and integrity. Those works that were the most problematic to understand, produced the greatest discomfort when listened to, and demolished the assumptions of most music lovers were regarded as the most sincere and having the highest integrity. To Howe, "the essence of modernism" revealed itself through these terms. When Randall Thompson examined Antheil's *Ballet Mécanique* in 1931, he spoke of its "passionate sincerity" in capturing "the quintessence of industrialism, undiluted, uncompromising." Ezra Pound praised Antheil's integrity in offending pieces like *Ballet Mécanique*, which meant, to Pound, the refusal to conform to current taste and kowtow to societal dictates, in short the artist's refusal to lie.[59]

What Modernism Reveals

Music as a manifestation of science or as a reaction to science and technology, music as a mirror of contemporary reality and the future or as a deliberate irrationality induced by the underlying absurdity in the world—these were four major revelations supposedly disclosed through music. Certain composers, like Varèse, assumed scientific method and research could provide musical knowledge and worthy artifacts. The composer articulated an idea, accumulated information about it by means of experiments with sound, reached a conclusion in a completed composition, and then publicized that conclusion by letting an audience hear it. Often, it was apparent that the idea behind the "scientific experimentation" was more important than the actual composition. This was true for Varèse and Cowell during the earlier part of the century and for Cage and his associates in the later part of the century.[60]

Varèse, who arrived in New York in 1915, gave a great deal of impetus to the experimental music movement then starting up in the United States. He had studied mathematics and science at the École Polytechnique. When he came to America he "dedicated himself to glorifying in music the modern triumphs of science," writes Adolfo Salazar. Copland, in 1926, singled out Antheil as an American young man of promise, referring to his "visionary" experimentation with mechanical pianos and electrical appliances. He described Cowell as "essentially an inventor, not a composer." Cowell has discovered "tone-clusters, playing piano with the fore-arm, and the string piano."[61] The next year, Henry Gilbert took in the Frankfurt, Germany, music festival sponsored by the International Society for Contemporary Music, where European and American works were heard. He noted that science, not art, guided the composers on exhibition. They were trying to emulate the achievements of scientists and to imitate scientific procedures. Although sincere, Gilbert said, these composers had produced bad art.[62]

Increasingly in the 1920s and 1930s, Charles Ives grew in stature among modernists. Yet, it was less the expressive content of his music that was mainly discussed and more the experimentation, a proclivity he had acquired from his father. "The off-rhythms and the off-key character of the music of popular bands and of church hymns played on a harmonium not very well tuned" spurred the incorporation of similar sounds in his compositions, for which he was much praised.[63]

Composers concentrated their experimentation chiefly on texture, on inventive configurations of sound. For Ives and Thomson, the texture resulting from a mix of seemingly incompatible melodic elements characterized their inquiries into sound. Copland seized on qualities available through the incorporation of jazz and blues elements into a brittle fabric of laconic melodic phrases and hard harmonic punctuations. What he pursued was the production of the "new sound images" suggested by Igor Stravinsky's *L'Histoire du Soldat* (1918) and Darius Milhaud's *La Création du Monde* (1923), two works that experimented with jazz.[64] For Ruggles, a unique texture resulted from an absence of tonality and the aggressive thrust of chords sounding seconds and sevenths. Cowell produced his experimental textures by strumming a piano's insides and swatting clusters of adjacent black and white keys of the keyboard with fists or pieces of wood. Varèse and Antheil probed the use of untraditional "instruments" and unorthodox "music," as in the wail of fire sirens, the roar of airplane propellers, and the clang of a variety of percussion mechanisms. Looking over the extensive textural trials of the twenties, Cowell spoke in admiration of the "evolution of harmonic appreciation." With rickety reasoning, he suggested: "Our trained ears should now feel consonance in seconds and sevenths. Evolution, and not any arbitrary domination of special intervals, determines what we feel to be harmonious."[65]

When *American Composers on American Music*, edited by Henry Cowell, first came out in 1933, Leah Adomian wrote, in the *Daily Worker* for 25 December 1934, that "the prime requisites for inclusion are: contemporary idiom, or some detail of technique that has been treated experimentally," however meritless was a great deal of the music discussed. Rosenfeld's review griped that the articles contained "meaningless technical 'criticism' and evidences of an obsession with the means of music and a neglect of the substance."[66]

In 1932, Alfred Meyer attended a Yaddo Festival concert, listening to works like Copland's *Piano Variations*, Piston's Sonata for Flute, Thomson's *Stabat Mater*, and piano sonatas by Sessions and Harris. He concluded: "This music of the present is apparently most concerned with texture. The experiments deal in the main with texture; the successes are successes in the management and manipulation of texture. This preoccupation too often relegates to a secondary place the equally pressing demands of form and content."[67]

Capturing the reality of the contemporary world was another desideratum behind musical modernism. When Copland, Louis Gruenberg and others used jazz, they wanted to generate its hard-boiled, present-day atmosphere. Then there are compositions whose titles indicate their contents, like Cowell's *Competitive Sport* and *Steel and Stone* for chamber orchestra (1931).

Van Vechten praised Ornstein's works because, like the finest painting and literature of the day, they resonate with the disquiet of the times which produced World War I. He also mentioned Ornstein's *Impressions of the Thames* for piano (1915), which attempted a realistic description of ponderous barges, workers on the river, and the screech of tugboat whistles. When Varèse completed *Amériques* in 1921, he said: "To be modern is to be natural, an interpreter of the spirit of your own time. I can assure you that I am not straining after the unusual."[68]

Thomson met Antheil, the protegé of Sylvia Beach, James Joyce, and Ezra Pound, at Beach's Paris bookstore and exposed himself to the "brutal charm" of Antheil's music. The brutality was largely the result of Antheil's writing "the machine music of the future," said Mary Louise Bok after she heard *Ballet Mécanique* in 1925. "It is the rhythm of machinery. . . . It is the life, the manufacturing, the industry of today," in America. Two years later, Richard Hammond commented that Antheil was trying to communicate "much of the mathematical beauty of machinery"—an ambiance realized in the *Ballet Mécanique* through player-pianos, xylophones, rattles, airplane propellers, bells, buzzers, and assorted percussion.[69] Around that time European composers were also interpreting the machine age. One has only to recall Erik Satie's *Parade* (1917), Arthur Honegger's *Pacific 231* (1923) and *Rugby* (1928), Prokofiev's *Le Pas d'Acier* (1926), and Alexander Mossolov's *Iron Foundry* (1927).

Mary Louise Bok mentioned music of the future. So did others in the twenties, giving as examples the works of Varèse and Antheil. They equated such music with the modern city and noisemaking. Amusing to note, after Van Vechten heard Ornstein play, in January and February of 1915, he considered him "the post-futurist composer."[70] However, in a broader sense, all compositions that eschewed consonance, lyricism, and predictable rhythm earned the designation "music of the future," especially when scarcely any listeners cared for them.

During the twenties, Thomson more than any other American composer, wished to divulge the underlying absurdity in the world. He rebelled against all conventions, including those of modernism. The music he wrote deflated the pretensions of "artists" past and present by exposing the sham heroism and empty profundities that invested so much of their music. His aim was to restore art's human perspective.[71] He was a master at recasting the cliché so it sounded fresh, at combining stately hymns with tango rhythms and ditties like "For He's a Jolly Good Fellow," at writing an opera, *Four Saints in Three Acts* (1927-28), full of consonant, diatonic oom-pa-pas. The opera featured an African-American cast and scenery glistening in cellophane. Its outwardly nonsensical libretto came from the hand of Gertrude Stein. Thomson enjoyed what he was doing, treated his musical material with affection, and offered the public sophisticated amusement.

The Disdain for the General Audience

From everything that I have said thus far, one gathers that whatever composers believed about depicting the raw content of contemporary life, they felt disdain for most Americans, past and present, and the culture they had wrought. We have already mentioned Pound as saying ordinary Americans were muttonheads and served as waste and manure for their aristocratic and artistic betters. We recall Copland labeling listeners as dumbbells, too dense to understand his music. This chapter concludes with a gloomy litany of the tirades that modernists have flung at the American public, including those listeners essential to the validation of their creative existence. Their acid words, often born out of frustration, would eventually hurt their cause. However routine the listing that follows may seem, it needs recording.

Even the most cultivated Americans, the noted New England writers, thinkers, and artists who for years had dominated literature and the arts, received condemnation. The younger creative sets no longer drew membership mainly from New England. New England came to represent the civilized past that needed wiping away. Needing a scapegoat, they made New Englanders the persons most to blame for their problems. They denigrated the region's "Puritan" way of life with irrational animosity and its "genteel" cultural contributions with persistent attacks. As Michael Kammen said, "It surely sounded as though all the other regions were ganging up on poor old New England."[72] For example, Arthur Berger, of New-York Jewish background, attacked Bostonians with some relish, in 1927, when they failed to appreciate Copland's Concerto for Piano. He describes the work as "unbridled not only in its cacophonies but in its 'hot' polyphonies as well." Yet, Berger could not excuse the "veritable cabal [that was] . . . formed against this work . . . among staid Boston listeners [read white Anglo-Saxon Protestants]."[73]

"Puritans," said Deems Taylor in 1922, asked if a work of art pointed a moral and, "if not, will it help me to kill time without boring me." He then declared that Puritanism ran rampant among all the "self-styled" music lovers of the country. These "highbrows, defined as [persons] educated beyond [their] intelligence," possessed no sincere understanding of music. Besides, they were intellectually dull-witted and pretentiously genteel. "Highbrow" and "lowbrow" were derogatory terms first advanced by Van Wyck Brooks in 1915 to cover Americans with false refinement and those with less than none, respectively.[74]

That same year, Thomson expostulated against the "unpleasant qualities" he found in all Americans—"their dullness and obstreperousness and waste and disorder." He rebuked equally their "completely tamed" virtue, and viciously inspired vice. He could not help but be "annoyed and ashamed" of his country.[75] Varèse, two years later, applied the French concept of the bourgeoisie to Americans: they were selfish, money-hungry, materialistic, and inferior in intellect and artistic taste. From this bourgeois class came so-called music lovers who listened only instinctively and had atrophied mentally after the age of twenty-five. He preferred an "aristocratic intelligentsia."[76] Admittedly, the United States had problems and some to spare. However, not one of these critics took a close look at the individual nations of Europe and the narrowness of vision that would bring on depression, dictatorship, and World War II.

Varèse echoed the same line as his friend Mencken, whose term "booboisie" had recently appeared in the *Mercury* as a preposterous distortion of the American people. This sort of characterization has continuously existed but as a fiction only. It was accurate on the surface but nonexistent in fact. Crudity, imbecility, and ill breeding appears in all eras, among all populaces, and within all civilizations. The typical member of the middle and upper class, say in Mozart's time, did not devote his free moments to thinking loftily, reading Shakespeare, viewing Rembrandt, or listening to symphonies by Haydn and Mozart.[77]

Regrettably, the distinguishing mark of the composer and his friends, during the twenties, was a disapproval of everything valued by the "booboisie." This stand, however, was inconsistent, because at that time the American middle class was showing an interest in art composers more than hitherto had been true. Besides, some composers had quietly joined the middle class themselves, even while denying they were doing so. The dread of not appearing adequately devoted to new ideas may be more germane to some noted musicians of the twenties than they desire to acknowledge.[78]

Fortunately, Copland provided further clarification of composers' attitudes during the twenties. Yes, he considered listeners hostile to his music to be "dumbbells," but realized most listeners were unaccustomed to hearing music in contemporary styles: "And, actually, there was a lot of fun in bucking the tide and feeling part of the avant garde out there fighting new battles. That feeling was very much a part of the excitement of the times."[79]

Behind a great deal of the castigation of Americans was the new theory of musical behaviorism. J. B. Watson, Clark Hull, and B. F. Skinner had introduced the idea of behaviorism around 1913 in order to refer to "conditioning," the molding of behavior, which forced the "subject" to grow passive and limited his freedom of choice. Now composers, taking their cue from these psychologists, spoke of the conditioned negative responses of listeners to the new musical styles. The thinking and tastes of audiences, after years of conditioning, had become rigidly fixed on the old and incapable of taking in the new. This manner of reasoning, when applied to music, was peculiarly likely to spawn erroneous conclusions. Witness Varèse's slogan of 1923, "New Ears for New Music and New Music for New Ears." According to Varèse, the slogan was to make clear what they expected from recalcitrant listeners: "The day is coming when the present modernists in music will be found as simple as we now find Schubert and Chopin. It's all in the point of view and in the training of the ear." Witness also Cowell's insistence that "dissonance and discord do not actually exist. They only exist because of our habit of thinking. It is a matter of biological and psychological development and not a question of acoustics or physics, harmony or counterpoint."[80]

In addition there was the bugaboo of societal mediocrity or worse snuffing out hope of a favorable reception for new works. In 1919, Carl Engel was already reporting in the *Musical Quarterly* about "the miraculous appeal of mediocrity," the herd instinct of "the Great Majority," the utter incapacity to appreciate originality, which the new American audiences for art music brought with them to the concert hall: "So long as the multitude was kept from sitting in the Areopagus, the judges pronounced their verdict with blind disregard for the opinion of the masses. Now [in the American democratic system] this is changed." Two years later, Copland wrote to a friend that he was sad because one of his compositions had "made quite a hit," and explained: "I say it is sad because I can't get over the idea that if a thing is popular it can't be good." Alexander Fried seconded Copland's observation by warning, in *Modern Music*, of the dangers to art music that attended popularization. With it came vulgarization and the promotion of the obvious. Music that won "popular success . . . must be artistically bad."[81]

Because the music public is lazy, Cowell said, the modernist composer had a duty "to jar" it "out of its state of mind." Even so, warned Sessions, the public's interest in music remained lukewarm, since it wanted nothing demanded of it. And Copland cautioned not to expect the public to be jarred into anything because of its docility. Whatever opinions it might express on the new American music were largely formed by the daily music critic was Copland's claim.[82]

Pronouncements about America's citizenry were usually made with the addition that Europeans invariably had a finer attitude and approach to the arts. American music lovers more than Europeans were supposed to revel in the cliché and to want an escape from real musical experience. They belonged to the masses who were not sure that any art was altogether legitimate. Beneath their doubt hid a contempt for art music and the oddities who created it. Thus, artists saw the United States as harboring a materialistic, machine society that had "stumbled upon music and found a dump."[83]

A more specific insult was directed at American women. They were said to dominate America's music world by making up the bulk of the audience and the committees that fostered art music. Ninety percent of music's support came from women, stated Taylor. They were the principal subscribers to musical performances, forced "reluctant husbands and fathers" to attend with them, and staffed the clubs that furthered art music. Their influence was detrimental to art because they made genteelness the test for acceptance. Their undue esteem of conventional expression, their sham delicacy of feeling, and their requirement that art be edifying corrupted any appreciation of music.[84]

Genteel effeteness was their principal contribution to culture. Even the "liberated" women of the time went along with this half-truth. Mabel Dodge Luhan, affluent and privileged, was one of the most emancipated of the New York crowd. The plentiful money supply available to her had helped in her enfranchisement. She provided the usual distorted picture of American womanhood when she wrote that the features of many American women were of "plebian cast," which resulted "from the material of their thoughts and the lack of tension in their culture." American women aspire to nothing, lacked nobility, and were incapable of great art. "All other races have really suffered and been molded by suffering in the past, but Americans have only been nervous. No culture results from nerves."[85]

Mabel Dodge Luhan played into the hands of male prejudiced against women. After reading the commentaries of the time, one concludes that emancipated males, including composers, were predisposed to define women's equality in terms of sexual relations outside of marriage and much less often in terms of artistic sensitivity or creative ability. Gertrude Stein was one exception that proved the rule.

Women agreed to their submissiveness, Rosenfeld said. They attended concerts, "purchased a little solace," and then drew "their skirts free of the bastard emotion" and returned "into bondage and emptiness." Through them, timidity, correctness, and intellectual anemia entered to emasculate the arts as they had never done in Europe.[86]

According to modernist belief, hardly an American man or woman existed who was free of ordinariness or effeteness.

Notes to Chapter 2

[1] Carl Van Vechten, *Music and Bad Manners* (New York: Knopf, 1916), 189-90.

[2] Aaron Copland and Vivian Perlis, *Copland, 1900 through 1942* (New York: St. Martin's/Marek, 1984), 55.

[3] Randall Thompson, "The Contemporary Scene in American Music," *Modern Music* 18 (January-February 1932): 10-15.

[4] Harold E. Stearns, ed., *Civilization in the United States* (New York: Harcourt, Brace, 1922), vii; Charles Seeger, "Carl Ruggles," *Musical Quarterly* 18 (1932): 578-92.

[5] Rita Mead, *Henry Cowell's New Music, 1925-1936* (Ann Arbor: UMI Research Press, 1981), 37; Martha L. Manion, *Writings about Henry Cowell* (New York: Institute for Studies in American Music, Brooklyn College, 1982), 6, 74.

[6] Carl Van Vechten, *Music after the Great War, and Other Studies* (New York: Schirmer, 1915), 29-30.

[7] The last sentence is indebted to Diana Trilling, *Reviewing the Forties* (New York: Harcourt Brace Jovanovich, 1978), 18, where she says: "False notions can be introduced by good writers, then made into folk myths by bad writers."

[8] Aaron Copland, "The Composer in America, 1923-1933," *Modern Music* 10 (January-February, 1933): 87.

[9] Arthur Berger, *Aaron Copland* (New York: Oxford University Press, 1953), 22-23.

[10] Oscar G. Sonneck, "Modernists, Classics and Immortality in Music," *Musical Quarterly* 11 (1925): 572.

[11] Arthur Mendel, as quoted in Manion, *Writings about Henry Cowell*, 98.

[12] Letter to Briggs Buchanan, dated 4 August 1925, in *Selected Letters of Virgil Thomson*, eds. Tim Page and Vanessa Weeks Page (New York: Summit, 1988), 63.

[13] Roger Sessions, *The Correspondence of Roger Sessions*, ed. Andrea Olmstead (Boston: Northeastern University Press, 1992), 211-12.

[14] Manion, *Writings about Henry Cowell*, 91.

[15] Edward T. Cone, "Conversations with Aaron Copland," in *Perspectives on American Composers*, eds. Benjamin Boretz and Edward T. Cone (New York: Norton, 1971), 137.

[16] Copland and Perlis, *Copland, 1900 through 1942*, 192-94.

[17] Spackman, *Wallingford Riegger*, 34-35.

[18] Mabel Dodge Luhan, *Movers and Shakers* (New York: Harcourt, Brace, 1936), 440.

[19] Information on Thomson's reading comes from letters written in 1922 and 1924; see *Selected Letters*, 51, 52, 55, 59.

[20] Frederick J. Hoffman, *The Twenties*, rev. ed. (New York: Free Press, 1965), 43.

[21] Henry May, ed., *The Discontent of the Intellectual: A Problem of the Twenties* (Chicago: Rand McNally, 1963), 4-5.

[22] Deems Taylor, in *Civilization in America*, 31, 212, 214; Paul Rosenfeld, *An Hour with American Music* (Philadelphia: Lippincott, 1929),

28-31; Lehman Engel, *This Bright Day: An Autobiography* (New York: Macmillan, 1974), 60. See also, Malcolm Cowley, *Exile's Return* (New York: Viking, 1951), 36.

[23] Aaron Copland, *Music and Imagination* (New York: Mentor, 1959), 111.

[24] Deems Taylor, in Stearns, ed. *Civilization in the United States*, 199-200; see also Irving Weil, "The American Scene Changes," *Modern Music* 6 (May-June, 1929): 8; Carl Van Vechten, *Interpreters and Interpretations* (New York: Knopf, 1917), 269-71, 278.

[25] Lou Harrison, *About Carl Ruggles* (Yonkers: Oscar Baradinsky at the Alicat Bookshop, 1946), 2-3.

[26] George Antheil, *Bad Boy of Music* (New York: Da Capo, 1981), 149-50.

[27] Peter Westergaard, "Conversations with Walter Piston," in *Perspectives on American Composers*, eds. Benjamin Boretz and Edward T. Cone (New York: Norton, 1971), 159.

[28] Roger Sessions, *Roger Sessions on Music: Collected Essays*, ed. Edward T. Cone (Princeton: Princeton University Press, 1979), 33-34.

[29] John Vinton, *Essays after a Dictionary* (Lewisburg, Pennsylvania: Bucknell University Press, 1977), 112.

[30] Arnold Schoenberg, "The Musician," in *The Works of the Mind*, ed. Mortimer J. Adler (Chicago: University of Chicago Press, 1947), 69-70.

[31] Eric Salzman, *Twentieth-Century Music: An Introduction* (Englewood Cliffs, NJ: Prentice-Hall, 1967), 4.

[32] Stephen Spackman, *Wallingford Riegger: Two Essays in Musical Biography* (New York: Institute for Studies in American Music, Brooklyn College, 1982), 36.

[33] Carl Van Vechten, *Music and Bad Manners*, 236, 239-40; see also, Paul Rosenfeld, *An Hour with American Music* (Philadelphia: Lippincott, 1929), 60-63.

[34] See Rudolf Wittkower, "Genius: Individualism in Art and Artists," in *Dictionary of the History of Ideas* 2, ed. Philip P. Wiener (New York: Scribner's Sons, 1973), 297-312.

[35] Suzi Gablik, *Has Modernism Failed?* (New York: Thames & Hudson, 1984), 79.

[36] See Edward Shils, *Tradition* (Chicago: University of Chicago Press, 1981), 11.

[37] John J. Becker, "Imitative Versus Creative Music in America," in Henry Cowell, ed., *American Composers on American Music* (New York: Ungar, 1962), 190.

[38] Copland and Perlis, *Copland, 1900 through 1942*, 55.

[39] W. Jackson Bate, *The Burden of the Past and the English Poet* (Cambridge, Massachusetts: Belknap Press, 1970), 3-4.

[40] Ibid., 104-05.

[41] Charles L. Buchanan, "Ornstein and Modern Music," *Musical Quarterly* 4 (1918): 175-78.

[42] Henry Cowell, "A Note," in Lou Harrison, *About Carl Ruggles*, 3.

[43] Charles Seeger, "Carl Ruggles," 590.

[44] Copland and Perlis, *Copland, 1900 through 1942*, 180.

[45] Robert Phelps, ed., *Twentieth-Century Culture: The Breaking Up* (New York: Braziller, 1965), 17-19.

[46] Sessions, *The Correspondence of Roger Sessions*, 66.

[47] Wittkower, "Genius," 308; Van Wyck Brooks, *An Autobiography* (New York: Dutton, 1965), 360, 262; Edmund Wilson, "Paul Rosenfeld: Three Phases," in *Paul Rosenfeld, Voyager in the Arts*, eds. Jerome Mellquist and Lucie Wiese (New York: Creative Age, 1948), 13.

[48] Howe, *Decline of the New*, 38-41.

[49] Bernard Bergonzi, *The Myth of Modernism and Twentieth Century Literature* (New York: St. Martin's Press, 1986), xii.

[50] May, *The Discontent of the Intellectuals*, 11-12.

[51] May, *The Discontent of the Intellectuals*, 20.

[52] Van Wyck Brooks, "The Literary Life," in *Civilization in the United States*, ed. Stearns, 193.

[53] Louise Varèse, *Varèse, A Looking-Glass Diary* (London: Davis-Paynter, 1973), 181, 188.

[54] Seeger, "Carl Ruggles," 579.

[55] Sessions, *The Correspondence of Roger Sessions*, 84.

[56] Rosenfeld, *An Hour with American Music*, 81-87.

[57] Seeger, "Carl Ruggles," 580; Arthur Farwell, "Roy Harris," 32; Harrison, *About Carl Ruggles*, 10.

[58] Irving Howe, *The American Newness* (Cambridge: Harvard University Press, 1986), 35.

[59] Howe, *Decline of the New*, 9-10; Randall Thompson, "American Composers, V: George Antheil," *Modern Music* 8 (May-June, 1931): 20; Hoffman, *The Twenties*, 193-94.

[60] John Rockwell, in *The New Grove Dictionary of American Music* 2, eds. H. Wiley Hitchcock and Stanley Sadie (London: Macmillan, 1986), s.v. "Experimental Music." See also, Phelps, in *Twentieth-Century Culture*, 217.

[61] Aaron Copland, "America's Young Men of Promise," *Modern Music* 3 (March-April, 1926): 15-16.

[62] Adolfo Salazar, *Music in Our Time*, trans. Isabel Pope (New York: Norton, 1946), 318; Henry Gilbert, "Notes on a Trip to Frankfurt in the Summer of 1927," *Musical Quarterly* 16 (1930): 36-37.

[63] Salazar, *Music in Our Time*, 319; see also Vinton, *Essays after a Dictionary*, 112-13.

[64] Copland, *Music and Imagination*, 40.

[65] Manion, *Writings about Henry Cowell*, 318.

[66] Mead, *Henry Cowell's New Music, 1925-1936*, 301; Paul Rosenfeld, *Discoveries of a Music Critic* (New York: Harcourt, Brace, 1936), 279-80.

[67] Alfred H. Meyer, "Yaddo—A May Festival," *Modern Music* 9 (May-June, 1932): 172.

[68] Carl Van Vechten, *Music and Bad Manners*, 235, 243; Fernand Ouellette, *Edgard Varèse*, trans. Derek Coltman (New York: Orion, 1968), 57.

[69] Virgil Thomson, *Virgil Thomson* (New York: Knopf, 1966), 75; Linda Whitesitt, *The Life and Music of George Antheil, 1900-1959* (Ann Arbor, MI: UMI, 1983), xviii; Richard Hammond, "Ballyhoo," *Modern Music* 4 (May-June, 1927): 32-33.

[70] See Irving Weil, "The Noise-Makers," *Modern Music* 5 (January-February, 1928): 25; Thompson, "American Composers, V: George Antheil," 18; Paul Rosenfeld, *By Way of Art* (New York: McCann, 1928), 13; Van Vechten, *Music and Bad Manners*, 233.

[71] Thomson, *Virgil Thomson*, 57-58; Kathleen Hoover and John Cage, *Virgil Thomson; His Life and Music* (New York: Yoseloff, 1959), 50-51.

[72] Michael Kammen, *Mystic Chords of Memory, The Transformation of Tradition in American Culture* (New York: Knopf, 1991), 211.

[73] Berger, *Aaron Copland*, 13-14.

[74] Taylor, in *Civilization in the United States*, 203-04, 208-09; Van Wyck Brooks, "America's Coming-of-Age" (1915), in Van Wyck Brooks, *The Early Years: A Selection from His Works, 1908-1921*, ed. Claire Sprague (New York: Harper & Row, 1968), 82-84.

[75] Letter of 12 September 1922, to Leland Poole, in *Selected Letters of Virgil Thomson*, 56.

Modernists and the Public I   49

⁷⁶ Varèse, *Varèse: A Looking-Glass Diary*, 218.

⁷⁷ David Manning White makes valuable comments on this matter, in Bernard Rosenberg and David Manning White, *Mass Culture Revisited* (New York: Van Nostrand Reinhold, 1971), 15.

⁷⁸ On this topic, see John Lukacs, *The Passing of the Modern Age* (New York: Harper & Row, 1970), 127.

⁷⁹ Copland and Perlis, *Copland, 1900 through 1942*, 123.

⁸⁰ Varèse, *Varèse: A Looking-Glass Diary*, 207, 211; Mead, *Henry Cowell's New Music, 1925-1936*, 137.

⁸¹ Carl Engel, "The Miraculous Appeal of Mediocrity," *Musical Quarterly* 5 (1919): 455-56, 459-60; Copland and Perlis, *Copland, 1900 through 1942*, 51; Alexander Fried, "For the People," *Modern Music* 4 (January-February, 1927): 33-35.

⁸² Manion, *Writings about Henry Cowell*, 6; Sessions, *Roger Sessions on Music: Collected Essays*, 108; Copland, "The Composer and His Critic," *Modern Music* 9 (May-June, 1932): 143.

⁸³ Van Vechten, *Music and Bad Manners*, 179, 207-08; Sessions, *The Correspondence of Roger Sessions*, 192; Brooks, *The Early Years*, 7; Taylor, in *Civilization in the United States*, 207. The quotation is from Paul Rosenfeld, *Musical Chronicle (1917-1923)* (New York: Harcourt, Brace, 1923), 63.

⁸⁴ Taylor, in *Civilization in the United States*, 205.

⁸⁵ Luhan, *Movers and Shakers*, 520.

⁸⁶ Rosenfeld, *Musical Chronicle (1917-1923)*, 64; see also the comments of Harold Stearns, in *Civilization in the United States*, 135, 141-42, 147-50.

Chapter 3

Music from a Lost Generation

Gertrude Stein said she had first heard the phrase "lost generation" concerning a young French mechanic who was making a slipshod repair on her car. She related this to Ernest Hemingway and warned that his hard-drinking, amoral crowd was also lost. Hemingway in turn prefaced his novel *The Sun Also Rises* (1926) with the phrase to describe the post-World War I young people whom he knew—disturbed, rootless, and estranged from society. Then in 1931, Malcolm Cowley published *The Lost Generation*, having in mind the American writers who had expatriated themselves to Europe, later to return to the United States to find themselves spiritually homeless in their former home.

American composers of modern inclination were not exempt from this designation. They also seemed to be loosing touch with the viewpoints and standards of most Americans including their musical predecessors. Many of them propounded a societally antagonistic art in contrast to the more companionable and dedicated art that would come in later, as the Great Depression intensified. Not surprisingly, their musical compositions displayed several "lost" qualities. For one, from the public's viewpoint, the music revealed an uncertainty of artistic direction. Each composer was bent on a novel stylistic course different from those of his colleagues. Moreover, important composers kept on switching their direction—Cowell, Antheil, and Copland, to name three. For another, much of the music from the twenties and early thirties lost a sense of the audience's physiological and psychological needs and the limits of its listening capacities. Altogether too much of the sound was provocative rather than conciliatory, an art of denial rather than acceptance. For a third reason, some music appeared lost to the listener because it had gone out of control. No recognizable guidelines invested what appeared to be the weird to hair-raising noises called up by Ornstein, Antheil, Cowell, Varèse, and others. Music was indeed becoming a "lost" art. Altogether too many compositions were no longer grasped by the public and no longer had any likelihood of acceptance into the standard concert and operatic repertoire.

Tone clusters, anti-lyricism, different chords piled on each other, abandonment of triadic chord construction, microtones, polytonality, atonality, twelve-tone music, percussion music, noise—this was the stuff of modern music that electrified the young American composers and switched off listeners. Taking a retrospective look at the early twenties, Copland said:

> I still retain an impression of fantastic sonorities after a first contact with Schönberg's *Pierrot Lunaire*, or a little later, the astonishing percussive imaginings of Edgar Varèse, especially in a piece called *Arcanes*, heard once but not again. Also from the early twenties I recall hearing the mysterious sound made by a string ensemble . . . a sound which was later identified as an Alois Hába quarter tone Quartet.[1]

The music critic and editor Oscar Thompson, however, voiced concern that composers were too preoccupied with technical matters but neglectful of the more profound properties by which music was judged when people heard it.[2] His own preferences in music may have influenced what he said. Yet he does underline the fact that most listeners cared not a jot about innovative chord structures and atonality. Instead, they asked where had melody as they understood it gone, why the unceasing dissonance?

Composers rebutted that they were deeply concerned about expression, but wanted it unhackneyed, vital, and responsive to the present age, which was so different from previous ages. The only way to achieve the expressive results desired was through techniques never previously attempted. They were living in an age when writers and artists were taking chances, in their lives and modes of artistic expression. They also did so.

The novel sounds they invoked were assuredly risky when it came to acceptance by listeners. What follows is a general description of prominent composers' styles, while keeping in mind the perspective of the first American audiences who were trying to assimilate them into their own musical experience. The listing, I hope, will prove informative. My discussion is necessary because from the styles to be described there developed every twentieth-century American style that ensued, from the more conservative to the more radical. It helps also to explain the reactions of music lovers, from the more approving to the more hostile.

Five Radicals

The most extreme of the modernists were either experimenters, prospecting percussive rhythms and outlandish sounds (Cowell, Varèse, Antheil), or atonalists, exploring intensely dissonant and chromatic tones unconnected with a tonal system (Ruggles, Riegger). Except for Antheil, these composers were loosely allied to each other. Leo Ornstein, born in the Ukraine in 1892 and musically educated in Boston and New York, was one of the earliest experimenters heard in America, achieving special notoriety for his frenzied *Wild Men's Dance* (1915). His career, however, was brief and came almost to a halt in 1920. Like a comet, he raced across the musical horizon and disappeared. The three experimental composers with whom we are now concerned had a greater capacity for endurance and a greater impact on their fellow composers, if not the music public.

From the age of thirteen, Henry Cowell, a Californian, put aside caution and began to make a name for himself as a seeker of novel sounds, though not necessarily as a bona fide composer. Bemused music lovers saw him clobber the keyboard with fist or forearm (*Advertisement*, 1917) or watched his head and arms disappear into a piano's insides to strum, pluck, or lightly finger its wires (*The Banshee*, 1925). In 1924, when Cowell was not yet twenty-eight years of age, a satirical poem appeared in *Musical America* called "Plaint of a Pedal-Point." It testified to his notoriety:

> I want to be a cluster
> And with the clusters stand
> Just like the other modern tones
> Played without use of hand!

> When youthful virtuosi
> Start banging keys with fist
> I sigh to think I'm orthodox.
> Oh my, what thrills I've missed![3]

Sometimes he grabbed up a Hopi thunderstick and whirled it about to produce a whir like a purling electric motor (*Ensemble*, 1924). Later, he helped Lev Termen produce the Rhythmicon, a device that permitted the simultaneous playing of several complexly intertwined rhythms. Cowell's composition employing it, *Rhythmicana* (1931), was never performed in his lifetime. Nobody was quite sure what to make of his compositions during the 1920s, neither audiences nor seasoned music critics like Paul Rosenfeld.

If Cowell evoked more bemusement than outrage, Varèse evoked more outrage than bemusement. He was out to liberate sound from its confinement to tones and demanded the freedom to make music out of any sounds. "After all," he said, "what is music but organized noises?" And what is noise to a listener but "subjectively . . . any sound one doesn't like." He refused to articulate logical musical structures, fearing that to follow any system would infringe on his independence. He accused Schoenberg and Stravinsky of growing so frightened by the freedom they had won that they resorted to the confining systems of serialism and neoclassicism, respectively. He scorned such cowardice.[4]

Listeners' ears took in hard, tensile "sound-masses" as obdurate as steel and concrete, as contemporary as the blast of factory whistles, the staccato clamor of automobile traffic, and the whine of elevators. To Varèse, musical instruments, orthodox or unorthodox, were machines. The traditional symphony orchestra was a conglomeration of machines called violins, flutes, trumpets, etc. "Each time a work is performed, it can only be so by means of a machine which produces sounds—the instruments composing our orchestras, which are subject to all the same physical laws as all other machines."[5]

His *Amériques* for orchestra (1921) included eleven percussionists. The title, Varèse said, was meant as a guide to the work's "spiritual impulse," which was "man's aspiration toward the unknown worlds that he interrogates."[6] Already we find a disinclination to set forth themes and to develop material. Blocks of contiguous, overlapping, or simultaneously sounding sonorities and streams of reiterated rhythms were dominant features. A variety of boldly stated sounds, among them the wail of a siren, stunned listeners, who discerned no spiritual impulse and ended up detesting the piece. His biographer Fernand Ouellette says nobody at the time, even prominent critics like Lawrence Gilman and Paul Rosenfeld, understood the composition: "It is precisely the absence of apparent logic and coherence that constitutes the work's power and originality. It is in this a complete break with the *Sacre du Printemps*, which reassures us with its logic."[7] Few people would accept Ouellette's notion that illogic and incoherence were meritorious.

In 1923, he completed *Hyperprism* for nine wind players and seven percussionists. It used an amazing array of noisemakers; among them were sirens, anvils, slapsticks, rattles, sleighbells, and Chinese woodblocks. The piece evoked first bewilderment, then laughter. In the same year, *Octandre* for winds and double bass came out. Two years later, he finished *Intégrales*, which called for winds and percussion. *Arcana*, in 1927, was for orchestra with a large battery of percussion. Then, in 1931, Varèse completed *Ionisation* for percussion instruments alone, none sounding any pitch at all. After Nicolas Slonimsky conducted it in Carnegie Hall, on 6 March 1933, *Ionisation* and the other Varèse compositions were rarely performed. No listeners agitated to hear them. Varèse was left to fret himself about the inadequacies of democracy.

George Antheil, born in Trenton, New Jersey, in 1900, was entranced by three aspects of Igor Stravinsky's music: its driving rhythms, emotional coolness, and "hard, cold postwar flawlessness which [he himself] wanted to attain."[8] He tried writing pieces that emulated these features. Eventually coming to sojourn in Paris (1923), Antheil won endorsement from the literary figures that met at Sylvia Beach's bookstore, "Shakespeare & Co," and especial support from Ezra Pound. His admirers included James Joyce, William Butler Yeats, and Pablo Picasso. Pound, in 1927, would publish *Antheil and the Treatise on Harmony* in confirmation of his backing. While Antheil remained an *enfant terrible* and turned the music world upside down, his gratified sponsors hailed him as the musical genius of his era.

Music from a Lost Generation

When he returned to tonality and a more amenable style, his erstwhile friends abandoned him.

He wrote a series of piano works, beginning with the *Airplane Sonata* and *Sonata Sauvage* (1921, 1923) that satisfied the rebellious appetites of his circle. His music was based on what he called a "time-space" principle. It relied on an unmelodic succession of dissimilar chords, organized into chordal units and energized through percussive rhythms. One hears abrupt shifts from one section to another and no spinning out of any material. Each unit has its own ostinato figures and brief reiterated motives. Whatever the activity within the unit, no sense of forward motion occurs. Antheil wanted the expression to remain impassive, even hard-boiled. An impersonal striking of the keyboard and broad stretches of one dynamic level produced a robotic effect. The pianist was made to resemble a machine in human form that performed without emotion and sensitivity.

The culmination of his experimental period arrived with the *Ballet Mécanique* (ca.1925), which was first envisioned for a large percussion ensemble, including sixteen pianolas (player pianos). It premiered in Paris, in 1926, with a reduced force that utilized only one pianola, but asked for two propellers and a siren. Antheil says: "It was finished before 1925, and it closed a period of my work and life. For, after I had written it, I felt that now, finally, I had said everything I had to say in this strange, cold, dreamlike, ultraviolet-light medium."[9]

Its New York performance took place on 10 April 1927 and earned *Ballet Mécanique* the reputation of being the crowning or the most infamous American avant-garde composition of the 1920s, depending on one's point of view. Altogether too much sensational ballyhoo preceded the concert. Newspapers played up the public uproar attending the Paris debut and promised that the forthcoming din would exceed the eruptions in a boiler factory. An augmented ensemble containing several pianos, a pianola, a large airplane propeller, and assorted noisemakers was visible on the stage. Then, suddenly, the performance began. Like a racketing engine, the piece roared relentlessly onward. A hidden electric fan (substituting for the visual propeller) blew air threateningly at the heads of apprehensive listeners. Next, the siren went out of control. Chaos reigned. At first, writes Deems Taylor, the audience listened attentively. Soon fidgeting and giggling began.

When a man raised a white handkerchief on a cane as token of surrender, "the entire house, simultaneously, gave up trying not to laugh."[10] The following day, reviewers committed mayhem on the work, judging it to be a disagreeable prank, foisted on the public by a charlatan. An ominously high number of the music lovers who attended wanted nothing further to do with avant-garde music.

Antheil left New York penniless and disgraced. There was no point in remaining, especially after he had "deeply and perhaps permanently antagonized the sedately respectable League of Composers, a most important concert organization for any young American composer."[11] Not until after World War II did the admirers of *Ballet Mécanique* grow to more than a few. For almost three decades, the fiasco of 1927 obscured the genuine merits of the piece—its jazzy élan and assured cockiness.

One could draw an analogy between Ruggles and Riegger and the Central-European composers Schoenberg, Berg, and Webern, but the comparison would prove inaccurate. The Americans wrote more emphatic rhythms, more differentiated counterpoints, and differently considered sonorities. Carl Ruggles, a New Englander born in 1872, met Varèse after he settled in New York in 1917. He soon had the International Composers' Guild sponsoring performances of his music. Charles Seeger and Cowell would also befriend him. A series of severe yet strong compositions came from his pen—*Angels* (1922), *Toys* (1923), *Vox clamans in deserto* (1924), *Men and Mountains* (1924), *Portals* (1926), and the notably outstanding *Sun-Treader* (1931). The employment of seven- to nine-tone rows, motivic fragments, melodic distortions via wide ungainly skips, and intrusive harmonies based on highly dissonant seconds and sevenths are Ruggles's hallmarks. These and the conveyance of vehement or potent but latent emotion qualify him for the designation expressionist. One finds in his scores no hint of American folk or popular music and no jazz rhythms. Nothing in the music aids effortless listening.

His defenders described his compositions as mystic and apocalyptic, beyond the ken of ordinary people. Charles Ives praised the strength evident to him in *Men and Mountains*. Nicolas Slonimsky found it enmeshed in devices well known to Schoenberg but liked its powerful string unisons "for striding men and bulky discords for marching mountains." Yet, when Cowell's

New Music Edition published *Men and Mountains* in 1927, half the subscribers canceled.[12] Presumably, they included men and women sympathetic to innovation. The powerful orchestral forces unleashed in *Sun-Treader* are awesome. From the accelerating drum thumps and searing brass cries of the opening onward, the piece allows no rest to the ear. Like *Ballet Mécanique*, it survives as a landmark in modern American music. Regrettably, few music lovers have taken to it.

Wallingford Riegger was born in Georgia (1885) and educated in Germany. After holding a few German and scattered American positions, he alighted in New York in 1928. It was just the year before that he abandoned conventional for atonal writing with *Study in Sonority* for ten violins or any multiple thereof. Charles Seeger gives a valuable insight into Riegger's thinking at this time. Seeger told Rita Mead that in 1929:

> I was sitting down to lunch at the Institute for Musical Art one day with Riegger. He was a nice chap who wrote very conventional music, perfectly good. He said, 'Charles, I want you to know something. I've decided to write modern music.' Well, that's very amusing, and I put him down as another faker. But I had enough respect for him—he was a very honest man and his integrity was unquestioned—so I said to myself, we'll see what happens. Becker may have done just the same thing—written a lot of very conventional, dull music and then said, 'Oh, I've got to be modern.' A lot of people did. But Riegger was a different matter. He was a very good musician, very well trained, and a fine teacher. It wasn't long before I had to admit that it could be done.[13]

Riegger decided that composers had exhausted tonality. Individually designed tonalities, the simultaneous use of several tonalities, and the complete avoidance of tonal centers would provide him with unlimited opportunities for fresh musical research. Besides, he thought experimentation typified contemporary attitudes in American music and atonality was "in the line of historical development."[14] The austere atonality of *Study in Tonality* and the use of tone-rows in *Dichotomy* for chamber orchestra (1932) carried out what he saw as his imperatives. The latter, one of his finest achievements, explored the conflict generated by the opposition of contrasting and antagonistic forces. Tortuous strings of melody and forceful repetitive figures within a serial context generate a considerable amount of perturbed feeling. On the other hand, he quickly learned that unremitting anguish was not suited to most listeners' tastes. Later works would not always be so stylistically severe. The Concerto for Piano and Woodwind Quintet (1953), for example, despite its stretches of atonality has passages where rhythms and melodies are attractive and expression is on the lighter side.

The works that these crusaders against the status-quo issued during the 1920s and early 1930s did shake up the thinking of other composers and the music public. They obliged a reconsideration of one's stand with respect to existing music. If at the end the majority of listeners refused to accept what these radicals proposed, they returned to the music they loved with a stronger sense of why they valued it. Meanwhile, the less radically inclined composers picked up here and there a hitherto untouched technique that invigorated their own compositions.

Neoclassicists

American neoclassicists have taken their lead more often than not from Igor Stravinsky. Detachment and reticence in emotional expression pervade their manner of composing. Aaron Copland speaks of his and his neoclassical colleagues' "new impersonal approach." This approach assumed that, contrary to the beliefs of almost all listeners and musicians reaching back over three centuries, music lacked the power to excite the emotions "beyond any of the other arts."[15]

Balanced structures, loosely focused tonalities, more translucent than opaque textures, and precise thematic content are stylistic attributes common to much of the music they wrote before the mid-1930s. Aggressive experimentation is not central to their thinking. Stylistic prototypes from the past, especially from the seventeenth and eighteenth centuries, may guide them. Older genres, like the symphony, concerto, and string quartet, still hold their attractions. Yet, the actual sound of their music is up-to-date and would never be confused with anything from the past. Nontriadic chord structures, prominent rhythmic patterns, and constant dissonance make their utterances genuinely contemporary.

Aaron Copland, born in Brooklyn in 1900, is a far more complicated person to describe than the five just discussed. This holds true for the music he wrote, the way he conceived of his relation with the public, and the listeners he attracted or repelled during his lifetime. For the moment, the early years of his career will come under scrutiny.

After his return in 1924 from France and study with Nadia Boulanger, he set about making a reputation for himself as a composer. His ballet *Grohg*, the *Organ Symphony*, and *Music for the Theatre* were all premiered in 1925, followed by the first performance of the Concerto for Piano in January 1927. His music struck sophisticated listeners as distinguished by somber weightiness, which now and again conveyed a measure of desolateness. This was the effect especially of the first two works, and to a lesser degree of the concerto. He imparted, more often than not, tart and harsh sensations. Passages that project anxiety, ironic wit, and hectic activity succeeded each other. On the whole, his was a rarefied expression, both urbane and abstruse. Warmly endearing tunes were not for him. Melodic ideas tended to be concise and energetic. They made no concessions to current tastes. The rich harmonic textures of romanticism were anathema. Therefore, resonances were precisely calculated, kept firm in texture, and never allowed to veer toward lushness. He avoided the dramatic rhetoric employed by composers in the recent past. There was no mellifluousness, no personal ardor to be found. Occasionally, the absence of contrasts made the music sound tedious.

One other element is detected in the music of the 1920s —jazz. Its rhythms and special sound techniques were more in evidence in *Music for the Theatre* and the Concerto for Piano, less in *Grohg* and the *Organ Symphony*. Copland was not a nationalist, certainly not in the same way that Henry Gilbert, John Powell, Arthur Farwell, and Scott Joplin were. The first three musicians had tried to identify with and encompass the spirit of a popular-music genre, an ethnic-American culture, or a particular region. By so doing, they were usually looking back to some tradition that had persisted into the present, and mining its musical resources—African-American folk music, Amerindian music, Virginia's traditional song and dance. Scott Joplin had closely identified with his own African-American background in his ragtime opera *Treemonisha* (1911). An aim of all four composers was to summon the mood of an era or manner of life different from theirs in a musical language that owed much to romantic scene painting.

Copland abstained from picturesque and romantic writing. He did believe that "Americans needed a kind of music they could recognize as their own. The jazz came by way of wanting to write this more immediately recognizable American music." It was identifiably au courant urban American and antiromantic. It even had a shock value with fairly staid symphony-goers. The use of jazz was internationally fashionable in the twenties. The Russian Igor Stravinsky and Frenchman Darius Milhaud had already demonstrated that it was compatible with modernity. Copland decided to incorporate jazz into his style.[16]

The *Organ Symphony* received a high compliment from Virgil Thomson when he told Nadia Boulanger: "The piece was exactly the Boulanger piece and exactly the American piece that several of us would have given anything to write and that I was overjoyed someone had written."[17] The work called for a large orchestra with six percussionists. Copland said that he himself got excited when he walked in on Walter Damrosch and the New York Symphony Orchestra rehearsing the Scherzo movement in January 1925, which was "very brilliant, brassy, and glamorous sounding" and had "a strong drive all the way through." He thought his rhythmic experimentation, including irregular note groupings and uneven accents, had gone very well: "The Scherzo was my idea of what could be done to adopt the raw material of jazz. I was not yet using jazz openly and directly; nevertheless, if you listen to the Scherzo even now [ca.1983], you hear rhythms that would not have been there if I had not been born and raised in Brooklyn."[18] He also felt that grandiose, dramatic, and tragic ideas were expressed to some degree in the rest of the work.[19]

Nevertheless, Copland did conclude that the symphony was "too European in inspiration" and tried to make amends in *Music for the Theatre*, where greater use of the jazz idiom helped it to sound as if only an American and a New Yorker at that, and not a European, could have written it.[20] He continued similarly with the Concerto for Piano. Unfortunately, few American listeners of the time were willing to accept jazz as a legitimate component of serious concert music, especially when it occurred in the many dissonant and polyrhythmic passages that Copland insisted upon. It was still considered a manifestation of American low-life and having no redeeming attributes. The liberation from repression that it connoted to modernists was alien to public thinking. Copland's music met with laughter or caustic remarks. Perhaps influenced by the lack of approval from listeners, Copland said: "With the Concerto I felt I had done all I could with the idiom, considering its limited scope. True, it was an easy way to be American in musical terms, but all American music could not possibly be confined to two dominant jazz moods: the 'blues' and the snappy number."[21] He also may have temporarily given up on the general music public.

One finds more serious introspection, an international rather than American stylistic orientation, and even less accommodation to prevalent tastes in the *Symphonic Ode* (1929), *Vitebsk Trio* (1929), *Piano Variations* (1930), and *Short Symphony* (1933). Chromaticism increases. Tonality grows very elusive. Expression turns more cryptic. Clues as to meaning are anything but forthright. Little by little what public he had began to fall away, in part put off by the music, in part deflected from concert attendance by the myriad problems attending the Great Depression. On the other hand, Copland is one of the few composers who can claim that a future audience was able to accept if not understand what a contemporary one could not. His *Music for the Theatre* and Concerto for Piano, especially, have gone over well with post-World War II listeners, to be sure not with everyone, but certainly with more than a scattering of men and women.

Like Copland, Virgil Thomson was one of the first American students of Nadia Boulanger, though he never completely accepted her teachings or thought himself a member of the Boulangerie. Unlike Copland, he stayed on in Paris until the onset of World War II, although he visited the United States from time to time. As was true of Copland, Stravinsky's neoclassicism excited his interest. However, from the beginning of his transatlantic sojourn, he gravitated toward the Dadaists, especially as represented by the French composer Erik Satie. In his first works, Thomson, like Satie, endeavored to belittle what he regarded as the pretentious and overly emotional music of the nineteenth century by satirizing it. He kept his own compositions succinct and uncomplicated. The deliberate impudence and bizarre juxtaposition of unconnected tunes and askew harmonies in his music allowed Thomson to startle snobbish people of conservative taste. The sophisticated deployment of pseudo-elevated rhetoric, stripped-down triadic consonance, and melodic, rhythmic, and harmonic clichés in strategically telling places contradicted what other composers of his own day took seriously. He seemed not even to take himself seriously.

Thomson's was also a nostalgic contemporaneity, evident when he recalled the homespun tunes and harmonies of shape-note hymns, the jazz and blues of his place of birth, Kansas City, Missouri, old folk songs of Anglo-Saxon America, and former and current American popular songs and dances. Paradoxically, his affection for all of this vernacular Americana emerges from the music. A third influence that shaped his outlook came through his friendship with Gertrude Stein, who supplied him with many of the texts he set to music. She honored words for themselves and their on-the-spot reverberations rather than just for what they meant. Thomson says that she and Satie changed his life.[22]

The *Sonata da Chiesa* (1926) for four winds and viola injected more dissonances into the musical fabric than his later pieces would. The listener is tossed outrageously from chorale to tango to fugue. Thomson hit his mark more squarely than perhaps he realized when he caused the ultra-serious Roger Sessions to react adversely to it with: "There is intellectualism, lack of clarity, diffuseness, and an uncomfortable sense of strain."[23] The *Symphony on a Hymn Tune* (1928) is both poignant and disconcerting. In addition, it radiates an engaging atmosphere of innocence. The hymn "How Firm a Foundation" forms the basis of the work, which also includes "Yes, Jesus Loves Me" and "For He's a Jolly Good Fellow." Sometimes the music intones solemn chorale-like passages; other times it turns into a jolly rollick. If the listener feels uncertain whether to laugh, sigh, or grit his teeth when listening to the *Symphony on a Hymn Tune*, he is not left in doubt in *Capital, Capital* (1927) for four male voices and piano, to a nonsensical text by Stein. Thomson delighted in the hilarity it conjured up among listeners. Jolly as it might be, the piece testified to the great care he exerted to realize the proper declamation of English words in his musical setting.

Gertrude Stein supplied him with the libretto for *Four Saints in Three Acts*, completed in 1928 and scored for orchestra in 1933. A shrewd eye for surprise and an urge to do things contentiously different guided his employment of an all-black cast and a dazzlingly-tinctured cellophane set. He recognized that this apparent story of religious life in medieval Spain was told in stream-of-consciousness fashion with words put together so that they defied anyone making sense of them. Thomson explains:

> My hope in putting Gertrude Stein to music had been to break, crack open, and solve for all time anything still waiting to be solved, which was almost everything, about English musical declamation. My theory was that if a text is set correctly for the sound of it, the meaning will take care of itself. And the Stein texts, for prosodizing in this way, were manna. With meanings already abstracted, or absent, or so multiplied that choice among them was impossible, there was no temptation toward tonal illustration, say, of birdie babbling by the brook or heavy hangs my heart. You could make a setting for sound and syntax only, then add, if needed, an accompaniment equally functional.[24]

Melodies are brief and hearken back to his Baptist-hymn religious upbringing. Thomson says that he had never been to Spain, nor did he try for an accurate historical recreation "when my librettist had assumed no such obligation. So I took my musical freedom, following her poetical freedom, and what came out was a virtually total recall of my southern Baptist childhood in Missouri."[25] These recalls alternate with stretches of speech-like patter, conversational or analogous to psalmodic recitation. Here and there are wisps of well-known American songs propelled by tango, waltz, and other American dance rhythms. Harmony remains unambiguous even rudimentary, content to remain in one key, and occasionally produces a bichordal clash. The opera's reception won it notoriety because of the astonishing nature of its contents. Several avant-gardists considered it a slap in their faces, owing to its utterly plain non-dissonant musical style.[26] It has not become a part of the standard operatic repertoire. Even today, audiences do not know how to interpret this and Thomson's other early works. Were listeners to take them as consequential and of lasting value or as witticisms and pertinent only to the period in which they were written?

A member of the neoclassic Boulangerie, Walter Piston did not own up to a direct jazz influence, as Copland did. Yet, he had played in dance bands during his youth, in order to make a living. Neither did popular music directly guide his pen. Music historians have described him as an internationalist, because sounds based on American jazz, popular, and folk music did not pop up at you in his scores. Yet all three Americanisms were allowed discretely to affect his style from the beginning. More open to view was Piston's adoption of Classical and Baroque structures and textures, like those of the passacaglia and fugue, and sonata-allegro form—in his *Symphonic Piece* (1927), Suite No. 1 for Orchestra (1929), Concerto for Orchestra (1933), String Quartet No. 1 (1933), and *Prelude and Fugue* (1934). His employment of dissonance is rarely strident. Intervals of the fourth and fifth subdue the harshness of seconds and sevenths. Tonality remains clear. The triad is not entirely banished from his harmonies. He was an extraordinary craftsman, knowing with certainty why he wrote every note that he did[27] and perceiving how to get what he wrote to sound exactly as he wished through an idiomatic handling of instruments.

For a long while, listeners did not embrace these early works, although they did not repudiate them either. Certainly a main deterrent to appreciation was the way Piston scrubbed most vestiges of romantic feeling out of his music. Otherwise, there was a great deal that was "old-fashioned" about his approach.[28] The public seems to be experiencing a change of heart now that the century is almost spent. Some music lovers have begun to understand that his first pieces were more emotionally neutral than neutered.

Unlike Piston, Roger Sessions was an uncomfortable neoclassicist from the beginning of his career. He was a student of Ernst Bloch rather than Boulanger, and an expatriate resident of Berlin, Florence, and Rome rather than Stravinsky's Paris, until his return to America in 1933. Yet his early ballet *The*

Black Maskers (1923) and to a lesser extent, the First Symphony (1930) and First Piano Sonata (1930) bear neoclassic Stravinskian markings. The ballet contained appealing music and was the most colorful score he ever wrote, but it was in a style from which he quickly decided to deviate. From 1923 on, his textures grow denser, his melodic lines longer, and his structural schemes more tightly argued than those of Stravinsky. So ordered and concentrated did his music become that it struck many as excessively prescribed by the intellect. The music was considered so stuffed with ideas that expression was imprisoned, so concisely precise in saying only what the composer had to say that it defeated understanding. He prized elevated musical thought, held musical humor in disdain, and abhorred any hint of nationalism, whether in sentiment or sound—and this included jazz. He would not direct an appeal to the senses, because it left a superficial impression. The result was music that was strong, firm, and tough to assimilate. It offered no instant gratification and, for most, no delayed gratification either—nothing that hospitably invited the public in to visit a while. Composers respected his earnestness and expertise. Very few people took kindly to his works.

The Contributions of Jazz

Several writers have characterized the years after World War I as the "Jazz Age" or "Jazz Epoch" owing to the surge in popularity of what had been the entertainment mostly of African-Americans. In the minds of most music writers of the 1920s, jazz was a more ubiquitous term than it became later in the century and comprehended both the music of the original jazz-oriented practitioners and the more highly rhythmic and syncopated popular dance music of the era. It is in this broader sense that the term is used here.

Until the Great Depression deepened, in the early thirties, all-white and all-black jazz ensembles freely roamed the United States and Europe finding eager listeners and dancers wherever they played. Deems Taylor, who noted jazz's end as a component of art music in the mid-1930s, said the music was amusing, exciting, and without emotion. Its best and worthiest examples, he said, sounded brilliant, exuberant, and "hard as nails." ("Hard was a favorite adjective for describing the latest music of the twenties. The word has already occurred in this chapter in connection with Varèse and Antheil.) Jazz allowed everybody "to forget everything but their bodies." Elie Siegmeister commented that the many American art composers who saw fit to introduce jazz into their music did so because it was fashionable. Jazz was "a plaything to be taken up for a while and then discarded in favor of the latest European style."[29]

Antheil's *Ballet Mécanique* and Copland's *Music for the Theatre* and Concerto for Piano have already received mention because they contained a significant coefficient of jazz. However, it was not the governing style in these works. More patently works derived from jazz and popular music were written by Antheil, Louis Gruenberg, George Gershwin, and William Grant Still. For example, Antheil in his Sonata for Violin, Piano, and Drum (1923) had a good time with a collection of diverse popular-tune fragments. His *Jazz Symphony* (1925) for piano and jazz band, though requested by Paul Whiteman, was premiered by an ensemble of W. C. Handy, with Antheil at the piano, before an enthusiastic audience. A good-natured work, it indulges in many humorous digressions, including musical bits by Scott Joplin and Igor Stravinsky. Like the audience attending the premiere, Virgil Thomson found it "terrific fun" to hear.[30]

After 1925, Antheil's style grew less mechanized, more melodic, and more inclined toward triadic harmonies. This direction is apparent in the *Symphony in F* (1926), the Concerto for Piano (1926) and the opera *Transatlantic* (1928). All of them are attractive works. The change displeased his militant backers, including Pound, and inaugurated a falling away of his support. Later, when he went ("sold out") to Hollywood and wrote music for films, almost all of the "serious" musicians disowned him and belittled his music. His pieces were criticized as derivative, uninspired, poorly crafted, and shallow. From then on, Antheil's performances were nil.

Yet, music lovers would have found a great deal of superior and pleasing music in his post-*Ballet Mécanique* works if obstacles had not impeded their reaching listeners. To give one instance, *Transatlantic* does not deserve oblivion. It is a bona fide American composition with a fertile use of jazz, traditional songs, and popular tunes or their facsimiles. Its cockeyed scene-shifts delineate a presidential election. A sure-footed sense of theater is always present. Elevated and vulgar moments succeed each other. Despite its splendid sound, it met with a predictable fate; critics with an animus against Antheil found it imitative of pieces by Shostakovitch and Gershwin, including their music written after the opera. One cannot blame Antheil for complaining:

> A few years later [after *Transatlantic*'s premiere] the Gershwins and their wonderful librettists put on a semi-opera called 'Of Thee I Sing.' Like 'Transatlantic,' it centered around an American election, and in much the same manner. But, as with my supposedly 'Shostakovitch style,' I should meekly like to re-emphasize here that 'Transatlantic' did not come after but before 'Of Thee I Sing.'[31]

For a while Louis Gruenberg almost specialized in jazz. Witness works with titles like *Daniel Jazz* (1924) for tenor, clarinet, trumpet and strings, *Jazz Suite* (1925) for orchestra, *Jazzettes* (1925) for violin and piano, *Jazzberries* (1925) for piano, and *Jazz-Masks* (1931) for piano. They were convincing and well-received pieces. Gruenberg was an earnest, straightforward, and somewhat cerebral composer, despite the wit that fizzes from his scores. His strong suit was adroit use of instruments and rhythm; his weak point, trepidation about sounding truly lyrical.

So long as he remained jazz-oriented, Gruenberg was regarded as in the musical vanguard.[32] When he removed himself from the vanguard in 1931 to write two stage works not directly tied to jazz, he began to lose the regard of many modernists. Then when he left for Hollywood, as with Antheil, he was dismissed altogether. Yet, *Jack and the Beanstalk* is a delightful "fairy opera for the childlike," equipped with sparkling and effervescent music. *The Emperor Jones*, a wild success at the Metropolitan with Lawrence Tibbett in the starring role, owes much of its triumph to Eugene O'Neill's play and the appearance of Tibbett. Most of the music remains in the background, accurately supportive of the drama but not really an entity in itself. One affecting musical moment is the spiritual-like song "Standin' in the Need of Prayer." Few music lovers are aware that he later wrote symphonies, orchestral rhapsodies, a violin concerto, chamber works, and musical stage dramas. He may not have composed any works indicative of consummate artistic achievement, but he did write fine music worthy of greater respect than it did receive and potentially of interest to more than a few listeners.

When he was young, the African-American composer William Grant Still faced a dilemma—which of his two diametrically different teachers should he heed, the experimentalist Varèse or the nationally-inclined George Chadwick? For a brief period, he emulated the former, feeling guilty for ignoring his own ethnic heritage and upset because no music lovers wanted to hear his avant-garde pieces, despite accolades from members of the International Composers' Guild. He commenced wondering if freedom from tradition had not placed him in the new prison of ultramodernism.[33] At the same time he was racking up a large amount of experience as an oboist, cellist, and arranger in the jazz and art-music world. Shortly, he decided to heed Chadwick's advice and became a voice for black America. William Grant Still then turned to a more orthodox style that was imaginative and, at the same time, sensitive to the emotional aspects of African-American history. Jazz, blues, and other musical material originating in America and Africa came into use or served to guide his own creativity. The symphonic *Africa* (1928), later withdrawn, tried to embody his changed outlook. His more successful ballet *Sahdji* (1930) followed. However, it was the widely approved *Afro-American Symphony* (1930), premiered on 29 October 1931, that won him deserved recognition as a serious and significant composer. Fresh, lyrical, individual, and skillfully orchestrated, it was a forerunner of many excellent pieces for concert hall and operatic stage. His music is potentially acceptable to a broad range of music lovers. Like so much other American music, little of what he wrote has remained in performance longer than the few months after the premiere.

George Gershwin was an anomaly in the art-music world. During his lifetime, "serious" composers conceded his abilities as a popular song writer. On the other hand, they either dismissed him as not worthy of the appellation of composer or hedged their acceptance so that people understood he was not a fully accredited member of the artistic fraternity. Nor did the conservative art-music critics care for the substitution of "vulgar" vernacular sounds for what was supposed to be a profound and earnest expression. He carried three strikes against him—he had not been educated to all the refinements of his art, his background was entirely in the popular-music field, and his concert music partook excessively of the commercial sounds with which he was usually associated. Worst of all, he was an entertainer, wrote to entertain, had won a huge following among ordinary men and women, and actually made a great deal of money from his music. To entertain was compatible with artistic excellence, he countered and pointed to the music of eminent nineteenth-century composers of songs, instrumental music, and opera. Regardless of what his critics have said, he was perhaps the most significant composer of the post-World War I period, certainly so to the thousands who gladly gathered to hear his music and his piano playing.

When he said that he regarded himself as "a modern romantic" who wrote unabashedly sentimental melodies, he was defying the proscriptions of the modern camp. He did not readily theorize or intellectualize about what he did. Once when asked about how he had come upon a complex rhythmic passage in his Concerto for Piano, he shook his head and said: "I feel things inside, and then I work them out—that's all."[34] This led to critics considering him musically naive, deficient not only in learning but in perception.

Gershwin furthered this impression among modernists when he asserted that the Machine Age was all right when it was applied to better music distribution through radio and recordings and to increasing the number of listeners. It was all wrong when it led to misguided composers writing machine music, which could never amount to anything of great significance. Composers had to write music as they always had. If music gave in to a machine mentality, it could no longer call itself art. Likewise, he wondered about the necessity for experimenting with sound. To musicians like Copland, jazz was a form of experimentation, employed as an intellectually driven critique of the Machine Age. To him, jazz was a natural and unfeigned means for expressing himself.[35]

He contradicted the pronouncements of the avant-garde when he declared his faith in the sensitivity of common men and women. Music was important to civilization because it was understood and enjoyed by people whatever their intelligence and education. Melody was the thing they valued most. That was why he tried to speak openly, plainly, and tunefully. Americans appreciated a down-to-earth, graphic idiom that was native to them. When people in small towns, who know little of symphonic music, failed to respond to, say, his *Rhapsody in Blue* or Concerto for Piano, they might lack experience with such music but not the possibility of understanding it eventually.[36] Nor did he think what he wrote was sacrosanct. If audiences refused to like his music, they were probably right. At any rate, he was always interested in listeners' reactions and open to suggestions for improving his works.[37]

A Gershwin biographer, Edward Jablonski, states that Gershwin was constantly being abused, when not ignored, in the pages of the *Musical Quarterly* and *Modern Music*. "Serious" composers and modernistically inclined critics continued their attacks throughout his lifetime. Not surprisingly, Paul Rosenfeld thought Gershwin was "of a lower order," with "little feeling for reality," and a receiver of "second-hand ideas and ecstasies." What he composed "scarcely transcends the level of things made to please an undiscriminating public." His ideas were "weak and cheap"; his structures were deficient; he lacked artistic conviction and insight. Gershwin was musical materialism personified.[38]

On 12 February 1924, Gershwin became famous or infamous in the art-music world, depending on the point of view. On that evening, Paul Whiteman presented the *Rhapsody in Blue*, heralding Gershwin's arrival at the art-music scene. The composer described it "as a sort of musical kaleidoscope of America —of our vast melting pot, of our unduplicated national pep, of our blues, our metropolitan madness."[39] The piece obviously stemmed from jazz and Broadway in both musical and instrumental performance techniques. The repetitive and meandering structure and awkward shifts from one section to another were equally obvious. The music public did not care. People loved the infectious melodies and rhythms.

The Concerto for Piano, first heard on 3 December 1925, hewed to the same vernacular idiom and assembled its sections somewhat better, despite his scarcely knowing anything about how to put a concerto together. The contrast of the Charleston passages of the first, the urban blues mood of the second, and the frenzied pulsations of the last movement proved highly pleasing to audiences. According to Merle Armitage, the capacity audience consisted of "one-third curious intellectuals, one-third conservative subscribers, and one-third Gershwin devotees."[40] Like *Rhapsody in Blue*, it became a perennial favorite with the music public.

Even better organized than the concerto, *An American in Paris* made a first appearance on 13 December 1928. Predictably, critics of modernist inclination found the composer deficient in knowledge and talent and the piece deficient in substance. Arthur Mendel, for one, wrote in *Modern Music* that the piece contained scarcely any estimable music. The orchestration was extraordinarily ugly. The taxi horns failed to amuse.[41] He, Oscar Thompson, and Herbert Peyser hated it. On the other hand, the public accepted it as their own.

The "American folk opera" *Porgy and Bess* received its initial performance on 10 October 1935. Although it opened to mixed reviews, the opera went on to become one of the glories of American music. Ostensibly about African-American life, it ultimately addressed an international humanity. Decade after decade, audiences all over the world have appreciated how the music gave expression to universal human feelings through affecting dramatic scenes and one captivating song after another. Gershwin was the American people's "art" composer par excellence, and the American people determinedly kept his music alive heedless of all criticism.

A Miscellany of Composers

Gershwin was one of the few composers of the twenties and early thirties to become widely popular. The four composers that are discussed next also succeeded in pleasing the general music public, though not to the extent that Gershwin did.

Assuredly, one unreconstructed romantic, Howard Hanson, stuck out from the crowd of American composers who started their professional lives in the 1920s. Hanson did not wander abroad for his musical education but was satisfied to study at home under Percy Goetchius. He was proud of his Swedish inheritance and admired the North-European composers Edvard Grieg and Jan Sibelius. His first garnering of considerable public attention came with his First Symphony, *Nordic* (1922). In it he sounds at his best and most characteristic. Pliant and eloquent songfulness, dark, modal and sometimes bitonal harmony, sumptuous sonorities, and suspenseful climaxes convey deeply perceived sentiments to listeners. His is true American music, he says, because it is written by an American, reflecting his descent from recently arrived immigrants, and capturing the grandeur of the prairies in his native Nebraska.[42] A sincere conservative, he would not leave his audience behind by adventuring into unexplored musical territory.

Another inspired early work was *The Lament for Beowulf* (1925), for chorus and orchestra. The epic text, rendered into contemporary English by William Morris and A. J. Wyatt, describes compellingly the burial of this hero. Hanson first sketched out his musical ideas in Scotland, "in an environment [that was] rugged, swept with mist." His intention was to achieve in the music "the austerity and stoicism and the heroic atmosphere of the poem. This is true Anglo-Saxon poetry and may well serve as a basis for music composed by an American."[43] The musical result was woeful, stirring, and majestic, and its first audiences found it so.

A third composition, the Second Symphony, *Romantic* (1930) was extremely well received by the music public. Hanson says that he named it *Romantic* as a protest "against the mode of belittling anything in the least beautiful by calling it 'romantic'."[44] He says further:

> [The Second Symphony] represents my escape from the rather bitter type of modern musical realism which occupies so large a place in contemporary thought. Much contemporary music seems to me to be showing a tendency to become entirely too cerebral. I do not believe that music is primarily a matter of the intellect, but rather a manifestation of the emotions. I have therefore aimed in this symphony to create a work that was young in spirit, lyrical and romantic in temperament, and simple and direct in expression.[45]

With this symphony, Hanson scored another success with the general public. By stressing melody and emotion, he was giving people the sort of contemporary music for which they had hungered and which modernists scorned.

We now come to two composers, Douglas Moore and Randall Thompson, whose first achievements were in instrumental music and who then went on to win much greater fame as writers of vocal music. Both were lyrical, tonal, sometimes modal, agreeable in harmony, and now and then given to heightened dissonance. Both hewed to simplicity and echoed the several vernacular musical languages of America. Moore attracted a great deal of attention in 1926 when the Cleveland Orchestra performed his good-humored suite *The Pageant of P. T. Barnum* (1924), in which one hears country fiddle tunes, spirituals, and marches. The symphonic poem *Moby Dick* followed in 1928, A *Symphony of Autumn* in 1930, and the *Overture on an American Tune* in 1932. However, Moore did not come to a full realization of his talents until 1938, with his one-act opera *The Devil and Daniel Webster*.

Randall Thompson, beginning in 1922, composed many instrumental pieces but did not achieve a notable triumph until 1932, when his Second Symphony (1931) was first heard. Music akin to jazz, it utilizes blues, spirituals, and Broadway tunes in its pages. Listeners loved its animation, wit, and absence of ostentation. Nevertheless, it was not until *The Peaceable Kingdom* (1936) and *Alleluia* (1940), both for unaccompanied chorus, that his true forte revealed itself. *Alleluia* has gone on to become an all-time favorite among choruses in the United States.

Hanson modestly claimed to mirror Nebraska in his music; Roy Harris, with an ego larger than that of most musicians, staked out the entire West as his claim. At its best, his music is expansive, proceeds in powerful flowing lines, and achieves a craggy potency. This was what listeners admired. At its worst, the music does not know when or how to stop, rhetoric turns bombastic, and sections and movements are awkwardly constructed. Listeners grew bored, especially when he often seemed to be writing the same piece over and over again. Harris valued tonality, but was not averse to employing two or more different harmonies simultaneously. He wanted to sound indigenous, but did not forthrightly incorporate musical Americana into his early works to the extent that Moore and Thompson did.

In 1925, Harris gave the public his first work, *Andante* for orchestra. Slowly his reputation built up, until genuine enthusiasm greeted his *Symphony 1933*. Like Moore and

Thompson, his greatest acclaim came later, in 1939, with his Third Symphony.

Supporters of the Vanguard

From the onset of the modern era, music lovers, not many to be sure, listened to specific contemporary works and liked what they heard. Their delight was more a response to the actual sound of a piece, less a result of careful study of the composer's intentions and his technical realization of those intentions. Nor did it originate solely from obedience to a set of aesthetic principles. In this fashion listeners could be said to have "understood" the music without necessarily having extensive knowledge of its structure, melodic contouring, harmonic construction, and rhythmic manipulations. Oftentimes it was this sort of intuitive reaction that moved Paul Rosenfeld, for example, to enjoy or abhor a work and to discover talent in unknown musicians. No wholesale endorsement of everything written by a group of composers followed. Taste was particular and appreciative. Such listeners represented the more sincere portion of the vanguard audience. They were a minority within a minority. The negative comments that follow do not apply to them.

The "Vanguard Audience" is a phrase that Harold Rosenberg uses to describe the new coalition that formed after the Armory Show in New York. Its components included forward-minded critics and loyal followers friendly toward artistic innovation in one or more of its forms. Newness soon became a mark of worth, and modernity a crusade for most of them. Composers might falter between atonality, neoclassicism, or outright experimentation; a hard core of believers did not usually share their uneasiness. Some segment of this coalition welcomed one musical novelty or another, however glaring its illogical suppositions and its conflict with other current novelties. The devotion of these supporters, restated with every newly arrived avant-gardist, insured the perpetuation of a shared attitude that advocated the desirability of change. It did not, however, insure genuine understanding of what an artist was attempting to accomplish. It did help solidify a folklore surrounding modernity. The avant-garde subscribers to this folklore in their approval of the new and condemnation of any backsliding revealed the involuntary reactions characteristic of an ongoing tradition. For almost a century this coalition battled for innovation in American music, urging listeners to accept anything current that some recognized leader proclaimed to be worthwhile.

It has witnessed crusade supersede crusade—to begin with, there were the composers endorsed by Pound, and others dedicated to newness immediately after World War I, who in turn succumbed to the jazzists and neoclassicists of the late twenties. The latter subsequently gave way to the humanistic Americanists of the thirties. Then the atonalists of the fifties overwhelmed the Americanists. Not for long—the atonalists soon gave way to the iconoclasts of the sixties. Iconoclasts like Cage proved that by the sixties any composer promising something utterly different could expect a constituency of some sort to back him in his battle for performance and demand for financial sponsorship. The sixties also completed a full circle for modernity as its iconoclasts returned to the precepts urged around World War I by Cowell and Varèse.[46]

Whether European or American, private or public, the vanguard coalition that turned out for concerts gradually grew smaller and smaller. When Cowell's music received performance in his home state, California, during the twenties, commentators observed that sometimes no large number of people attended. One must keep in mind that Cowell was relatively unknown to the public and what music lovers thought he offered were demonstrations of musical experiments rather than finished artistic works. The few people who did appear at the concerts consisted chiefly of music critics, University of California faculty members, and students. Cowell also gave concerts that were better attended, which meant not by thousands but by three or four hundred. By the early thirties, however, tiny audiences at contemporary concerts had become the rule. Elie Siegmeister, after surveying the music world of the early thirties, explained that: "Modernism galvanized the young composers, but was royally rejected by major orchestras and the broad musical public, and survived in those tiny concerts attended by 100—always the same 100—people." Even, New York, the center for American modernism, failed to produce a respectable sized group of attendees. Speaking of conditions around 1930, Lehman Engel admitted that no composer he knew had any considerable constituency and could not earn a living from his music. There were many special concerts given by the League of Composers, the International Society for Contemporary Music, and the New School, but few attended these concerts. Moreover, the attendees were "so to speak, 'in the family'—and certainly nobody earned a penny from such performances. Even the prestige gained from such programs was en famille prestige about which the general public could not have cared less. This factor, I think, also accounted for the cultish quality of the music itself."[47]

With sarcastic wit, Lucius Beebe has described the vanguard coalition that attended the premiere of Thomson's *Four Saints in Three Acts*, in a 299-seat theater in Hartford, Connecticut. He describes "the art enthusiasts" arriving by Rolls Royce, airplane, and Pullman compartments and making grand entries into the theater ("some of the more enterprising got around [to entering] as many as five times"). During intermissions, the most au courant cried tears of joy because of how beautiful it all was. Soon everybody was "letting down their back hair and crying in corners for beauty." John Houseman, who reproduced the Beebe comments in *Run-Through: A Memoir*, added that when the opera opened in New York, the men and women who attended opening night consisted of "the press and the fourteen hundred 'members of the Social Register and Intelligentsia'."[48]

Several writers on the music of the time have concluded that the intellectuals constituting a large part of the vanguard coalition often had little understanding of the music they were supposed to be appreciating. They were a band of literate, informed, and articulate men and women, self-conscious about their position in society and appropriating for themselves the advisory position proper to cultural leaders. Thomson claimed many intellectuals were hung up on aesthetic theories and searched for something he scornfully describes as the "manifestation of the Modern Spirit." This band also never hesitated to lecture to musicians about correct taste and was more certain of what was musically right and wrong than the composers themselves. If the composer deviated from its notion of rightness, he was apt to become ostracized—as was Ornstein and Antheil after they modified their radical styles.

Nor were the composers present at concerts always supportive of each other. At New York's concerts given by the International Guild, the composers, when their own music was not being performed, could be seen, according to Louise Varèse, "running up and down the aisles, greeting friends, chatting loudly, clapping one another on the back." At concerts given by the League of Composers, the concert-goers comprised "a rather high leaven of the 'musical intelligentsia'." Yet, when confronted by "the newest trends," it fidgeted and tittered. "There was a temptation to be on the qui vive for some sensational effect to laugh at" even though that was not what the composer intended, said Claire Reis.[49]

When the League of Composers once gave an all-Schoenberg concert, Reis, sitting close to Schoenberg, saw him get extremely upset at the admirers of modern music on hand, who presumably included sophisticates of every sort, including critics and composers. A song was performed with the piano accompanist playing in the wrong clef. Schoenberg winced throughout the rendition. Yet, an enthusiastic burst of applause greeted its conclusion and an annoyed Schoenberg was forced to rise and take a bow: "The audience [and probably Reis] had not been aware, however, of any departure from the original score. Perhaps that, in itself, disturbed Schoenberg."[50]

The music public as a whole had gradually proved indifferent to modernity; large segments of the vanguard coalition were suspect. Every American composer whose music revealed a noteworthy modification of the prevalent styles quickly realized the reality of this. What he therefore found essential was acceptance by some coterie willing to bolster his aspirations. Since so many Americans were trying to make their reputations in Paris during the 1920s, acceptance by a Parisian salon was a major requirement, if only because European acceptance opened the door to American acceptance. Antheil said that fortunately he had Ezra Pound to champion him in Paris during the early twenties and direct his path to the Parisian salons. Because European music critics expected bribes for decent reviews and claques cheered on whoever paid them, the audience's response to new music was not trustworthy. Hence acceptance by the musical salons, whose members passed sentence and bestowed status, was important.[51]

Thomson said that an all-Thomson concert introduced him to Parisians, but the dominant musical circle (which included Jean Cocteau, Darius Milhaud, Georges Auric, and Arthur Honegger) would not let him enter. Commissions for new works never materialized. One result was that it kept him an American composer and eliminated enticements toward becoming someone different. He did, however, eventually become part of a Parisian circle, one that included Gertrude Stein, especially, but also Sylvia Beach, Lincoln Kirstein, the painter Marcel Duchamp, the sculptor Jo Davidson, the writers James Joyce, Ezra Pound, and Max Jacob, and the composers George Antheil, Theodore Chanler, Vittorio Rieti, Igor Markevitch, and Paul Bowles.[52] Whether the circle was interested or dominant enough to further the ambitions Thomson entertained was another matter.

When Thomson visited New York in the winter of 1928-29, Carl Van Vechten introduced him to several important opinion-makers—Mabel Dodge Luhan, Emily Clark, Muriel Draper, Blanche Knopf, and Ettie Stettheimer, among them. Nothing came of the introduction. He was asked to evening socials where he was expected to provide musical entertainment, but nobody would pay him for his trouble.

A group that could have provided much needed support, the League of Composers looked at Thomson's scores but accepted none for performance; so did Alma Wertheim's Cos Cob Press, but it accepted none for publication. This was New York's way of "letting me know I was no part of their power-group." Later, both opened the door a crack for him. Part of his problem, of course, was that his base at the time was Paris and not New York.

In 1931, Copland got Thomson to write articles for *Modern Music*. While so doing, Thomson had to keep in mind the political viewpoints of, and the differences between, New York's coteries and those of Paris. After *Four Saints in Three Acts* premiered in 1934, he made modernist circles angry:

> After twenty years of everybody's trying to make music just a little bit louder and more unmitigated and more complex than anybody else's, naturally everybody's sounded pretty much alike. When we went them one better and made music that was

simple, and harmonious, the fury of the vested interests of modernism flared up like a gas-tank. That fury still burns [1939] in academic places. In my own case it is strongest where I was educated. At Harvard and among the Nadia Boulanger coterie in Paris I am considered a graceless whelp, a frivolous mountebank, an unfair competitor, and a dangerous character.[53]

When Thomson became the music critic for the *New York Herald Tribune*, in 1940, he held a powerful position. Composers and performers saw him now become a strong coterie of one, able to make or break them. Disapproval of his music quickly abated while performances increased.

Copland, who returned from Paris to live in New York, was far more successful at the early stage of his career in joining an important coterie, one that revolved around Alfred Stieglitz's gallery and Paul Rosenfeld's apartment. In one or the other place, Copland said, he met with the photographer Paul Strand, the painters John Marin and Georgia O'Keeffe, and the writers Waldo Frank, Edmund Wilson, Hart Crane, Lewis Mumford, and e. e. cummings. Edmund Wilson augments the list of Rosenfeld's familiars to include Ornstein, Varèse, Marianne Moore, and the Stettheimers.[54]

What did composers need: coteries for strength and patrons for money. Fortunately for composers, money and willing patrons of the arts were relatively plentiful in the twenties. Thomson, for example, despite what he claimed was a lack of backing, did receive financial aid from Mrs. Chester Whiten Lasell and Emily Crane Chadbourne. Antheil had a liberal patron in Mrs. Mary Louise Bok. Copland got money from Alma Wertheim; then influential supporters helped him to win Guggenheim Fellowships; when the fellowships ran out, Rosenfeld secured him a lecturer's position at the New School for Social Research.[55] Several other prominent composers could have told similar stories. Through patrons, they could live and work segregated from the larger American populace, which dismissed them, and the regular musical establishment, which disregarded them.

Patrons who helped composers financially did not necessarily enjoy the music. They might believe that aiding modern composers was an obligation for the affluent. Obligation did not necessarily entail a love for their compositions. As a case in point, Mary Louise Bok for years supplied Antheil with money but showed little affection for his music. When wealthy Mrs. Christian Gross, wife of the First Secretary of the American Embassy, wished admission into Paris's intellectual circles, she solicited the advice of Thomson. He got together with Antheil and devised a plan of inviting the intelligentsia (writers, painters, composers, and assorted thinkers) to her home for a series of concerts. Thomson and Antheil allowed only their own works any space on the programs. Mrs. Gross had her entrée and was satisfied. Enjoying the music (*Sonata da Chiesa*, *Ballet Méchanique*) was not part of the deal.[56]

After examining all of the evidence, one must conclude that the composers and most of the vanguard coalition (including intellectuals, literary figures, patrons, etc.) were frequently at variance with one another. Composers hoped for listeners who would show real understanding of the music itself and for an audience that "would patronize the concerts for more serious reason than just to be shocked" or to keep up with fashion, wrote Reis. Some of the music played "did cause hearers to have disagreeable reactions," she added. "Because our 'inner group' was somewhat inclined to be fanatic in the cause of modern music, we did not always sympathize quickly with those who did seem actually to suffer." She witnessed Walter Naumberg, who had funded the Naumberg Music Foundation, gag at the performance of a Schoenberg piece. He exclaimed: "Claire, this is the first time in my life that music has nauseated me!" Instead of offering sympathy, she replied: "In my zeal to uphold modern music at all costs, perhaps I reacted a little spitefully, for I replied, 'Well, I'm glad at least to hear you admit that contemporary music had so much effect on you'."[57]

From everything that has been said, it is apparent that the composer's relation to most supporters of modernity was not all that he wanted it to be. Scarcely anyone of them really understood what the musical artist was trying to do. Indeed, composers had problems trying to understand each other.

The General Public for Music

Finley Peter Dunne's Mr. Dooley, a man of the people, once posed as one of the newfangled intellectuals crossing the cusp of modernity. This wise man looked over the American citizenry and found only the unredeemable masses: "An' who ar're th'mob that directs this country? A lot iv coarse, rough people, who ar're sawin' up lumber an' picklin' pork, an' who niver had a thought iv th' Higher Life that makes men aspire to betther things an' indijestion. They ar're ye'er fathers an' mine, young gintlemen. Can I say worse thin that? An' to think iv' th' likes iv thim runnin' this governmint!" Dunne's widespread readership would have known exactly what sort of person he was lampooning.

Dunne personifies the intellectual in a "Pro-fissor Windhaul" who had unleashed a savage attack on Abraham Lincoln, then declared: "Me own opinyon iv th' arth is that it is about twenty-eight years old. That is as far as I go back. . . . Th' opinyon I have iv Shakespeare is so low that I will not express it befure ladies. I ain't sayin' that his wurruks have not been pop'lar among th' vulgar. An' he might have amounted to something if he had been ijjicated, but his language is base, an' he had no imagination. Th' gr-reatist potes th' wurruld has projooced are Ransom Stiggs an' J. B. Mulcoon iv Keokuk. . . . J. B. Mulcoon has discovered more rhymes f'r dear thin Al Tinnyson iver heerd iv."[58]

Dunne had satirically invoked the views of modernists that I have previously described and indicated that the ordinary American knew quite well what these views were—the dismissal of the common people, repudiation of history, ignorance about the past, forsaking of tradition, and elevation of untested contemporary figures in arts and letters above former giants. Louis Filler says that people, not ideas, interested Dunne and his Mr. Dooley. Both thought that the common run of Americans basically longed for decency and dignity, "and—despite World War I—were rather worthwhile and meriting regard."[59] Dunne, through Mr. Dooley, might also have added that when the public saw a musical work had come out supposedly in the spirit of science, and that happened pretty frequently, they felt in their bones the result had nothing to do with art; furthermore, they thought that a democratic composer wanted a work to communicate with the public and accepted responsibility if he failed to do so. On the other hand, an artist was a snob who wrote to please himself and belabored the public if it was not pleased by the outcome.[60] For this reason (though not the only reason), they took Gershwin to their hearts and spurned Varèse. The belaboring of the music public was far more consequential than that of other art publics since the composer needed performers and audiences numbering more than a handful. Equally baffling, he refused to accept that symphony orchestras, opera companies, and most chamber ensembles somehow had to retain the affection of this public in order to remain viable as institutions.

Nevertheless, there are no grounds for believing that the public had entirely blocked its ears to contemporary music. During the first decades of the century, most men and women would have known next to nothing about art music. Only a few cities boasted professional performing groups. Those fortunate urban Americans who could attend concerts and operatic presentations were mostly new to art music. Bach, Mozart, Beethoven, Brahms, and other prominent European composers of the past were recent discoveries and, in a special way, struck them as contemporary. They had not completely made up their minds about musical modernity.

My discussion of the vanguard coalition tells only half the story of the turnout for contemporary concerts. During the twenties and, to a lesser extent, the early thirties, some members of the ordinary music public were also represented at these performances. And of course they were present in much larger numbers at performances of new music by established ensembles like the Boston Symphony Orchestra. Several writers have commented on the public's exceptional willingness to hear and consider innovative compositions of every kind that prevailed then. Listeners might laugh at the results, as they did once when Cowell was twirling his thunderstick and it accidentally went sailing over the heads of the audience. Yet, the public for a while was fascinated by Cowell's musical offerings.[61] Or they might laugh alongside the composer, as they did when Thomson's *Capitals, Capitals* was heard in February 1929. The bravos of the public, the entertainment the piece gave, and the intellectual excitement it aroused pleased Thomson. His attitude was the exception rather than the rule among modernists. In addition, when contemporary concerts featured the less revolutionary modernists, the public might come in droves, as they did for the American Composers' Concerts that Howard Hanson commenced giving at Rochester in May 1925. The composer William Grant Still sums up the public's reactions during the twenties and early thirties by saying that the American audience of the past was willing to listen to something new, citing the audiences for Dr. Hanson's American Composers' Concerts, in Rochester, who "performed a great service for native composers by that willingness." Still also praises the audiences who attended the concerts of the International Composers' Guild in New York's Aeolian Hall. He states, "They provided sharp and immediate reactions: Sometimes approval, sometimes disapproval. As the years went on and the music that was offered continued to be, in a large degree, the same sort of music which had been disapproved, the audiences lost much of their early interest, and even lost the energy to hiss and protest." They would not listen to it over the radio, nor by attendance at concerts.[62]

What had happened was that the necessary balance of art between composer's and public's requirements, which was discussed in Chapter 1, had ceased to be a self-renewing process. The modernist viewpoint had disturbed the balance and the composer brashly capitalized on his perception of freedom by refusing to answer to any outside party. The composer's responsibility to himself alone rather than to the music community sanctioned the continuation of off-putting techniques. The public was allowed no active role. By 1933, Roger Sessions saw modern music as in a crisis, with a "reactionary tendency observable in every country." The public, he wrote, was finding itself out of touch not with one or another composer but with modern music in its entirety.[63]

By the thirties, a large number of music lovers wanted nothing to do with modernity. As a straw in the wind, Cowell had tried sending some copies of his *New Music* publications gratis to places all over the United States. On 19 April 1930, Dene Denny wrote to him, saying that people disliked having the issues forced upon them: "Peoria Public Library asked us to kindly cease the subscription—they were returning last year's copies for which they had not subscribed."[64] The unsettling music and assertive behavior of modernists was causing the defensive withdrawal of music lovers.

In 1932, Thomson warned his fellow musicians that "our high-brow music" was "dull," "notoriously ineffective," and "the bane of audiences at home and abroad." Five years later, Taylor said that audiences were getting used to musical discords but did mind "the absence of any discernible inevitability of relationship between these discords."[65]

Possibly for the first time in cultural history, composers were faced with a choice—they could live liberated and alone or help develop a workable if not viable musical environment. The music public craved equity, appreciation, sympathy, sounds that did not seem to abjure their civilization. However flawed their civilization, it was all they had. As the Great Depression deepened, human society was coming undone.

Composers began to feel that they could no longer afford the luxury of irritating others, although no one would deny them the right to do so. There was misery enough as it were. While hunger and joblessness had the upper hand, the oratory of modernists sounded preposterous. It was not an imposition on artistry to request that the needless maligning of ordinary men and women cease—which was the first step to be taken if a sense of unity was to grow. By the mid-thirties it was becoming clear that there was one fundamental criterion by which all parties had to live—if the composer could not exist completely independent of his society, he had to meet it halfway. In truth no artist could accomplish something durable if he and the public that came to hear him did not consent to honor some particular rules.

Those who refused these terms faced exile, sometimes without remission. Antheil provided an early example. He lamented in 1945: "If the public still thinks of me at all, it probably thinks of me as the composer of this damned 'Ballet Mécanique.' . . . It is frankly my nightmare, this in spite of the fact that since 1925 I have never again touched the idea of 'mechanism' in music." However, he could not accept the fact that the American public had disliked the piece for its music: "It has . . . been in bad repute in America only because it once endured a wrongly advertised and badly represented performance in Carnegie Hall."[66]

By the mid-thirties, the problem for many American composers was how to rid themselves of the impedimenta of modernism and how to reshape their music to win over an audience more than suspicious of any of their musical offerings.

Notes to Chapter 3

[1] Aaron Copland, *Music and Imagination* (New York: Mentor, 1959), 33.

[2] Martha L. Manion, *Writings about Henry Cowell* (New York: Institute for Studies in American Music, Brooklyn College, 1982), 98.

[3] Manion, *Writings about Henry Cowell*, 2-3.

[4] Edgard Varèse, "The Liberation of Sound," in Benjamin Boretz and Edward T. Cone, eds., *Perspectives on American Composers* (New York: Norton, 1971), 28-29, 32; see also Louise Varèse, *Varèse, A Looking-Glass Diary* (London: Davis-Paynter, 1973), 240.

[5] Fernand Ouellette, *Edgard Varèse*, trans. Derek Coltman (New York: Orion, 1968), 90.

[6] Sanborn Pitts, "The 1925-1926 Season," *Modern Music* 4 (May-June, 1926): 5-6.

[7] Ouellette, *Edgard Varèse*, 89.

[8] George Antheil, *Bad Boy of Music* (1945, reprint New York: Da Capo, 1981), 29.

[9] Antheil, *Bad Boy of Music*, 137.

[10] Deems Taylor, *Of Men and Music* (New York: Simon & Schuster, 1943), 83-84.

[11] Antheil, *Bad Boy of Music*, 190.

[12] Nicolas Slonimsky, "Composers of New England," *Modern Music* 7 (February-March, 1930): 26; Rita Mead, *Henry Cowell's New Music, 1925-1936* (Ann Arbor, MI: UMI Research Press, 1981), 77.

[13] Mead, *Henry Cowell's New Music, 1925-1936*, 141-42.

[14] Riegger states these conclusions in *American Composers on American Music*, ed. Henry Cowell (1933, reprint New York: Ungar, 1962), 180-81. The Riegger quotation comes from Stephen Spackman, *Wallingford Riegger: Two Essays in Musical Biography* (New York: Institute for Studies in American Music, Brooklyn College, 1982), 37.

[15] The first quotation is from Aaron Copland, "Music Since 1920," *Modern Music* 5 (March-April, 1928): 19; the second, from Copland, *Music and Imagination*, 19.

[16] Edward Cone, "Conversations with Aaron Copland," in *Perspectives on American Composers*, ed. Boretz and Cone, 138.

[17] Virgil Thomson, *Virgil Thomson* (New York: Knopf, 1966), 71.

[18] Aaron Copland and Vivian Perlis, *Copland, 1900 through 1942* (New York: St. Martin's/Marek, 1984), 103.

[19] Cone, "Conversations with Aaron Copland," 138.

[20] Aaron Copland, *Our New Music* (New York: Whittlesey House, 1941), 225-26; Copland and Perlis, *Copland, 1900 through 1942*, 124. The reference to his sounding like a New Yorker was made by Henry F. Gilbert, in "Notes on a Trip to Frankfurt in the Summer of 1927," *Musical Quarterly* 16 (1930): 26-27.

[21] Copland, *Our New Music*, 227.

[22] Thomson, *Virgil Thomson*, 46.

[23] Roger Sessions, "An American Evening Abroad," *Modern Music* 4 (November-December, 1926): 35.

[24] Thomson, *Virgil Thomson*, 90.

[25] Virgil Thomson, in the jacket notes to "Virgil Thomson: *Four Saints in Three Acts*, for the LP recording Nonesuch 79035.

[26] Virgil Thomson, *The State of Music* (New York: Morrow, 1939), 216.

[27] When I began study with him in his composition seminar, he examined a score I had brought in, then isolated a measure on the third page, and said: "Defend that measure. Why is it there?"

[28] Piston used this term to describe his writing for instruments; see Peter Westergaard, "Conversations with Walter Piston," in *Perspectives on American Composers*, 163.

[29] Deems Taylor, *Of Men and Music*, 75, 78; Elie Siegmeister, jacket notes for the LP recording Vox Turnabout TV-S 34640: *Elie Siegmeister: Flute Concerto, Clarinet Concerto*.

[30] Linda Whitesitt and Charles Amirkhanian, in *The New Grove Dictionary of American Music*, eds. H. Wiley Hitchcock and Stanley Sadie (London: Macmillan, 1986), s.v. "Antheil, George."

[31] Antheil, *Bad Boy of Music*, 250.

[32] See Randall Thompson, "The Bartered Cow," *Modern Music* 9 (November-December, 1931): 32.

[33] *William Grant Still and the Fusion of Cultures in American Music*, ed. Robert Bartlett Haas (Los Angeles: Black Sparrow, 1972), 115.

[34] Edward Jablonski, *Gershwin* (Boston: Northeastern University Press, 1990), 123; see also the "Preface," x.

[35] *The American Composer Speaks*, ed. Gilbert Chase (Baton Rouge, LA: Louisiana State University Press, 1966), 144-45; jacket notes on LP recording Seraphim S-60174: *Gershwin: Rhapsody in Blue, An American in Paris*.

[36] Charles, Schwartz, *Gershwin, His Life and Music* (Indianapolis, IN: Bobbs-Merrill, 1973), 93; Isaac Goldberg, *George Gershwin*, supplemented by Edith Garson (New York: Ungar, 1958), 354; *The American Composer Speaks*, ed. Chase, 143; Claire R. Reis, *Composer, Conductors, and Critics* (New York: Oxford University Press, 1955), 50.

[37] Jablonski, *Gershwin*, 101-02.

[38] Jablonski, *Gershwin*, xii-xiii; Paul Rosenfeld, *An Hour with American Music* (Philadelphia: Lippincott, 1929), 138-39; Paul Rosenfeld, *Discoveries of a Music Critic* (New York: Harcourt, Brace, 1936), 265-66, 270-72.

[39] Schwartz, *Gershwin*, 77.

[40] Merle Armitage, *George Gershwin, Man and Legend* (New York: Duell, Sloan, and Pearce, 1958), 47.

[41] Arthur Mendel, "First Fruits of the Season," *Modern Music* 6 (January-February, 1929): 31.

[42] John Tasker Howard, *Our American Music*, 4th ed. (New York: Crowell, 1965), 74-75; Milton Cross and David Ewen, *The Milton Cross New Encyclopedia of the Great Composers and Their Music*, I, rev. (Garden City, NY: Doubleday, 1969), 452.

[43] Madeleine Goss, *Modern Music-Makers: Contemporary American Composers* (New York: Dutton, 1952), 228.

[44] Edward Royce, "Howard Hanson," in *American Composers on American Music*, ed. Cowell, 98.

[45] Harold Gleason and Warren Becker, *20th-Century American Composers*, 2nd ed. (Bloomington, Indiana: Frangipani, 1980), 81.

[46] My discussion of the vanguard audience owes a great deal to Harold Rosenberg, *The Anxious Object* (New York: Horizon, 1964), 191-92. I differ from Rosenberg in one respect. He found the "Vanguard Audience" to be monolithic, nondiscriminating, and enthusiastic about every modern style. In music, this was not completely so.

[47] Elie Siegmeister, "Three Points of View," *Musical Quarterly* 65 (1979): 282; Mead, *Henry Cowell's New Music*, 55; Lehman Engel, *This Bright Day: An Autobiography* (New York: Macmillan, 1974), 44.

[48] John Houseman, *Run-Through: A Memoir* (New York: Simon & Schuster, 1972), 110, 122.

[49] Virgil Thomson, *The State of Music* (New York: Morrow, 1939), 9; Varèse, *Varèse, A Looking-Glass Diary*, 212; Reis, *Composers, Conductors, and Critics*, 50-51.

[50] Reis, *Composer, Conductors, and Critics*, 198.

[51] A. Walter Kramer, "American Composers, III: Louis Gruenberg," *Modern Music* 8 (November-January, 1928): 3; Antheil, *Bad Boy of Music*, 118-19.

[52] *Selected Letters of Virgil Thomson*, ed. Tim and Vanessa Weeks Page (New York: Summit, 1988), 68.

[53] Thomson, *The State of Music*, 116, 134-35, 137-38, 207. The quotation may be found on page 216.

[54] Copland and Perlis, *Copland, 1900 through 1942*, 101-02, 125; Jerome Mellquist and Lucie Wiese, eds., *Paul Rosenfeld, Voyager in the Arts* (New York: Creative Age, 1948), 9.

[55] Copland, *Our New Music*, 225; Kathleen Hoover and John Cage, *Virgil Thomson: His Life and Music* (New York: Yoseloff, 1959), 67; Antheil, *Bad Boy of Music*, 19; Cone, "Conversations with Aaron Copland," 136 and 139.

[56] Hoover and Cage, *Virgil Thomson*, 55.

[57] Reis, *Composers, Conductors, and Critics*, 53.

[58] Finley Peter Dunne, *The World of Mr. Dooley*, ed. Louis Filler (New York: Collier Books, 1962), 83-84.

[59] Louise Filler, "Introduction," to Dunne, *The World of Mr. Dooley*, 19.

[60] Dunne, in the voice of Mr. Dooley, makes analogous observations, in *The World of Mr. Dooley*, 29, 73.

[61] See, for example, John Rockwell, in *The New Grove Dictionary of American Music*, ed. H. Wiley Hitchcock and Stanley Sadie (London: Macmillan, 1986), s.v. "Experimental Music"; Reis, *Composers, Conductors, and Critics*, 29; Arthur Berger, *Aaron Copland* (New York: Oxford University Press, 1953), 11-12.

[62] *William Grant Still and the Fusion of Cultures in American Music*, ed. Robert Bartlett Haas, 118-19.

[63] *Roger Sessions on Music: Collected Essays*, ed. Edward T. Cone (Princeton: Princeton University Press, 1979), 27.

[64] Mead, *Henry Cowell's New Music*, 140.

[65] Virgil Thomson, "Aaron Copland," *Modern Music* 9 (January-February, 1932): 70; Taylor, *Of Men and Music*, 97.

[66] Antheil, *Bad Boy of Music*, 138.

Chapter 4

Modernists and the Public: The Second Contact

Copland looked back to the twenties from the vantage point of the 1980s, and said tradition had amounted to nothing and innovation everything then.[1] However, both forgetfulness and an altered perspective from the eighties guided his recollection. He did not mention the seed of traditionalism planted in him. In the twenties, alongside his interest in innovation, he had given consideration to shaping a style that stemmed from his own background—his being Jewish and American, and his growing up to the sound of synagogal cantilation and urban music, including jazz and blues. He had emphasized then that he wanted to be taken as an American composer who had evolved an American musical language. However, his Americanism was entangled in modernist attitudes that denied him a large public and directed him into restricted expressive channels. For a while, in the early thirties, he deviated greatly from this attitude and adopted an international atonal style. But the seed was still there and ready to germinate into a substantial plant by the mid-thirties. In Chapter 3, I mentioned that other composers, though not all, harbored the same seed or, by the late twenties, found it already sprouting—Virgil Thomson, George Antheil, George Gershwin, Roy Harris, Douglas Moore, Randall Thompson, William Grant Still, to name six. Every one of them experienced the need to clarify his position as an American composer and to generate a music reflecting the American locale. In addition, traditionalists galore continued active, whether Americanly or otherwise inclined—six of them, Howard Hanson, Henry Gilbert, Arthur Farwell, Charles Wakefield Cadman, Frederick Shepherd Converse, and John Alden Carpenter. No modernist, impenitent or repentant, would forthrightly acknowledge their existence and some continued to disparage them when they did. On the other hand, traditional music by living American composers persevered alongside more stylistically enterprising music. Moreover, American audiences liked it much better than the offerings of the modernists.

All of what I have just said shows that the actual record of thoughts and actions of the past is more complex than at first appears, even to those who have participated in that past. It also shows that the disenchantment with the excesses of modernism and the existence of approachable musical styles were already present before the Great Depression. The economic disasters that followed the "crash' facilitated the escalation of these views and the nourishment of these styles with extraordinary swiftness.

Revised Values and Perceptions

The Great Depression occasioned change of a sort different from what modernists had predicted. We have seen that the change was in part a continuation of a viewpoint and style that had been aborning while modernism took hold in the twenties. In part, it was forced on composers by the new reality. During March 1933, when the Great Depression was at its height, Robert Carter wrote in his diary that he and a friend, Jola, found themselves penniless and went on the road looking for work. Jola was a musician, painter, "and defender of modern art." Yet nobody had any use for his artistry or any curiosity about his modern outlook: "It's a hard grind going from house to house and saying: 'We're artists and will draw your picture for a quarter.' No one responds."[2] Modern artists, like Jola, had to confront their uselessness, the knowledge of a public that cared not a whit about what they said or did.

Composers lacked the resources to defy that public, nor did they all want to do so any longer. More and more of them were becoming affected by the crisis affecting huge numbers of destitute Americans. Copland said he felt compassion for and identification with the predicaments of ordinary men and women and no longer wanted to write "self-engendered" works that no one asked for. He and his fellow composers needed to reestablish contact with the rest of the country and develop a healthy relationship with a "real audience." The first step was "to simplify musical language as much as possible."[3]

We find Roy Harris, in 1933, asking how a composer could serve a society in need, become recognized as a contributing citizen, and reestablish contact with other humans. He later said that he had never wanted to be an experimentalist, nor did he approve of experimental music like that of Ives, Varèse, and Ruggles. Yes, experimenters were necessary to keep music from growing stale, but "real composers" then had to follow through and create genuine music.[4]

The compositions that modernists had touted as masterpieces came under increased attack. For example, Mark Brunswick returned after several years residence in Central Europe to contend, in the pages of *Modern Music* no less, that Verdi's *Falstaff* (1893) was "the last true masterwork of this age." He dismissed *Pelléas et Mélisande*, *Le Sacre du Printemps*, *Les Noces*, and *Pierrot Lunaire* for lacking the breadth, vitality, and inevitability that distinguished a masterpiece. There had followed a fatal absence of communication between composer and public, he claimed, which was the result not of social conditions but of the composer's innate deficiencies. Schoenberg had over-emphasized minutiae and relied on willful intellectual reasoning. Stravinsky's attempt to reestablish a relationship with a more objective pre-nineteenth-century style had vitiated itself into an insignificant mimicry of the past, rescued at times "by wit or the flavor of an aristocratic personality but none the less inherently sterile."[5]

After Roosevelt became president and the WPA Arts Projects took hold, an outpouring of imaginative compositions, many of them showing awareness of our native soil and capable of reaching a broad public, would take place. The distrust of society prevalent in the twenties subsided. As Diana Trilling said in 1943, during the twenties and early thirties, society had been held responsible for the unhappy condition of the author-hero; in the era of social consciousness the author-hero was now held responsible for the unhappy condition of society.[6] The same could be said of the composer-hero. More than a few composers began to regard the views of the previous decade as too frivolous, agitated, and facile. Overthrowing these attitudes, they believed, would expedite a move toward the fuller development of American music.

When, in 1936, Gershwin spoke against the "machine-made music" of the twenties and the thinking behind it, he had in mind the men and women who yearned for music that related to them. These were ordinary people that composers spurned at their peril. Why insult them and call them insensitive ignoramuses, Gershwin asked? They should be allowed to reap the benefits of music through every means available and would soon learn to criticize and evaluate it properly.[7]

The confidence of the composers in the thirties may also have been overly facile. However, encouragements of a consequential kind had fallen into place. There was a burgeoning expectation of material and spiritual social recovery, which alleviated the former perception of a doomed humanity. For the first time in American history, government was taking the arts into consideration and actually keeping artists afloat financially. Surprised composers found themselves asked to write music. What is more, instrumentalists and vocalists performed what they composed, and audiences seemed more interested in their offerings. Moreover, composers, one of them William Schuman, now were saying that they could gain from the criticism of audiences. Schuman had in mind the question period that followed performances of contemporary music at the Composers' Forum-Laboratories of the WPA Federal Music Project, which started in the fall of 1935.[8] At least two American art composers, amazing to note, would shortly start earning a living by composing—Aaron Copland and Samuel Barber. As Granville Hicks wrote, in 1940, of "the fighting decade," what American arts and letters could not survive was "pessimism as a pose, as a form of sophistication and snobbishness, or as an excuse for inertia."[9]

Many writers, painters, and composers active during the latter half of the thirties had been cultural escapees. Most of them had expatriated themselves to Europe in the 1920s to escape the sensate and artistic aridity of home. Without money to sustain them in the thirties, and with Nazis, Fascists, and Falangists erupting savagely out of the soil of what had seemed a civilized Europe, Americans abroad found their homeland turn attractive again. They came back contrite about their former feelings and glad to lighten an ideological burden that now seemed oppressive.

At one time they had given themselves completely to complex and incomprehensible creativity. Now they had the embarrassed feeling that the artistic answers they had offered, to counter their disaffection with conventional society, had been self-centered and futile. They began to long for an affirmative creed and a renewed set of social values. A made over Copland declared: "I must believe in the ultimate good of the world and of life as I live it in order to create a work of art. Negative emotions cannot produce art; positive emotions bespeak an emotion about something. . . . You cannot make art out of fear and suspicion; you can make it out of affirmative beliefs."[10] The statement has additional significance because it shows Copland admitting to personal sentiments as legitimate aspects of a composer's approach to composition.

As might be expected, the articulate Thomson had a few words to say on this subject. He observed that with the "crash" the time for isolation and experimentation passed. Those who were expatriates, penniless and uncelebrated, had to return home:

> Among the artists and writers, too, exodus went on, those vowed to preserving the gay twenties being the first to leave, since it was clear by the end of 1929 that the postwar time was over. To those of us no longer living in that aftermath, no shock came with its demise. We had long since lost our taste for its bar-stool discussions of courage, its pride in banal misbehaviors, and had moved into a range of sentiment that seemed to us far fresher. Our new romanticism was no nostalgia for the warmth of World War I or for the gone-forever prewar youth of Stravinsky and Picasso, but an immersion complete in what any day might bring. Mystère was our word, tenderness our way, unreasoning compassion our aim.[11]

Composers like Elie Siegmeister took notice of the birth of a commanding new art, like Picasso's *Guernica*, Thomas Mann's *Dr. Faustus*, and Eugene O'Neill's plays. Most important, it was communicating with an extensive humanity. In music, Prokofiev's *Lieutenant Kije* Suite and Second Violin Concerto, Gershwin's *Porgy and Bess*, and Shostakovich's Fifth Symphony were winning over large audiences with their engaging melodies, sensible harmonies, and understandable rhetoric. Bartók, Milhaud, Honegger, Britten, Ginastera, Revueltas, and Copland were now interested in creating lucid comprehendible works that would draw modern music out of quarantine and into normal musical life. Stravinsky was falling into line with his *Symphony of Psalms* and Schoenberg with his Suite for Strings and Theme and Variations for Orchestra.[12]

Indicative of the values in the thirties was Thompson's assertion that "a composer's first responsibility is . . . to write music that will reach and move the hearts of its listeners in its own day"; and Moore's that "the history of art shows that musical composition flourishes best when the demand is the greatest."[13] Such statements would have amounted to sacrilege in the twenties. Thompson and Moore were, of course, not out-and-out modernists. Yet, observe Antheil's comment that at the Yaddo Festival of September 1933, the outstanding young composers busily discussed the danger of not cultivating the public. Thompson reported on the same Festival: "The radical kicking and screaming of last year have turned to a stately tread and decorous speech. Gone the non-conformity, gone the hearty satisfaction of smashing everything in sight; gone the passionate conviction, gone the spirit of the Mohawk Trail."[14]

In the twenties a polarization of music positions had occurred between left-wing modernists and right-wing conservatives. Though some composers had maneuvered between the two poles, the split had nevertheless been there. The two commentaries on the Yaddo Festival of 1933 gave evidence that musical centralists, hewing to no extreme, were coming to the fore. They were moderates, advocates for an approachable music midway between the extremes, despite being scorned by the doctrinaire like Varèse and chided by the idealists like Sessions. They heeded Hanson's warning that there was no "ought" in music. Creating a successful indigenous art would be an impossibility, if the composer were forced to accept the tenets of any theory. A spirit of complete tolerance was necessary.[15] These centralists believed not only in self-control, but also in the merit of respecting others and considering their needs. By so concluding, the centralists generated a commitment as profound and as much founded on integrity as that professed by zealots who pressed for their own cramped dogmatisms and operated at the avant-garde or reactionary extreme. There was, however, a new force, one entwined in Marxist values and critiques, which the centralists had to consider. Marxist attacks were sometimes launched at them by leftists in the audience that attended the Composers' Forum-Laboratory concerts. Surely this was one reason Elliott Carter disliked the quizzing he received at these concerts. Thomson stated that at one concert, in 1936, whose program he shared with Roy Harris, Goddard Lieberson, and Isadore Freed, communists were prominent among the listeners. They asked "loaded questions" to show how questionable or tainted were his social affiliations, politics, and music. Marxism surfaced strongly in the thinking of the composer Marc Blitzstein around 1935, brought around to this viewpoint by the ideas of Hans Eisler and Blitzstein's wife, Eva Goldbeck. Eva Goldbeck denounced all music not designed to further the cause of "the people." Criticism of Thomson's music provides an instance—she said that "emotional impact" on listeners was "outside Thomson's range or intention," his works had "the relaxed mood of a well-carpeted cocktail hour."[16] Thomson, obviously to her, served no purpose in furthering the elevation of the masses. When Mark Blitzstein heard Still's *Afro-American Symphony*, he blasted its African-American ambiance that only proved Still's servility to his white overlords and his acquiescence to perverting the life and spirit of his people in order to entertain the decadent white upper class.[17] Fortunately, Marxists could muster large forces in New York alone and even then only occasionally. On the other hand, the greater attention that artists, including musical centralists, began to give to the collective destiny of humanity was surely fostered by their thinking. Marxism forced modernists to confront their past, in particular the doctrines that had fed and maintained their devotion to the new. This scrutiny, in part, helped cause a transformed perspective on the character of Americans and society, and the place of the artist in that society.

To give an instance, it caused Elie Siegmeister, who for a while was a dedicated socialist, to want to reach "the wider audience of people who never came to modern music concerts—never even heard of them, in fact." He devoted his energies to organize "a chorus of shipping clerks, house painters, stenographers, and college students (their enthusiasm was greater than their note-reading ability)" and to give "concerts of newly written American works in empty lofts and abandoned stores." Siegmeister discovered a "fresh audience of common people" who "insisted on getting their money's worth" after paying 25¢ admission. When the program ended, "members of the audience would rise and fire questions at the composers: 'Where is the melody in your work?'—'Why did you write that composition?'—'What has your music to do with us?' " Siegmeister said that he grew angry at times, but after the question-session ended, he realized that he "had gotten the most honest and direct music criticism of all."[18]

After attending Marc Blitzstein's *The Cradle Will Rock*, in 1937, a populist musical drama that attacked capitalism as the vilest form of prostitution, Thomson realized how immensely successful it was. He then gave a description, laced with Marxist thought, of what he called the three publics for art music. One was "the luxury-trade, capitalist Toscanini public"; still another was "the professor-and-critic conspiracy for internationalist or 'contemporary' music, which prizes hermetism and obscurantism and makes a cult out of the apparent complexities in systematically discordant counterpoint"; the third was the "public of the leftist-front, a public of educated, urban working people who want educated, urban spokesmen for their ideals." This last public was the one that went for *The Cradle Will Rock*.[19]

Musical Centralism

The foundation of the centralists rested on tradition. They valued it less because it helped them evade the unpleasant reality surrounding them, though that tendency was undeniably present, more because of the positive artistic effect of remembrance. It helped forge suitable and inventive schemes for musical thought and musical composition. President Roosevelt for the sake of national cohesion called on Americans to "cherish their customs and collective memories."[20] To this summons most writers, artists, and, as the next chapter will show, composers responded. One has only to recall Copland's *Appalachian Spring* and *Lincoln Portrait*, Thomson's film music for *The Plough that Broke the Plains* and *Louisiana Story*, and Harris's *Folksong Symphony* and *Gettysburg Address Symphony*. These works demonstrated that the comprehension of music was no longer to be denied the public owing to caprice, intricacy, and the shedding of all shared symbols in the music, nor owing to the necessity for comprehending the singular patois of modernism. The music cherished custom and collective memory, which made communication of the musical substance and its interpretation, far easier than had previously been true.

The act of remembrance went outside the cities and into the huge stretches of agrarian America. Indeed, we find Charles Seeger, in a significant article published in 1939, writing about the essential link between the composer's style and the life of America's rural districts. The American composer had to rid himself of prejudice and study his own folk and popular heritage, Seeger said. It was salutary to get away from the cities and the summer colonies which recreated the urban atmosphere, in order to learn how all sorts of people lived and what they sang. The composer then had to digest the experiences thus gained in order to shape a new musical language: "Plainly, if we are to compose for more than an infinitesimal fraction of the American people, we must write in an idiom not too remote from the one most of them already possess—their own musical vernacular."[21]

We hear Copland praising the "downright plain" music and "simple tunes and square rhythms and Sunday-school harmonies" written by Thomson and Moore. Their compositions, in a "midwestern style," evoked "the homely virtues of rural America" through revivalist hymn, sentimental ditty, and country dance.[22] Theirs was a regionalism as fascinating as the paintings of Grant Wood, Thomas Hart Benson, and John Steuart Curry.

The first problem for centralists was to strike a balance between tradition, originality, and national identity. Music in every period of history has exhibited national traits to some degree. Similarly, original ideas and their musical realization have contributed to the excellence of master works from all periods. We have only to remember Bach, Mendelssohn, and Brahms, whose music was as special and inventive after its own fashion as that of the modernist. Even Mozart was orthodox in his approach to music and never plunged ahead with radical ideas. Their music, however, achieved this perception of specialness and inventiveness by means of a commonly understood musical language natural to them and not artificially acquired.[23]

The centralists toned down the modernist clamor for originality at all costs, saying the emphasis on sounds never before heard was counterproductive and peculiar only to the twentieth century. Moore asked why music had to be completely unconventional to be worthwhile. However much Bach and Brahms struck their contemporaries as reactionaries, they had produced great music. Standards, ideals, and conventions, he said, never remain static but are constantly modified. Similarly, Antheil advised composers not to feel the need to "trade-mark" their music with idiosyncrasies that would establish them as unique. It produced sterile works. He also reported on a conversation he had with Copland, in 1939, over Harris's then new Third Symphony. Although Copland thought it sounded like Sibelius, he liked the work and found it straightforward, honest, and in Harris's own manner.[24]

Harris's Third Symphony had one supreme virtue—it was preeminently a centralized composition. To concert-goers, it achieved a counterbalance between the pull of custom, innovation, and the underlying character of America. Listeners found that it had achieved another centralization expressing the composer himself and the nation as filtered through Harris's sensibility. It conveyed a variety of affinities and preoccupations which he had not verbalized in his mind. Those music lovers who admired it heard personal emotion, an understanding of human emotions and impulsions in general, and a concentrated expression of universal human experience. Harris seemed intensely immersed in the essence of an America that had a rich past and inspired trust for the future. Such were the altered criteria for evaluating music.

The centralists also attempted a balance between art as an aesthetic entity and art intended for use. Thomson, Copland, and Antheil wrote film music without thinking they had compromised their integrity. They and others wrote pieces for presentation on radio or by students. They turned out scores for dance companies and incidental music for plays. Copland said composers no longer wanted to write just for themselves, producing scores nobody asked to hear. He himself had assumed a vernacular and more accessible style that was in no way a calculated writing down to an audience so that everyone could understand the music, nor a compromise on quality. Music for use, which is to say functional music, called for a less complicated style. He was merely responding to the task that faced him. Thomson prized his own pieces for film, dance, and stage. He had achieved a position of distinction in these areas "by treating show business as communication, never as glamour, religion, or ideology." Antheil pointed out the worth of functional music—it taught the composer to write quickly and surely, to write universally understood melody, and to cultivate real and continuing contact with a large public. These sentiments would have been abominations to him at the beginning of the twenties.[25] Finally, we find American composers, in the thirties and forties, taking a small step toward redressing the wrongs they had done to native composers of the past. For the first time they admitted the claim that a valid creative American presence had predated the twenties. It was surprising and encouraging to hear admiration for and read positive words about George Chadwick, Henry Gilbert, Horatio Parker, Edward MacDowell, and others. The accusation that they wrote pretentious music for a genteel class of Americans lost some of its strength, though it was still there. Van Wyck Brooks, who did an about face from his earlier thinking, wrote that the phrase Genteel Tradition had "too long a run. It has been stretched in so many directions that it is as lifeless as an old elastic." He was "heartily sick" of the phrase. Besides, those who had employed "this phase confound the noble and the genteel. They will be calling Marcus Aurelius genteel next."[26]

A Changed Valuation of the General Audience

The music public's indifference to modernists' indictments and music caused a shrinking of the resources to continue defying this indifference. The empathy that composers now felt for their fellow Americans in need and the growing desire to write music that could communicate with them was certainly forced on some musicians but, as certainly, sincerely felt by most. Furthermore, all of them noted, with growing envy, the vast crowds that turned out for band concerts and Broadway musicals as compared with the few who attended art music concerts, let alone the infinitesimal number at modern concerts.[27]

During the twenties, the younger modernists had been inclined to sneer at the older advocates of nationalism and their use of vernacular music in art works. These older composers were still active in the twenties and thirties—witness Converse's *Flivver Ten Million* (1927), *California Suite* (1928), and *American Sketches* (1935), Cadman's *Dark Dancers of the Mardi Gras*

(1933) and *Suite on American Folktunes* (1937), Shepherd's *Horizons* (1927), and Mason's *Lincoln Symphony* (1937). Possibly taking their lead from these men (although they would scarcely have admitted it) and from musicians of the next generation, like Gershwin, Moore, and Thomson, several outstanding musicians who had inhabited the modernist camp, accepted the idea that art, folk, and popular music could come together in honest works of broad appeal—notice Copland's *Billy the Kid* and *Rodeo* ballets (1938, 1942); Cowell's *Old American Country Set* (1937) and *American Melting Pot* (1939); Still's *Kaintuck (Kentucky)* and *Ebon Chronicle* (both 1936); Harris's *When Johnny Comes Marching Home* Overture (1935). Most consequential of all, these composers recognized in these works the urgent need of a standardized language that enabled a dialogue in music to take place between them and their listeners. A collection of musical signals shared by composer, performer, and listener, and an already established convention on how to react to those signals, made possible the necessary communication. If American audiences held back from accepting some native products meant for them, Harris said, it was because their tastes were developed by foreign conductors and performers ("imported music and imported interpreters"), by pro-European music educators and commercial critics, and by obtuse music publishers and recording firms. How could New Yorkers otherwise have allowed Toscanini to tour Europe with the New York Philharmonic without playing a single American work? Give Americans more than a passing acquaintance with a "live indigenous style" and they would grow "robust and wholehearted" in their endorsement of native music compositions.[28]

Foreign-born musicians had neither the patience, desire, nor interest to study American compositions, Harris said. If pressured to play an American work, performing groups usually put a concert together haphazardly, after limited rehearsal. The result was anything but satisfactory. The audience could not help but conclude that the work was poor, dull, and of uncertain workmanship.[29]

The molding of tastes to prefer, and the advocacy of performers for, transatlantic works, and the infrequent and indifferent presentation of American works were two reasons why the public responded as it did to native art music. This was a universally accepted analysis among composers in the thirties. A third critique was added: it was not that the public was inherently unable to understand art music, more its lack of self-confidence and experience that made it uncertain. To their credit, American concert-goers did not exhibit hostility or boredom toward their own composers, only hesitation. This, Sessions once said of Mexican audiences in 1937, but it could equally have applied to audiences in the States.[30] All of what has just been said, though hardly a complete acceptance of the audience, was an improvement over the attitude from the twenties that the music public was unredeemably vulgar and without capacity for aesthetic sensitivity.

Sessions, and Copland from time to time, did believe that the public needed education in music in order to listen more intelligently. As an example of Copland's continuing unease about putting the general audience first is his statement, in 1934, that the audience was a problem for "every composer of serious intentions." The problem involved the way an audience demanded and rejected music and acted as a stimulus and brake on the composer. He implies that any composer of stature should come first (he cites Ives) and that for him an "audience must be found or American music will never be born." Needed was an informed audience willing to make an exertion to study the music and understand why the composer acted as he did.[31] This pronouncement sailed close to the modernist notions of the twenties. It would crop up again in 1939.

Thomson disagreed. In a letter to Copland, he evaluated Copland's *What to Listen for in Music* (1939). Brashly, he described the book as tedious and false in its insistence that "analytic listening is advantageous for the musical layman." After all, even professional musicians found such listening difficult to accomplish. The listener would benefit more by following the emotional alternations in the music, something easily done. He would derive no benefit from trying to analyze a piece.[32]

In the same year that Copland's book was published, so was Thomson's *The State of Music*. Thomson begins by saying that music was "an auditory thing, the only purely auditory thing there is. It is comprehensible only to persons who can remember sounds. Trained or untrained in the practice of the art, these persons are correctly called 'musical'. " He maintained that criticism and applause from the "consumer" was more clear-eyed than that from trained musicians. A layman's enthusiasm more than compensated for his lack of expertise. Intuition directed his understanding. His judgment might be defective, but it required respect. Of one thing the composer could be certain, the layman could get "pretty upset sometimes by music he doesn't understand."[33]

Thomson's was a position held by several musical populists of the late thirties and forties. The division on this matter between Copland and Thomson was over where musical meaning was to be obtained. Was it to come from the work itself through knowledge of its internal arrangements, which was the affair of the composer, or was it to come from the music's conveyance of emotional states, which was the affair of the listener?[34] The question would continue to be asked in the post-World War II years.

Individual listeners can err; the audience in its entirety is usually correct when it passes judgment on a musical composition, so thought more than a few composers of the time.[35] The composer had to speak through his music as clearly as he could, then hope the concert-goer listened more than superficially. But whether the listening was deep or superficial, the verdict of the listener was paramount. A summation of all listeners' verdicts decided the fate of a composition.

Redefining the Vanguard Audience

When Copland complained that the supporters of the vanguard had melted away after the early thirties, he was referring to the small group of devotees that had turned out for the Copland-Sessions concerts, which started in 1928 and went on for three years. It had consisted mainly of composers, academics, and "youthful highbrows." Newspapers had falsely reported that the concerts were thronged with enlightened music lovers who were very supportive of the modern crusade. At the beginning of 1932, Sessions observed that instead of the special audience for modernity increasing, a "reactionary tendency" in Europe and America was noticeable. Less and less people felt in touch with any kind of modernity. By 1935, Copland wondered if there was any public at all left for his sort of music. Those who could pay were not interested in attending. Music seemed to them unimportant during a time of economic and social turmoil.[36]

Around 1938, modernism seemed almost dead. For example, a disastrously small audience attended a concert of modern piano music at Boston's Jordan Hall in 1938. In attendance to report on the concert was a Harvard student named Leonard Bernstein. One composition heard was a badly executed dissonant work of Copland, his uncompromising *Piano Variations* of 1930. "Some fifty curiously assorted people" were in the hall, among them "some aspiring composers, some budding piano talents, two critics (another one came in very nonchalantly half an hour later), three dilettantes, several avant-gardists." People looked condescending, guilty, or embarrassed about attending, said Bernstein. "Everybody was watching everybody else. One felt the emptiness of the place as one feels a chilly draft."[37]

The year Bernstein heard the *Piano Variations*, others were speaking of an unparalleled apathy toward challenging music and of a public that cared not at all about any contemporary music. The music director of Columbia Broadcasting, responsible for a program to commission new American works, said: "The honest men who are writing for themselves admit they find it cheerless. Some still write for their clique, but the clique is very tired of claquing."[38]

Seeing the failure of modernism to take hold, some musicians who had shown great interest in, and had written about, the experimentation and iconoclasm of the twenties took a second look. Charles Seeger had decided in 1939 that a tie was necessary between a writer's and artist's style and the life around him, that a simplification of style and a turning to the vernacular was advisable. An unwavering modernist writer or two refused to budge from their previous positions, among them Paul Rosenfeld. He immediately rebutted Seeger, saying that an artist need not follow Seeger's recommendations and should, if he wanted, leave the world behind him, remain in his ivory tower, and write as he always had, if only for the future. An artist of integrity had to be true to himself and indifferent to outside pressures and material things.[39]

Although the older ultramoderns, like Ives, Varèse, Ruggles, Rudhyar, Cowell, Riegger, and Becker, and the younger ones, like Ruth Crawford, Gerald Strang, and Adolph Weiss, found only negligible support for their sort of music, one crucial publication kept some of their scores in circulation, Henry Cowell's *New Music Edition*, which had begun life in 1927.[40] It was their misfortune that hardly anyone took them seriously until the end of World War II.

Linking the Twenties to the Fifties

As an indication that variations on the attitudes of the twenties persisted in the thirties, we have only to read Arthur Berger's review of a Boston concert given by the Federal Emergency Relief Symphony in 1935. The pieces played, Moore's *Pageant of P.T. Barnum*, Schelling's *Victory Ball*, and McKinley's *Masquerade*, were weak and aimed solely to garner the public's approval, he said. Fortunately for music, the committee to select future programs would include not just Carl McKinley but also Piston, Copland, and Hugo Leichentritt. This, he thought, would insure the selection of superior compositions for performance. He then closed with an assertion insulting to democratic principles: "The project has many advantages, most notable of which is the absence of any obligation to social patronage and a paying audience. Theoretically, under these circumstances the committee should be in a position to dictate public taste, rather than the opposite."[41]

Paul Rosenfeld, who lived until 1946, was one of the tiny number of significant people who kept the torch of the twenties burning in order to hand it on to the modernists of the post-World War II era. For his entire lifetime, he despised the drift of composers away from the modern principles of the twenties and toward a music that the music public might enjoy. Composers like Copland, whom he had thought up-and-coming, offended him, when they wrote for radio or Hollywood, or published books that popularized music.[42] He scolded Copland sharply, in 1939, for composing *An Outdoor Overture* and *Billy the Kid*. These he called a species of "playboy" music, superficial and without distinction. The composer had settled for shallow entertainment rather than the serious probing of life evident in his uncompromising earlier works, like the *Symphonic Ode, Short Symphony*, and *Piano Variations*. Then he deplored "the evil times," which "are not specially propitious to the human translation of the divine moments—the mystic moments of the soul—which we call beauty."[43]

When a work that was difficult to comprehend failed to win the public's favor, he was on hand to encourage the composer to keep firmly on his course. William Schuman's Second Symphony proved a failure with listeners, in 1938—the Baltimore audience caused "a near stampede" trying to flee the hall, and the Boston audience found it one of the "most hated" symphonies it had heard. The composer considered abiding by the criticism and rewriting the piece, but Rosenfeld convinced him not to try.[44]

Helping to sustain the Rosenfeld view and to rescue modernism from total eclipse were the émigrés who fled to the United States from Europe, among them the composers Schoenberg, Stravinsky, and Ernst Krenek. The last, an Austrian, said in an article, of 1938, entitled "The Transplanted Composer" that on arrival in America he found many European musicians who were conductors, instrumental and vocal soloists, and members of professional performing groups. Their repertoire was mostly European. Nevertheless, Europe's music had achieved superior merit in part because it had aristocratic sponsors and could adhere to artistic principles, whereas America's music was tainted because it relied on commercial sponsorship and on pleasing the public as quickly as possible. Furthermore, "the curse of nationalism" had fallen on American composers, destroying everything that might have been worthwhile in their music. Only through interfertilization with different civilizations could American music reach "the highest artistic and spiritual levels, and set forth new and original ideas in the greatest technical perfection."[45] He and the other émigrés would pass their convictions on to their American students.

Meanwhile, several old-line modernists, by adamantly refusing to budge from their previously held positions, kept the principles of modernism alive. Ruggles, for one, carried on stubbornly with his dramatic dissonant style, though ignored and finding scarcely any outlet for his compositions. Varèse kept his head above financial waters through his wife's earnings as a translator. In 1945 he looked back over the previous decade and said: "I haven't made enough money from my compositions even to pay for my funeral." Nevertheless, the term "the masses" still was anathema to him, when he stated it was a degradation to write for the taste of plebeians, to write for an insensate public without will or vision. Roosevelt's New Deal was a mistake, especially when it came to the arts projects and their endorsement of the mediocrity concomitant with mass culture.[46] His assertions would again have meaning for a host of American composers in the post-World War II period.

He reiterated his stance about the similarity between scientific development and musical progress and between musical instruments and machines. Composers, he claimed, were forgetting that the essence of artistic accomplishment resided in irreverence and bold experimentation. He looked forward to the day when music could be precisely designated in the score and the score could be routinely entered into a machine that would accurately deliver the sounds to the listener.[47] This was unquestionably an anticipation of the future.

Sessions, in contrast to his friend Copland, veered away from neoclassicism toward increased complexity, extensive chromaticism, and a dissonant style that gave no hint of an American origin. In fact, he considered a national style simply a mannerism empty of "significant human content."[48] Sessions's music affected his centralist peers as "professor's music," too labored, recondite, and charmless.[49] Possibly so, but his ideas, adherence to atonality, and teaching at Princeton University would abet the atonal movements of the fifties and sixties.

False notions growing out of isolation entered his thinking in similar fashion to the way they had entered modernist thinking in the twenties. In the winter of 1934-35, he asked Koussevitzky to play his Violin Concerto, claiming his music was widely played in America and Europe and that "there is a real desire here [New York City] to know my music better." This illusory fantasy was in contrast to the Copland assertion that the Concerto made extraordinary demands on the listener and performer and won few friends. "It is not a question of giving an audience what it wants," Copland said, "but of not giving it more than you can reasonably expect it to be able to digest."[50]

After he joined the Princeton faculty in 1944, Sessions warned students against courting immediate success and box-office appeal. Isolation, though not always healthy, might be for the best. It could preserve artistic purity and make the composer strong, he concluded. The sincere artist had to go after "vital musical experience," however difficult it was for the public to comprehend him. Demanding nothing of listeners, offering them "panem et circenses" alone, led to a situation that, if it became general, indicated "Fascism is around the corner whether we like it or not."[51]

The views of Rosenfeld, Varèse, and Sessions were shared by the young Elliott Carter, even while he was half-heartedly composing music that complied with the notions of the centralists. (Carter would later become one of the most prominent American art composers.) Sessions, he said, had kept his music honest and serious by not compromising with the public. The younger man denounced listeners who got upset over a composition that "threatens to afford a new experience," and he praised the ideal listener who was fascinated by absolutely new, difficult, and unusual music, knowing it was "a living message to him" and that it helped "him to understand the people around him,"[52] a contention that surely ends on a non sequitur. After World War II, Carter would cease his attempts to accommodate the public and shift to an intricate atonal style, one that was exclusionary rather than inclusionary.

Also instrumental in keeping the movement toward traditionalism of the thirties and forties from continuing to flourish were the derogatory criticisms of influential reviewers inclined toward European music. Several major American compositions that audiences heard and liked were savaged. After studying the newspaper and magazine reviews, one has to conclude that American music of any sort was not usually recommended to the listener. Olin Downes of the *New York Times*, for example, attacked Samuel Barber's delightful Overture to *The School for Scandal*, in 1938, finding it too Italianate in tone, trifling in substance, and easily forgettable. When, eleven years later, Still's opera *Troubled Island* was scheduled for performance in New York, the composer refused to heed Downes' opinion that revision was essential. Shortly after that, if Verna Arvey is correct, a friend "warned Billy [Still] that plans were then underfoot for `the boys' to pan the opera, even before they heard it." Another well-known reviewer, Bernard Haggin, in 1940, reviewed Harris's Third Symphony by tearing it apart and proclaiming: "I have confidence in my own ability to hear greatness in music and the lack of greatness." He also found Menotti's music "trashy" and Barber's "empty."[53]

Critics, in 1936, dismissed Thompson's *The Peaceable Kingdom*, music that was distinctive, expertly written, and inviting to listeners. Reviewers found it completely unoriginal, every measure identifiable as coming from somewhere else. Here was the bugaboo of originality rearing its head again. Thompson wrote to his friend Douglas Moore and asked with bitter sarcasm: "Come now, are you a tune detective? and did you trap me in 30 minutes of unmitigated plagiarism?" He said the importance of originality was exaggerated. He wondered how critics who valued originality were "able to accept any of the classics? Are any of them 'original' in the sense that they bear no resemblance to previous works?"[54]

Another work that reviewers failed to praise was Copland's Third Symphony (1946). The composer said he was accused of stealing from others and of being "too popular to be a great composer."[55]

The test of originality, so insisted upon in the twenties, was certainly kept alive by critics and ready at hand for a new batch of modernists when the fifties arrived. In the decade and a half before the fifties, however, the battle lines were clearly drawn. Victory for the centralists seemed assured. A distinctive home-grown musical style seemed in the offing. The centralist would soon learn that they had won only a battle and not the war.

Notes to Chapter 4

[1] Aaron Copland and Vivian Perlis, *Copland, 1900 through 1942* (New York: St. Martin's/Marek, 1984), 55.

[2] *The Strenuous Decade, A Social and Intellectual Record of the 1930s*, eds. Daniel Aaron and Robert Bendiner (Garden City, New York: Anchor, 1970), 46.

[3] Aaron Copland, *Our New Music* (New York: Whittlesey House, 1941), 117-18; *The New Music, 1900-1960*, rev. and enlarged ed. (New York: Norton, 1968), 161.

[4] *American Composers on American Music*, ed. Henry Cowell (New York: Ungar, 1962), 164 (the book was first published in 1933); Rita Mead, *Henry Cowell's New Music, 1925-1936* (Ann Arbor: UMI Research Press, 1981), 350.

[5] Mark Brunswick, "After Munich," *Modern Music* 16 (November-December, 1938): 4-5.

[6] Diana Trilling, *Reviewing the Forties* (New York: Harcourt, Brace Jovanovich, 1978), 30.

[7] Merle Armitage, *George Gershwin, Man and Legend* (New York: Duell, Sloan & Pearce, 1958), 79.

[8] Ashley Pettis, "The WPA and the American Composer," *Musical Quarterly* 26 (1940): 109. The article also mentions that Elliott Carter hated the "pitiless questioning of the audience." After World War II, Carter would turn into a "pitiless" modernist.

[9] Originally in *The Saturday Review of Literature*, the quotation is reproduced in *The Strenuous Decade*, 512.

[10] A discussion of this change in attitude is found in John Patrick Diggins, *The Rise and Fall of the American Left* (New York: Norton, 1992), 147-48; the Copland comment came from the Norton Lectures he gave at Harvard in 1951-52—see Aaron Copland, *Music and Imagination* (New York: Mentor, 1959), 117-18.

[11] Virgil Thomson, *Virgil Thomson* (New York: Knopf, 1966), 155-56.

[12] Elie Siegmeister, "Three Points of View," *Musical Quarterly* 65 (1979): 282-83.

[13] The Thompson quotation appears in the jacket notes to the recording Columbia MS 7392: *Randall Thompson: Symphony No. 2/ William Schuman: "To Thee Old Cause."* Thompson said it in a lecture "Music, Popular and Unpopular" given at Princeton University in 1946; see Caroline Cepin Benser nd David Francis Urrows, *Randall Thompson, A Bio-Bibliography* (Westport, CT: Greenwood, 1991), 29-30. The Moore quotation is from Douglas Moore, *From Madrigal to Modern Music* (New York: Norton, 1942), 258.

[14] George Antheil, "Opera—A Way Out," *Modern Music* 11 (January-February, 1934): 93; Randall Thompson, "The Second Year at Yaddo," *Modern Music* 11 (November-December, 1933): 41.

[15] Howard Hanson, "American Procession at Rochester," *Modern Music* 13 (March-April, 1936): 23.

[16] Thomson, *Virgil Thomson*, 254.

[17] Mark Blitzstein, "New York Medley, Winter, 1935," *Modern Music* 13 (January-February, 1936): 38.

[18] From the jacket notes of the recording Desto DC 6467, *Elie Siegmeister: A Musical Profile*.

[19] Virgil Thomson, "In the Theatre," *Modern Music* 15 (January-February, 1938): 114.

[20] Michael Kammen, *Mystic Chords of Memory* (New York: Knopf, 1991), 502.

[21] Charles Seeger, "Grass Roots for American Composers," *Modern Music* 16 (March-April, 1939): 144, 147-48.

[22] Copland, *Music and Imagination*, 100-01.

[23] This argument was set forth by conservatives like Cecil Gray; nevertheless, it permeated composers' thinking from the mid-thirties through the forties; see Cecil Gray, *Predicaments or Music and the Future* (London: Oxford University Press, 1936), 141.

[24] Moore, *From Madrigal to Modern Music*, 254; George Antheil, *Bad Boy of Music* (1945, reprint New York: Da Capo, 1981), 324. Antheil criticized Copland for still thinking that an individual style was important.

[25] Edward Cone, "Conversations with Aaron Copland," in *Perspectives on American Composers*, eds. Benjamin Boretz and Edward T. Cone (New York: Norton, 1971), 139; Thomson, *Virgil Thomson*, 276; George Antheil, letter to Mrs. Bok, dated 8 March 1938, in Linda Whitesitt, *The Life and Music of George Antheil, 1900-1959* (Ann Arbor, MI: UMI University Press, 1983).

[26] Minna Lederman, *The Life and Death of a Small Magazine (Modern Music, 1924-1946)*, I.S.A.M. Monographs: Number 18 (New York: Brooklyn College, 1983), 43; Van Wyck Brooks, *From a Writer's Notebook* (New York: Dutton, 1958), 14.

[27] See Hans Heinsheimer, "Challenge of the New Audience," *Modern Music* 16 (November-December, 1938): 31.

[28] Harris, in *The American Composer Speaks*, ed. Gilbert Chase (Baton Rouge: Louisiana State University Press, 1966), 152-53; also see *American Composers on American Music*, 157.

[29] *The American Composer Speaks*, 155-56.

[30] *The Correspondence of Roger Sessions*, ed. Andrea Olmstead (Boston: Northeastern University Press, 1992), 267.

[31] Aaron Copland, "One Hundred and Fourteen Songs," *Modern Music* 11 (January-February, 1934): 59-64.

[32] *Selected Letters of Virgil Thomson*, ed. Tim Page and Vanessa Weeks Page (New York: Summit, 1988), 127-28.

[33] Virgil Thomson, *The State of Music* (New York: Morrow, 1939), 4, 8.

[34] Leonard B. Meyer, *Emotion and Meaning in Music* (Chicago: University of Chicago Press, 1956), 1, discusses this division as one between an "absolutist" and a "referentialist."

[35] This statement about listener and audience is attributed to George McKay, in Verna Arvey, *In One Lifetime* (Fayetteville: University of Alabama Press, 1984), 122. I heard Elie Siegmeister make the same observation during a luncheon conversation.

[36] Carol J. Oja, "The Copland-Sessions Concerts and Their Reception in the Contemporary Press," *Musical Quarterly* 65 (1979): 224; Roger Sessions, "Music in Crisis," *Modern Music* 10 (January-February, 1932): 63-78; Aaron Copland and Vivian Perlis, *Copland, 1900 through 1942* (New York: St. Martin's/Marek, 1984), 237.

[37] Leonard Bernstein, *Findings* (New York: Simon & Schuster, 1982), 23.

[38] Davidson Taylor, "Why Not Try the Air?" *Modern Music* 15 (January-February, 1938): 86-87.

[39] Charles Louis Seeger, "Grass Roots for American Composers," *Modern Music* 16 (March-April, 1989), 144, 147-48; Paul Rosenfeld, "Variations on a Grass Roots Theme," *Modern Music* 16 (May-June, 1939), 218-19.

[40] Elliott Carter, "Expressionism and American Music," in *Perspectives on American Composers*, 219. Ruth Crawford married Charles Seeger in 1931. By 1939, when he wrote the article "Grass Roots," she had stopped composing almost completely.

[41] Arthur Berger, "Boston Hears American Works," *Modern Music* 12 (March-April, 1935): 144.

[42] Edmund Wilson said this, adding that Rosenfeld was eclipsed in the thirties; see *Paul Rosenfeld, Voyager in the Arts*, eds. Jerome Mellquist and Lucie Wiese (New York: Creative Age, 1948), 14.

[43] Paul Rosenfeld, "Current Chronicle," *Musical Quarterly* 25 (1939): 372-74, 376.

[44] William Schuman, "Virtuosity in Discernment," in *Paul Rosenfeld, Voyager in the Arts*, 106-07.

[45] Ernst Krenek, "The Transplanted Composer," *Modern Music* 16 (November-December, 1938): 23, 26-27.

[46] Fernand Ouellette, *Edgard Varèse*, trans. from the French by Derek Coltman (New York: Orion, 1968), 127, 160; the quotation is from an interview published in *Newsweek*, 11 June 1945.

[47] *Contemporary Composers on Contemporary Music*, eds. Elliott Schwartz and Barney Childs (New York: Holt, Rinehart & Winston, 1967), 198-99.

[48] Roger Sessions, "On the American Future," *Modern Music* 17 (January-February, 1940): 72-73.

[49] See Frederick Jacobi, "In Defense of Modernism," *Modern Music* 17 (May-June, 1940): 222; and the 1947 review of Sessions's Second Pi-

ano Sonata, in Virgil Thomson, *Music Reviewed, 1940-1954* (New York: Vintage, 1967), 211.

[50] *The Correspondence of Roger Sessions*, 230; Aaron Copland, "Scores and Records," *Modern Music* 15 (May-June, 1938): 244-45.

[51] *The Correspondence of Roger Sessions*, 335.

[52] Elliott Carter, "Orchestras and Audiences, Winter, 1938," *Modern Music* 15 (March-April, 1938): 167; *Modern Music* 17 (January-February, 1940): 95.

[53] Barbara B. Heyman, *Samuel Barber* (New York: Oxford University Press, 1992), 92; Arvey, *In One Lifetime*, 142-43; Bernard H. Haggin, *Music in the Nation* (Freeport, New York: Books for Libraries, 1971), 41.

[54] Caroline Cepin Benser and David Francis Urrows, *Randall Thompson, A Bio-Bibliography* (Westport, CT: Greenwood, 1991), 23.

[55] Aaron Copland and Vivian Perlis, *Copland Since 1943* (New York: St. Martin's, 1989), 68.

Chapter 5

Music for a Burdened Homeland

Throughout the 1930s and most of the 1940s, American men and women were burdened and beset, first by the Great Depression, next by the threat of war, and finally by war itself. Composers were caught up with the crises of these years and acted accordingly. I cannot take up all composers or the great variety of sounds with which they revealed their fellow feelings, only the prominent composers and those compositions most indicative of the mind-set of the era.

Certain considerations of paramount importance preoccupied composers. They were aware of two approaches to understanding what culture meant. One approach identified the way people conducted their lives, understood to be a comprehensive scheme of activity. It revealed itself in belief, discourse, occupation, leisure, and products—Japanese culture, tribal culture, etc. The other approach looked to the humanities and the achievements of literature and the arts, those activities of a group that illuminated and ennobled human experience as contrasted with the activities of business and industry. From this latter viewpoint, culture provided an avenue, in heightened measure, to a social life pregnant with meaning other than the mundane. It embraced an entire society, not just the artist, and embodied both the creative individual's and the society's profoundest expressions. Culture thus understood included the modes for dealing with and explaining reality, the special mind-set for interpreting the circumstances of human existence, and the artistic institutions that made available this interpretation to the community. In this way, individuals could direct their thinking to matters beyond and above themselves. In short, this viewpoint meant that composers interpreted culture through artistry of communal worth. These composers soon perceived the modernism of the twenties as having failed to allay the cultural anarchy and alienation of their decade, instead contributing to both. Not only that, but because the modernists worked apart from the cultural mainstream and often apart from each other, they had lacked a meaningful power base at home and thus allowed Europeans to view them, when they gave thought to American composers at all, as an insignificant assortment of persons composing second-rate pieces in a social vacuum and for a country with no artistic culture of consequence.

How would they reform themselves? What then was the music they should write? Could they attract a major audience and draw strength from a sizable number of dependable music lovers? Composers believed, indeed had to believe, that they could. First, they had to heed the warnings that modernism was cutting off discourse during a period when discourse with an audience had become of pressing importance. If successfully realized, a reshaped sound might possibly win over a vast uncultivated audience waiting for an art that would speak clearly to it and its needs. Their problem was to address old and new music lovers more directly, without condescension or any weakening of the vitality of their message. Beauty, open emotion, largeness of expression—ideas proscribed in the twenties—reentered composers' thoughts when writing music. Again, composers asked themselves what made a work beautiful, and not just what did it express. They would not reject the perception of beauty out of hand, as had the modernists, for some illusive vision of truth. Nor would they accept the idea that there was no such thing as beauty, that it was merely a statement of liking something, no more. Again it became an axiom that an exceptional composition somehow moved the listener, whether the response was awakened through sheer pleasure, or through aesthetic reasoning, or roundaboutly through the inspiration that came with discovering something meritorious and moral in the musical tones. To achieve such communication and simultaneously sound contemporary without sounding hopelessly obscure was the aim.

By the mid-thirties, composers knew that almost all listeners willingly accepted dissonance only so far, before what goodwill was felt toward the piece started to disappear. Constant application of strident tones came across as stagnant and ugly harmony, so needlessly provocative for the layman. They therefore lessened the aggravating clash of minor seconds and major sevenths, assessed carefully the sonorous effects of novel tone combinations, and reintroduced conventional triadic chords. Nor could composers see total chromaticism and atonality replacing diatonicism and tonality. The former might be acceptable if sparingly and judiciously used, but inevitably anchorage in the latter was necessary, at least to the post-Crash audiences. Recognizable tonal centers and cadences reappeared. In 1941, Copland, who had relinquished his atonal stance of the early thirties, said he found atonal and twelve-tone music to be hopelessly dated, monotonous, and much too subtle to intrigue American ears, save for those of a handful of specialists.[1]

Melody to the music public was not just a carefully designed string of tones set forth with artistic discrimination and exactness—say the sculpted lines of Sessions. The more it sounded natural, simple, lyrical, spontaneous, and with a readily identifiable shape and expression, the more it would win over listeners. Melodies contoured with diatonic stepwise progressions increased, along with skips following triadic or perfect-interval configurations. Thomson said: "Music never lives by its professional quality. It lives by its tunes. . . . *La Traviata* and *Il Trovatore* are full of simple melodies that depict character and feeling in elementary but universally acceptable music. Wagner, at his best, and Mozart wrote melodies that express the same broad values but that comment more profoundly on the drama at the same time."[2] When Copland worked on his groundbreaking *Billy the Kid* ballet, he tried to discover fresh harmonies to support plain melodies, at the same time giving the music his "own touch." He knew nothing complex would serve to successfully reach a sizable audience. All the same, what he wrote had to be sincere and honestly phrased. Copland thought it no easy matter to realize all of this.[3]

Yet, there was no wholesale retreat to nineteenth-century positions. The composers intended to accommodate the breakthroughs of modernism to what they found of value, given their reformed outlook, in traditional practices. Consolidation not retrogression was the goal.

The Compatriotic Composers

The compatriotic composers were those who showed sympathy with, and wished to find a musical voice for, their native land. In several important respects, they took up where the earlier nationally-inclined composers, like Chadwick, Gilbert, Farwell, and Carpenter, had left off. However, the nineteenth-century romanticism that had invested much of the earlier music was largely absent. As never before, American musicians drew on native myth, folktale, legend, poetry, literature, history, geography, and philosophy for their subjects. On hand was a vast array of secular and sacred, traditional and popular, songs and dances to study, use, or pattern one's own music after. They aimed at, and succeeded in winning over, audiences much greater in number than the paltry few that had previously attended concerts of contemporary music. Not too many native works written before the thirties or since the forties have had the potential durability of this compatriotic outpouring.

Note what Morton Gould had to say about writing the *Fall River Legend* ballet with the advice of Agnes de Mille. The subject was a tale embedded in American history, he said. Composer and choreographer discussed the dramatic and evocative possibilities of the legend for Americans, and the dance patterns to introduce into the ballet, like waltzes and cotillions. New England hymn tunes and dance music of the period suggested how Gould could achieve the desired atmosphere. He then "attempted to create in" his "own invention, evocations of these expressions."[4] Gould's *Spirituals* for orchestra (1941), *American Concertette* for piano and orchestra (1943), later converted into the ballet *Interplay*, and *Fall River Legend* (1947) were three of a host of well-liked works written in the thirties and forties by excellent American composers.

Turning to a composer older than Gould, who was once considered a nefarious radical, George Antheil left Europe permanently behind along with the residue of his former extremism, in 1933, to return to the United States. He soon found employment as a Hollywood film composer and thereby lost his cachet as a principled musician in the opinion of serious-minded artists. Suspect in their minds was his fine score for *The Plainsman*, composed in 1937, however publicly well-received the film and the accompanying music. During the years after his reappearance in America, he continued writing for the concert hall and music stage, slowly realizing a style that was strongly personal, imaginative, heroic, emotionally appealing, and characteristic of the America with which he now identified. The stylistic changeover was well along the way in his *American Symphony* of 1936-39. He felt he had arrived at maturity with his Fourth Symphony, 1942, premiered by Stokowski and the NBC Symphony on 13 February 1944. It is not obviously American, in that no America-focused subject matter or musical idiom makes itself known. One or two tunes, however, resemble native folk tunes or suggest the ambiance of Latin America. The patches of raucous vulgarity, the occasional sentimentality à la popular music, and the refusal to be ultrarefined are also native characteristics. What the composer tried to do was to look on the war raging throughout the world with the eyes of an American devoted to democratic principles—quite a turnaround in Antheil's attitude from that at the close of World War I. The first movement projects the anxious, anguished emotions of someone observing the worldwide fight for freedom. The second, the horror of a humanist at the atrocities of Lidice. The third, the savage and cruel "joke" played on the human race by war. The finale, the expectation of liberty for all people and of ultimate triumph over the drive to tyrannize the world.[5] Melodies are contagious; some swell with feeling almost to bursting. Rhythms come alive with the blaring martial tramp of war or remain subdued with the soft tread of tragedy. The audience thoroughly approved the work.

Reviewers relentlessly called attention to the music's similarity to that of Shostakovich. Their adverse reviews also called attention to the way American composers were viewed, and, in particular, those who placed some value on tradition. Every new work, like Antheil's Fourth Symphony, invited a hunt for precedents. To be linked to the past, by too many critics, invariably meant to be accused of filching from now this or now that European composer, and of saying nothing original, substantial, or worthwhile. Antheil countered the criticism by saying the musical material originated in his opera *Transatlantic* (1928), particularly from the last act, and thus had preceded Shostakovich. Whatever the merits of either argument, the work was competently put together, sounded contemporary, incorporated excellent ideas into the score, and elicited a popular response. At least four other well-received works followed: the Concerto for Violin (1946), Fifth Symphony, *Joyous* (1948), Sonata for Piano No. 4 (1948), and Sonata for Violin No. 4 (1948). Antheil proved he was a gifted musician, who could write compositions of considerable allure with unaffected ease.

Once, like Antheil, an ardent espouser of the modernist cause, Henry Cowell replaced his former iconoclasm with some conformism, beginning in 1936. Another change took place in the 1940s, when he became engrossed in Celtic-American music and the rough-and-ready works of the eighteenth-century Yankee tunesmiths and William Billings in particular. The result was a *Gaelic Symphony* (1942), a series of *Hymn and Fuguing Tunes*, starting in 1944, and the *Short Symphony* (1946). The hymn and fuguing tunes caught people's fancy, but on the whole he was not as successful as Antheil in winning over the music public.

In the last chapter I made references to Copland and his awareness that he was living in an era inimical to outlandish artistry. He also fretted, as he modified his modernist manner, because ardent antipopulists like Roger Sessions and Arthur Berger did not approve of what he was attempting. The first real evidence of an altered style appeared in 1936 with *The Second Hurricane*, a musical-stage work for students, and with *El Salón Mexico* for orchestra. Immediately the die-hard artistic types pounced on the revisions in his musical practices. To allay their reproaches, he tried to explain that music could be born either complex or simple, and that neither was better nor worse than the other. Yet, Copland's was always a bifurcated allegiance: "After *El Salón*, I occasionally had the strange sensation of being divided in half—the austere, intellectual modernist on one side; the accessible, popular composer on the other."[6] He would never cease producing "austere, intellectual" modern compositions. However, the most enduring music he would write was found in the compatriotic works that reached out to the general listener—especially, the ballets *Billy the Kid* (1938), *Rodeo* (1942), and *Appalachian Spring* (1944), the *Fanfare for Common* (1942), the *Lincoln Portrait* (1942), and the film score for *The Red Pony* (1948). This is true despite the antipathy shown them by elitist critics.

When he worked on *The Second Hurricane*, the libretto by Edwin Denby, he undertook to discover how uncomplicated, how ordinary, he could become while maintaining his artistic personality. Copland decided on lyricism, relaxed rhythms, and gentle and agreeable harmonies. It was the first of his works, he said, to incorporate "a North American folk tune—the revolutionary song, 'The Capture of Burgoyne'." Above all, it was music for use, and it excited him to hear the composition first sung "by an enthusiastic group of youngsters." It was Copland's first "musical contact with an entirely new audience—the youth of America." The Epilogue contains the message of the school-opera, one especially fitting for the times:

> We got an idea of what life would be like with everybody pulling together. If each wasn't trying to get ahead of all the rest. What it's like when you feel you belong together. With a sort of love making you feel easy. We'll remember that feeling even if we six drift apart. A happy easy feeling, like freedom, real freedom.[7]

Copland felt more secure in his altered approach to musical creativity when, in 1938, he wrote the ballet *Billy the Kid*. From this work on, he appears to have anchored into solid ground the components of his new compositional method. Orchestration, though tidy and spartan, proves resourceful and captivating. Rhythms, when not obviously so, at least suggest established American dance and march prototypes, relieved now and again with unusual stresses. Homophony prevails. Counterpoint, when employed, is discreetly laid out and easily taken in by the ear. Euphonious triadic harmony appears, along with pleasingly open textures based on fourths, fifths, sixths, octaves, and tenths. Dissonance invariably moves on to balancing consonance. The composer convinces the listener that he voices ideas having emotional implications.

Copland at first was leery of writing *Billy the Kid*, believing that a musician born and raised in Brooklyn could not identify at all with the Wild West. Then Lincoln Kirstein presented him with two collections of cowboy tunes, several of which he decided to use. At the same time, Copland remembered that *El Salón*

Mexico had provided him with some experience in this sort of writing. He plowed through to the completed score for Kirstein's Ballet Caravan. After he extracted an orchestral suite out of the ballet music, in 1939, it became one of his most frequently performed pieces.[8]

Its success encouraged Agnes de Mille to commission another cowboy ballet from him. The result was *Rodeo*, in 1942, out of which he assembled, for concert purposes, *Four Dance Episodes from Rodeo*. This music was also exceedingly successful with audiences.

The United States entered World War II with the Japanese attack on Pearl Harbor, on 7 December 1941. American composers had an overriding cause to occupy all of their creative attention, the cause for freedom and against three brutal tyrannies. In 1942, Copland completed the *Fanfare for Common Man*, for brass and percussion, a work requested by Eugene Goossens and the Cincinnati Symphony Orchestra. Its message was direct. Its music was clear-cut, distinctive, and strong. Although bichordal harmonies and some irregular rhythms occur, they contributed a keen incisiveness to the sound. To Copland's amazement the *Fanfare* grew into an international hit, an unprecedented experience for an American composer of art music.[9]

In the same year he completed *Fanfare*, Copland also completed the *Lincoln Portrait* for a speaker and orchestra. Listeners heard selections from Lincoln's public addresses and music suggesting Lincoln's personality. The main traditional tune used was *Springfield Mountain* (*The Pesky Sarpent*). Another tune, but given lesser emphasis, was Foster's *Camptown Races*. Scornful music critics tore the work to pieces; American audiences loved it at the premier and have loved it since.

In 1944, a third outstanding ballet score, probably his most outstanding, saw completion, *Appalachian Spring*, which he wrote for Martha Graham's dance company. Paradoxically, it was one of his plainest yet most richly imaginative compositions. Poetic music summons forth the atmosphere of a traditional rural marriage eternally suspended in time. Toward the end of the work Copland inserts a set of variations on the Shaker sacred song "Simple Gifts" as a summing up. Widely spaced chords and intervals of the fourth and fifth allow plenty of air into the harmonies and melodic lines, thereby producing a convincing pastoral mood. It was another triumph for Copland, who was then accounted one of the finest composers America had yet produced by the music public.

Virgil Thomson was also a composer who wrote simply and directly, indeed was doing so long before Copland. However, he was never taken as seriously as Copland by writers on music and as much to heart by the public.[10] Yet, the slices of authentic Americana he conveys in the film scores for, and, later, the orchestral suites from, *The Plough that Broke the Plains* (1936), *The River* (1937), and *Louisiana Story* (1948) are succinctly and effectively realized. His employment of Southern white spirituals and other traditional tunes from the South and West can enthrall the listener. One of the most profound and gripping moments in all American music occurs at the close of *The Plough*, where drought and the other consequences of devastation are portrayed in solemn canonic passages over a tango beat. The ballet *Filling Station* (1937) and the suite drawn from it are charming. (Thomson set a great store on charm.) The composer comments: "I wrote a score made up of waltzes, tangos, a fugue, a Big Apple, a holdup, a chase, and a funeral, all aimed to evoke roadside America as pop art."[11] His sympathetic and nostalgic opera, *The Mother of Us All* (1947), on Susan B. Anthony and the women's rights movement, has in it a large measure of widely known hymns, marches, and popular songs and dances. In 1968, another opera would come from him, *Lord Byron*, in which he introduces traditional music of the British Isles.

Thomson deserves praise for his artistic achievements and insistence at every stage of his career that the composer had to communicate with a public numbering more than one or two people. As a writer, he was frequently a gadfly to modernists, his stings often infuriating them.

Alongside Thomson, Douglas Moore also furthered the cause of American opera and with notable results. Looking over the operas of the past and citing *Figaro*, *Tannhaüser*, and *Aida*, he said their main objective was to entertain, not merely to satisfy overly serious aspirers to culture. Three successful American operas, Gershwin's *Porgy and Bess*, Thomson's *Four Saints*, and Blitzstein's *The Cradle Will Rock*, were distinguished by their contemporary and arresting libretti, and their dramatic and musical appeal to the theater audience. Whether spoken or sung, the words could be understood, the drama relived.[12]

Moore had always believed that artists were too obsessed with questions of style and artistry and too fearful that their music might entertain. He had said this in the twenties and continued to say it until he died. Most of the musicians he knew were torn between the dread of being insufficiently modern or too modern. They brooded over whether their pieces accurately reflected America, or were fittingly international, so that one or another bloc would accept them. As for himself, Moore wished to write music that showed him at ease with the style he employed. He hoped his compositions would manifest the exhilarating features of American events and customs, and the spirit of the populace that he himself felt acutely. Why not write a catchy melody, conjure a magical ambiance, or reintroduce romantic warmth into music if one was so inclined?[13]

In 1938, Moore completed the first of his noted "folk-operas" on a legendary subject, *The Devil and Daniel Webster*, to a libretto by Stephen Vincent Benét. Although no conscious quotation of folk or popular melody takes place, the customary procedures and the lucidity of melody, harmony, and instrumental scoring do invoke the atmosphere of a mythical past. Audiences, from its first performance in May 1939 onward, found its songfulness, persuasive expression, and forceful drama spellbinding. Moore himself wanted it "to interest and appeal to the average American who likes music and likes the theater, but is not necessarily experienced as an opera-goer."[14]

Later, another opera, *The Ballad of Baby Doe* (1956) would catch the American fancy. It followed American tradition and had all the engaging musical qualities of *The Devil and Daniel Webster*. Its musical seasoning, however, is that of the old West rather than New England. A final opera, *Carrie Nation* (1966), although written in the vastly different postwar era, fastened on the same virtues. At the least, Moore proved that successful American operas on American subjects could be written to please an American public.

Moore's belief in the entertainment value of music was echoed by another composer, William Grant Still, from the middle-twenties until his death. He followed up on his *Afro-American Symphony* (1930) with other concert and operatic works that embodied his desire to recreate and delight listeners while simultaneously regenerating their being—symphonies, suites, tone poems, ballets, and operas, beginning with *Troubled Island* (1939) and *A Bayou Legend* (1940). Nothing to excess was his motto—no extreme noise, no immoderate cerebration, no unreasonably complex textures, no complete absence of tonality, no intemperate pursuit of originality, no overorchestration. He said yes to arousing emotion, to making simple combinations of melody with well-defined harmony and perhaps one arresting countermelody, to employment of the American musical vernacular, and to writing compositions based primarily on the African-American experience but also on the experience of all Americans. He would try to reach the public. Yet, if the public's verdict was negative, he would willingly accept its determination, provided it was actually the public who gave the ruling and not those impostors who claimed they spoke for the public.[15]

Still was not the first African-American composer of art music. There had been a few others, for example Robert Nathaniel Dett, born in 1882. From 1912 to 1938, Dett used the idiom of his ethnic group in some ambitious choral works and several attractive piano suites, among other compositions. However, he never garnered the high esteem nor achieved the popularity granted Still.

Not much more need be added to what already has been said about Randall Thompson, whose splendid Second Symphony, and two choral works, *The Peaceable Kingdom* and *Alleluia*, have already been mentioned. To these, we should add the radio opera *Solomon and Balkis* (1942*)*, *The Testament of Freedom* (1943) for men's voices and orchestra, the compelling Third Symphony (1949), and a number of smaller choral works of great charm, of which the seven choruses in *Frostiana* (1959) are typical examples. Fastidious workmanship, exactitude of utterance, and dignity of expression are three of Thompson's musical attributes. No other American composer has surpassed him in the idiomatic writing for chorus.

Not much more need be said, also, about Roy Harris. He tried to think big thoughts about America and capture them in fifteen symphonies, concertos, ballets, cantatas for solo voice or chorus, and various individual orchestral pieces. Two of his most successful works are his Third Symphony and Fourth (*Folksong*)

Symphony. In these pieces, he commands listener's interest from beginning to end. Other compositions have their magnificent moments and undoubtedly inspired passages, but they also may harbor clumsy transitions, garrulous spinning out of already exhausted material, and, when Harris is uncertain what to do next, an unanticipated resorting to counterpoint, canon, or fugue.

One of the very few composers to write an out-and-out political composition (music as "propaganda") during this period was the social radical Marc Blitzstein. Almost all such musical statements date quickly and are soon forgotten. Not so the musical play *The Cradle Will Rock* of 1937, the libretto by the composer, which has experienced revival after revival in the decades since its completion. It discourses on the nature of evil and the various "good citizens" of fictional Steeltown, U.S.A., who prostitute themselves to powerful Mr. Mister and with him act against the humble workers of the town. Satire, parody, barbed commentary, and characters as stereotypical symbols fill out the scenes. Ingenuous artifice is applied to chorale, college song, popular ditty, bluesy and jazzy sections to hammer out a genuine artwork greater than its parts. The passion of the composer and the attractiveness of the music are everywhere apparent. We listen to a sanctimonious minister's mealy-mouthed sermonizing, a parasitic artist and musician singing about "art for art's sake," silly and naive college faculty members whose forte is empty speech, a Polish husband and wife Sadie in an endearing love duet just before a bomb destroys them, the children of Mr. Mister as empty-headed as the Hawaiian mockery of a song that they sing, Ella Hammer and her impassioned protest against exploitation of ordinary people, and a mendacious policeman, doctor and newspaper editor. Not least, there is the captivating song "Nickel Under My Foot."

Blitzstein went on, in 1949, to complete his opera *Regina*, based on Lillian Hellman's play *The Little Foxes*. Again, evil is omnipresent; again, Blitzstein composed a winner. Reviewing it in the *Saturday Review*, in 1959, Virgil Thomson wrote: "Time has already told us that *Regina* . . . is a repertory piece. Its story line is strong; its characters have reality; its music animates and enlarges them all, as good opera music must. Here is a work that fills an operatic stage and fulfills the listener."[16] The dramatic stage action is convincingly set to music. The composition is beholden to various kinds of American music: rag, spirituals, two-steps, waltzes, among them. An ingratiating tunefulness infiltrates the singing of the stage characters.

The Nonaligned Composers

The nonaligned composers taken up here were musicians who did not think their compositions had to directly reflect America, whether in subject matter or in sound. They presumed that whatever American qualities their music exhibited, it was because they were composers working in America and therefore could not help but reflect their environment in their compositions. None of them retained a style sympathetic to that of the persistent modernists like Varèse, Ruggles, or Sessions. This is not to say that they did not occasionally write works on an American theme or with predominantly posttriadic techniques, only that such works were the exception not the rule.

Walter Piston is the first composer to come to mind. What he had to say about himself is equally applicable to other nonaligned composers: "It is not one of my aims to write music that will be called modern, nor do I set out to compose according to any particular style or system. I believe my music is music of today in both manner and expression, since I am inevitably influenced by the art, thought, and daily life of the present."[17]

Piston did remain alert to any new compositional qualities that he could amalgamate with the more established constituents of musical discourse. Whatever creative methods he employed, he directed toward producing an integrated and exceptionally well-crafted final product. During the twenties and early thirties he had written neoclassical compositions quite circumspect in emotional content. He grew less reserved after that. His sparkling wit is still apparent in his highly successful ballet *The Incredible Flutist* (1938), but also two new factors enter, emotional warmth and a greater commitment to orthodox technical procedures. The ballet, and the concert suite in twelve sections that he drew from it, brought him national fame after Arthur Fiedler and the Boston Pops performed it on 30 May 1938. Vivid spectacle (the entry of the circus), tunefulness (the flutist's melody), well understood dance (polka, waltz, circus march, etc.), and evocative atmospheric scene painting (the nighttime tryst) made the work an audience favorite. His intense, reflective, and solid Second Symphony (1943) is a deeply felt personal statement that easily telegraphs its expressive content to the listener. Hints of musical Americana emerge in some syncopated rhythms and in fiddle-tune passages. Nevertheless, Piston continued to oppose deliberate endeavors to achieve a national identity and attempts to be more American than one really was, believing they hindered the creation of a healthy and distinctive American style.

Other distinguished works include his Third and Fourth Symphonies (1947, 1950) and the *Three New England Sketches* (1959). The latter, in three movements entitled "Seaside," "Summer Evening," and "Mountains," presents the composer's own special sense of his native region without tagging his impressions with a program or traditional American tunes. Most of his creative output consisted of abstract instrumental compositions, for chamber or orchestral ensembles. It is not music that overwhelms the listener at first hearing. However, repeated encounters with one or two of his best works uncover a rich substance matched by few of his American peers.

Unlike Piston, Howard Hanson did not alter his approach to composition after the twenties. The Second Symphony (*Romantic*), of 1930, looks back to the First Symphony, *Nordic*, of 1923, and forward to the Third Symphony, of 1936, which was a tribute to the Swedish pioneers who settled in Delaware and the West. In all, feeling is unapologetically foremost, intellectualization in abeyance. His Fourth Symphony, *Requiem* (1943), eulogizes the memory of his dead father in a poignant twenty minutes of music. He would write seven symphonies altogether. Hanson's one opera, *Merry Mount* (1933), stems from a Hawthorne story *The Maypole of Merry Mount*. The Metropolitan Opera House presented it in 1934. Although thoroughly enjoyed by the attendees and praised by some, though not all, critics, the work received twelve performances and then was put aside. The writing for solo voices is lyrical, for chorus virile. The modal style first aired in the *Nordic* symphony here effectively captures the mood of Puritan times. Hanson's integration of musical segments into scenes, and the musical integration of scenes into acts reveal a sound faculty for craftsmanship. What the opera sometimes lacks is dramatic urgency. Nevertheless, its eclipse is unjustified.

Piston and Hanson began their careers in the 1920s, Paul Creston in the 1930s. The modal lyricism that characterized Hanson's music was one side of Creston's duality—the other side was dance. The composing of communicative music uniting song and dance represented a spiritual act to him. The expressions he valued most depicted spiritual states, especially those associated with elation, gladness, and ecstasy. The result was sound in direct opposition to the machine-sounding modernism of the twenties.

He, like Piston, was against providing any program as a guide to what the music depicted. The orchestral *Threnody*, of 1938, alerted the music world to the emergence of a major talent. No explanation attended its first performance, although the death of a first child may have prompted the piece. Muted strings intone a theme reminiscent of medieval plainchant. A more fervent subjective statement follows and grows in intensity to a vehement climax. The piece ends in plaintive quietness to the sound of a flute and muted strings. Also in 1938, Creston summed up his inclinations toward dance in *Two Choric Dances*, where rhythms remain flexible, moods diverse, and musical materials attractive and skillfully enlarged upon. When Ormandy and the Philadelphia orchestra did his First Symphony, Creston gained national attention. Indicative of his thinking, the four movements focus on moods: "With Majesty;" "With Humor;" "With Serenity;" "With Gaiety." Within each movement there are at least two distinct expressive contrasts, which he carefully balances to form a convincing whole. Creston's Second Symphony, in two movements (1944), more candidly reveals the composer's musical thinking in its designations: *Introduction and Song, Interlude and Dance*. Song and dance combine with his tendency toward the spiritual in the Third Symphony, *The Three Mysteries* (1950)—the movements entitled "The Nativity," "The Crucifixion," and "The Resurrection." Plainchant takes on the quality of passionately felt, personal lyricism, which is at times meditative, at times given compelling urgency through rhythms akin to dance.

Creston wrote other works, some clearly religious, like the *Missa Solemnis* (1949), some on Biblical or philosophical subjects, like *Corinthians XIII* (1963) and the *Chthonic Ode* (1966) for orchestra, and some obviously a response to his musical inclinations, like *Invocation and Dance* (1953) and *Dance*

Overture (1954), both for orchestra. In many ways he resembled the builders of the ancient cathedrals, masons who were solid workmen, utterly devoted to their task as an act of worship, and laboring to inspire others with things of the spirit. Without question, alongside Gershwin and Copland, the two art composers that the American public most favored were Gian Carlo Menotti and Samuel Barber, both born within a year of each other (1911 and 1910, respectively), both attending Philadelphia's Curtis Institute together, both becoming lifetime friends, and both steadfast romantics in music. Menotti was of Italian birth and concentrated on the writing of operas to his own libretti. Menotti's musical antecedents were Schubert, Brahms, and the legion of effective Italian opera composers from Pergolesi to Puccini. He was attentive to the writing of stage works with convincing dramatic action, sensitive musical characterization, and vocal melodic lines that the public loved. The light, floating, and catching *Amelia Goes to the Ball* came out in 1937, followed by *The Old Maid and the Thief*, a contemporary comic opera, in 1939. The Curtis Institute produced the first and NBC broadcast the second work. Several reviewers criticized the absence of modernity in his style; listeners loved it. Momentously, when the Metropolitan Opera produced his grand opera, *The Island God* (1942), it failed to please. It was refreshing to hear Menotti's assessment of his failure. He makes no mention of the audience's stupidity or of awaiting future understanding, instead: "Hopelessly trapped by the theater, I thought I would at least try my hand at a heavy and tragic opera. What I wrote was a big bore." The music was "uninventive" and a foolish try at impressing others.[18] In the future, he would avoid thinking in terms of the Metropolitan Opera.

He scored an astounding success with *The Medium* (1946), a bleak drama that premiered at Columbia University, after that experiencing a long run on Broadway. In the same year, the vivacious, comical and compassionate *The Telephone* reached the public, and in 1949, the unsettling *The Consul*. Public enthusiasm for his productions continued. Without question, the best received musical drama in America was his Christmas play *Amahl and the Night Visitors* (1951), written for American television. It has achieved an incredible popularity throughout the world.

Predictably, reviewers of modernist inclination damned Menotti's popularity as a betrayal of artistry and found his music glib, trite, and slovenly in construction. They were offended by his repeated assertion that he would not be "original" just for the sake of being different. He enraged them by saying that "what people consider originality is nothing but a tiresome mannerism that enslaves the artist to the point of sterility."[19] On the other hand, audiences enjoyed the thrilling accessibility of his music, the savory melodic quality of his vocal lines, and his commanding knowledge of the requisites for good theater. He wrote a string of operas after *Amahl*, but none achieved the fame of the earlier ones. Yet, all have their attractive moments and, at least for this writer, three have excellences from beginning to end, *The Saint of Bleecker Street* (1954), the children's opera *Help! Help! the Gobolinks* (1968), and *Goya* (1991).

Menotti's friend Samuel Barber (1910-1981) was born in West Chester, Pennsylvania. He was unsympathetic to the post-triadic avant-guardism of his day and persisted in writing fairly assimilable music not far removed from its nineteenth-century romantic antecedents. Asked toward the close of his life why he never embraced the modern experimental styles, Barber replied that he could never think of a reason why music should be made difficult for an audience to understand. His craftsmanship and sense of form were always impeccable. His enormous musical talent and individual expression found outlets in pronounced lyricism, warm harmony, an approachable style, and grateful, idiomatic writing for instruments and voices: factors that made him a favorite with performers and the general music public. He was preeminent as a composer of art songs and engaged in this activity during his entire creative life. The example of his aunt, the noted singer Louise Homer, his training as a vocalist, and his love of melody predisposed him to the genre. The first songs, *Sometime* and *Why Not?* saw the light in 1917; his last songs, *Now I have Fed and Eaten Up the Rose*, *A Green Lowland of Pianos*, and *O Boundless, Boundless Evening*, date from 1974. After 1944, he introduced more dissonance, nontriadic harmony, chromaticism, and simultaneously sounding multiple tonalities into his works, but he remained primarily a conservative artist.

While attending Curtis Institute, he composed his first piece to achieve public approval, the *Overture to the School for*

Scandal (1933). Works from his student years include the touching *Dover Beach* (1931), to a poem by Matthew Arnold, for voice and string quartet, and the lyrical Sonata for Cello (1932). Two other early compositions were well received, *Music for a Scene from Shelley* (1933) and the strongly felt Symphony No. 1 (1936), in one movement, written in Rome after he was awarded the Prix de Rome. The symphony received its initial performance in Rome, in December 1936, and was heard in Cleveland a month later, conducted by Artur Rodzinski. Barber revised the piece in 1942.

The Great Depression was at its height when Barber first won public attention. He, like Copland and Thomson, wanted to reach a broad audience with his music. However, he did not try to give a national identity to his works. It was enough for him to reach music lovers whose preferences centered on the sounds of the nineteenth century. His credo was contained in a public statement made at the time of a radio broadcast of *Dover Beach* and just before the premier of *Music for a Scene from Shelley*:

> Skyscrapers, subways, and train lights play no part in the music I write. Neither am I at all concerned with the musical values inherent in geometric cerebration. My aim is to write good music that will be comprehensible to as many people as possible, instead of music heard only by small, snobbish musical societies in the large cities. . . . The universal basis of artistic spiritual communication by means of art is through the emotions.[20]

Barber met the famous conductor Arturo Toscanini in Italy, in 1935, and showed him his music. Though noted for bypassing contemporary music in general and American music in particular, Toscanini liked Barber's compositions and conducted the NBC orchestra in the *First Essay for Orchestra* and *Adagio for Strings*, in 1938, an event that brought Barber lasting fame. The latter work, arranged from his Quartet for Strings (1936) and soon recorded by Toscanini, has proved to be an enduring international success. Audiences have appreciated its beautiful singing passages and have been moved by its intimations of deep sadness.

Yet, composers, whether modernists or former modernists, could not accept his romantic bent and would not forgive him for not being one of them. Socially aware musicians lamented the lack of any underlying "message" in his compositions. Copland, in 1936, said Barber lacked musical substance and was too emotionally conventional. Goddard Lieberson described Barber's works as without content, his melody and harmony as uncreative, and his every musical thought a proof that he servily imitated the works of other composers.[21]

Ashley Pettis, then an influential musician and writer active in the Federal Music Project, complained of Barber's popularity in the *New York Times*, 13 November 1938. To Pettis, public approbation meant nothing. In his criticism, rampant subjectivity and the arbitrary deductions found in too many writers on musical matters glare out at the reader:

> There are important American composers and important American compositions of every type of thought and tendency. But . . . neither Mr. Barber nor his works may be termed so. One listened in vain for evidences of youthful vigor, freshness, or fire, for use of a contemporary idiom (which was characteristic of every composer whose works have withstood the vicissitudes of time). Mr. Barber's was 'authentic,' dull, 'serious' music—utterly anachronistic, as the utterance of a young man of 28, A.D. 1938! Such a choice by the great musical Messiah [Toscanini] in our midst can only have a retarding influence on the advance of our creative musicians.[22]

The Pettis declaration disturbed Barber's close friend, Menotti, who replied a week later:

> I am afraid Mr. Pettis is still very passé and still accepts as the modern idiom the Parisian style of twenty years ago. If Mr. Barber dares to defy the servile imitation of that style (which has been called American music) and experiments successfully with melodic line and new form, is he not to be praised for his courage? . . . Isn't it high time that a young David appeared and struck on the forehead that in-

flated monster which still parades under the anachronistic name of modern music?[23]

Two more *Essays* followed in 1942 and 1978. In recognition of his creative achievements, the National Institute of Arts and Letters elected him a member in 1941, as did the American Academy of Arts and Letters in 1958.

Drafted into the U.S. Army in 1943, Barber joined the Air Force, for which service he wrote and dedicated a Symphony No. 2 (1944), a creation that met with criticism after its premier by Serge Koussevitzky and the Boston Symphony. In it, he introduced a novel electronic instrument that imitated the sound of radio signals. Although he revised the symphony and moderated its realistic effects, in 1947, the work never satisfied him. However, he did extract its second movement, now entitled *Night Flight*, for independent performance. Unusual for Barber was the higher coefficient of dissonance and weakening of tonal feeling that characterized much of the symphony's music and signaled a turn to a bolder style.

In the years following his return to civilian life in 1945, Barber was the recipient of several important prizes, including two Pulitzers, and substantial commissions. The composer was also a target for those who believed art music should challenge the listener and that artistry meant taking chances. Note Arthur Berger's statement, in 1951, that audiences could not help liking Barber's music and "experts" (meaning musicians of Berger's persuasion) could not help viewing it suspiciously owing to "its improblematic nature." Berger found the technique to be polished and the music envied by other composers, but Barber took too "few chances" and needed to "struggle more with the musical medium."[24]

Barber also composed the ballet *Medea (The Cave of the Heart)* for Martha Graham, the operas *Vanessa*, in four acts, libretto by Menotti, and *Antony and Cleopatra*, in three acts, the libretto by Franco Zeffirelli, for the Metropolitan Opera. *Vanessa* proved to be intricate in form and remarkable for the variety of feelings it evoked. Highly wrought dramatic scenes came alive through free use of dissonance, ambiguous tonality, and some singing neither definite in pitch and neither speech nor song. It was revised in 1978. *Antony and Cleopatra*, commissioned to inaugurate the new Metropolitan building at Lincoln Center, fared less well. The ponderous libretto and the elaborate production by Zeffirelli were its undoing. Its premier, in 1966, was marred by mishaps on the stage and by inferior acoustics. Critics and audiences endorsed it halfheartedly. A new version was completed in 1975, with revised music, shortened acts, and simplified staging. When put on at the Juilliard School of Music, it won much more public support.

Outstanding works in their own right are the extremely moving *Knoxville: Summer of 1915* (1948) for voice and orchestra, text by James Agee; the Sonata for Piano (1949); the Concertos for Violin (1941), for Cello (1946), and for Piano (1962); the *Hermit Songs* (1953) on ancient Irish texts, for voice and piano; and the *Prayers of Kierkegaard* (1954) for soprano, chorus, and orchestra. It was regrettable but to be expected that, later, musicians of modernist persuasion, especially during the fifties and sixties, would reject his updated musical romanticism as merely just one more avowal of cultural reactionism, even though it emanated from an intense belief in values that had largely vanished from modern creative life. To be sure, his works can be interpreted cursorily as anticontemporary declarations. However, such an interpretation is wrong. Barber's highly developed and sophisticated mind completely understood how great was the denigration that nineteenth-century romanticism has had to endure, as much because of its strengths as because of its weaknesses. From the public's point of view, modern composers miscalculated terribly when they quickly erected a wall between themselves and expression like Barber's by giving it a repugnant cultural stamp. There existed a cultural emptiness in twentieth-century life that militants, ready ferociously to attack intrusions from the reactionary camp, have not fully appreciated and which Barber's music fills. He, more than they, was conscious of the debasement of humane feeling that came from the radical camp. Moreover, he perceived that part of the void in people's existence could be filled with melody. Throughout his lifetime, Barber composed music distinguished by its unflagging songfulness. Music lovers found his genius for lyricism, its effortless spinning out and vast expressive amplitude, in few contemporary European and American composers. Add to this an acute sensitivity to structure and a coherent unfolding of the emotional content and one can understand the singular merit of his compositions in the opinion of the unbiased.

A Second Look at the General Audience

By 1940, it was plain that most listeners rejected the experimental, atonal, and detached neoclassical sounds of early modernism.[25] Although the critic Bernard Haggin had conservative tastes and had little good to say about almost any American music, he does put a finger on the pulse of the time when he writes that the music-loving public did not care what any composer said in explanation of his musical style. Nor did anybody worry about the claim that the general audience had lost the aesthetic battle to forward-looking artists—if people disliked what they heard, that was it; they would not return to hear new music again. Their attendance at or absence from the concert hall or opera house spoke volumes.[26]

It was equally plain that audiences receptive to art music, including music by Americans, were growing. In part this was owing to the Federal Music Project, which provided music education for ordinary men and women, sponsored a number of new musical ensembles, including symphony orchestras, that presented concerts at no or minimal cost to Americans, and actively encouraged the performance of American compositions. In part it was because outstanding composers who had been modernists, like Copland, modified their styles in order to reach a broad audience. And finally, it was in part because extraordinarily gifted conservative composers, like Barber, were producing works whose stress on lyricism and romantic feeling appealed directly to public taste. As Eugene Goossens concluded, in 1943: "We can honestly say that as compared with 1930, eighty percent more American music is today being written and performed for a public many times more numerous and, sometimes, as sympathetic as existed at the close of the twenties." One thing that composers should have learned from recent experience was that listeners could be "at one and the same time deeply moved and likewise entertained by music," and this was "the secret way to the hearts of their audience."[27]

After CBS radio broadcast new music by Hanson, Piston, Still, Copland, Harris, and Gruenberg, in 1937, the network received thousands of letters from listeners of all ages. Amazingly, few people objected; the great majority wanted to continue hearing art music, especially by Americans. Furthermore, they did not care if the piece was new or old, "great" or fashionable, or by a well-known or unknown composer. The test was in the listening.[28] Whether it was music by the Americans Gershwin and Barber or the Russians Rachmaninov and Shostakovitch, it was the music public, not "serious" musicians, that insisted their music was meaningful and elevated it to importance.

One recalls how full of dislike for Gershwin were most musicians in the art world, and how full of liking were most Americans, during the twenties and thirties. No music lovers needed music education or coaxing to get them to hear his Piano Concerto or *American in Paris*. When Hanson's opera *Merry Mount* was premiered by the Metropolitan, in 1934, its success was immediate and huge. The audience enjoyed the theatrical scenes, lyric vocal lines, pleasing dance music, and stirring climaxes. In contrast, influential reviewers in newspapers and magazines spoke rather slightingly of the multitude of operatic devices employed to retain the interest of the opera-goers. (Ironically, if they had approved the opera, they would have praised an aptitude for good theater.) Reviewers found most of the music uneven in quality. (That is to say, it did not conform to their standards of excellence.) They then resorted to their favorite game, which was to detect reminiscences of other composers' music in the score.[29] This game, they could have played with any composer's music, European or American, but somehow they exempted Europeans. At the end, the verdict of the critics and the propensity of the Metropolitan's leadership for things European ended presentation of the work. As usual in the music world, nobody thought to undertake a serious investigation of what in the opera's music had proven effective with listeners and why. Finally, one recalls Barber's rise in the estimation of the public and, eventually, of the music world, while composers dedicated to contemporaneity sniffed at him.

By 1940, the music public had heard a great deal about what it was supposed to like and dislike in music, and why—not much of it flattering. Unreconstructed modernists like Varèse, of course, continued their frontal attack on "the masses." Even composers like Copland who desired to comprehend the problems of ordinary men and women and wished to reach Americans, on several occasions, appeared to be more condescending than truly sympathetic. Twenty years after the inception of modernism and after five years of backtracking by some prominent composers, more than a few music lovers remained suspicious. The words that artists had uttered over the past twenty years bothered listeners. Some could not help but ponder what the musical world would have changed into if artists had their way. Art musicians were the subject of news reports and articles in, and wrote letters to, popular music journals like *Musical America*, newspapers like the *New York Times*, and sometimes general periodicals like *Times* and the *New Yorker*. Reading about these people, members of the public would detect certain composers who were unpretentious and acted responsibly, and others with swollen egos, a propensity for behaving undependably, and a habit of blaming everyone but themselves for their failings. Not all of this adverse publicity was the fault of the composers. In many instances an editor or writer was trying to make his subject more interesting (or perhaps sensational) by coloring the composer other than he really was. The romantic notion of the artist as societal rebel, isolated in his aerie and aloof from the world, still persisted in the world of journalism—despite the evidence to the contrary of contemporary art composers. Music educators also persisted in perpetuating the same fiction. There was, for example, that familiar myth of the deaf Beethoven, a demi-god quarantined from his community and shaking his fist at the world and at fate. When they mentioned Copland, writers loved to quote, out-of-context, Walter Damrosch's warning at the premier of Copland's *Symphony for Organ*, in 1925: "If a young man can write a piece like that at the age of twenty-three, in five years he will be ready to commit murder."[30] There was the disastrous episode of the unfortunate Cowell sentenced to San Quentin in 1937 on a morals charge. In that same year the question of the alliance between art composers and left-wing anti-Americanism arose (and would remain to the fore for around thirty years) with the premier of Blizstein's *The Cradle Will Rock*.

Audiences might admire the music of one or another American composer but would also suspect how disagreeable their own status might be if dictated to by narcissists unforgiving when any of their music was disliked and ceaselessly striking out at anyone who reproached them. The way artists chattered about and tattled on each other in newspapers and magazines amused readers. However, the gossip did not enhance their image as humans. On the contrary, too many Americans still thought that the mores and social habits of unassuming farm hands and factory workers contrasted advantageously with those of composers as a group. It would require more than a few years to allay the misgivings and to demolish the several falsehoods about contemporary American art music and the composers who wrote it. Progress toward this end was made during the thirties and forties. The reverse would be true after the forties, when a reinvigoration of the forces of modernism would take place.

Had American composers won over a large and permanent audience? "Large" is correct, if compared with the audiences of the twenties; incorrect, if compared with the total population of the United States. Moreover, there was no assurance that the audience would remain comparatively large. However much they thought they had accommodated the public from the mid-thirties on, the composers on the whole still attracted a modest number of listeners when all American men and women were taken into consideration.[31] Only if a renowned conductor and a major orchestra, like Serge Koussevitsky and the Boston Symphony Orchestra, performed an orchestral work would a truly large audience appear for their music. Otherwise, the growth in concert-goers was not what the composers had hoped for. Moreover, because so many men and women were new to all art music and uncertain of how to take contemporary sounds, it would not take much to discourage them. They would abandon the contemporary cause in droves after the forties when composers' attitudes were fully captured in the title "Who Cares If You Listen?" which *High Fidelity* gave to a Milton Babbitt article, in 1958, and composers' music reinstated with a vengeance the unapproachable sounds of the early twenties.

Notes to Chapter 5

[1] Aaron Copland, *Our New Music* (New York: Whittlesey House, 1941), 56-57.

[2] Virgil Thomson, *Music Reviewed, 1940-1954* (New York: Vintage, 1967), 22. Thomson wrote this on 8 December 1940.

[3] Aaron Copland and Vivian Perlis, *Copland, 1900 through 1942* (New York: St. Martin's/Marek, 1984), 279.

[4] Morton Gould's explanation may be found in the jacket notes to the recording RCA Victor Red Seal LSC-2532: *Gould: Ballet Music*.

[5] For a discussion of this symphony, see Linda Whitesitt, *The Life and Music of George Antheil, 1900-1959* (Ann Arbor: UMI Press, 1983), 145.

[6] Copland and Perlis, *Copland, 1900 through 1942*, 248, 251.

[7] Ibid., 257, 260-61.

[8] Ibid., 278-79, 284-85.

[9] Ibid., 368.

[10] Copland, in *Our New Music*, 189, says that he found it difficult to convince his fellow musicians that Thomson's music amounted to more than something amusing.

[11] Virgil Thomson, *Virgil Thomson* (New York: Knopf, 1966), 275.

[12] Douglas Moore, "Our Lyric Theatre," *Modern Music* 18 (November-December, 1940): 5-6.

[13] Madeleine Goss, *Modern Music-Makers: Contemporary American Composers* (New York: Dutton, 1952), 162.

[14] John Tasker Howard, *Our American Music*, 4th ed. (New York: Crowell, 1965), 89.

[15] *William Grant Still and the Fusion of Cultures in American Music*, ed. Robert Bartlett Haas (Los Angeles: Black Sparrow, 1972), 99-100, 103-04, 108-09, 112-15, 117-19, 121-23.

[16] David Ewen, *The World of Twentieth-Century Music* (Englewood Cliffs, NJ: Prentice-Hall, 1968), 89.

[17] David Ewen, *American Composers* (New York: Putnam's Sons, 1982), s.v. "Piston, Walter Hamor."

[18] John Ardoin, *The Stages of Menotti* (Garden City, NY: Doubleday, 1985), 32-33; also see John Gruen, *Menotti* (New York: Macmillan, 1978), 44-45.

[19] Ardoin, *The Stages of Menotti*, 10.

[20] Originally printed in the *Philadelphia Bulletin*, 24 March 1935; quoted in Barbara B. Heyman, *Samuel Barber* (New York: Oxford University Press, 1992), 130.

[21] Aaron Copland, "Our Younger Generation: Ten Years Later," *Modern Music* 13 (May-June, 1936): 11; Goddard Lieberson, "Over the Air," *Modern Music* 16 (November-December, 1938): 65-66.

[22] Ashley Pettis, "From the Mail Pouch: Important American Music," *New York Times* (13 November 1938): Section 9, p. 8.

[23] Gian Carlo Menotti, letter printed in the *New York Times* (20 November 1938): Section 10, p. 8.

[24] Berger's statement, which appeared in the *Saturday Review*, 26 May 1951, is quoted in Don A. Hennessee, *Samuel Barber: A Bio-bibliography* (Westport, CT: Greenwood, 1985), 132.

[25] See, for example, Aaron Copland, "Scores and Records," *Modern Music* 14 (January-February, 1937): 98; and the comment by Virgil Thomson, in *Music Reviewed*, 251.

[26] Bernard H. Haggin, *Music in the Nation* (Freeport, NY: Books for Libraries, 1971), 190. Haggin's observation was first printed in *The Nation*, 8 July 1944.

[27] Eugene Goossens, "The Public—Has It Changed?" *Modern Music* 20 (January-February, 1943): 74, 76; see also Hans Heinsheimer, "Challenge of the New Audience," *Modern Music* 16 (November-December, 1938): 32.

[28] Davidson Taylor, "Why Not Try the Air?" *Modern Music* 15 (January-February, 1938): 87-89.

[29] Burnet C. Tuthill, "Howard Hanson," *Musical Quarterly* 22 (1936): 149-50.

[30] See, for instance, Ewen, *American Composers*, s.v. "Copland, Aaron."

[31] Heinsheimer, "Challenge of the New Audience," 28.

Chapter 6

The Resurgence of the Avant-Garde

This chapter offers an overview of the two decades or so of modernism's revival after World War II. What is taken up in what follows will be discussed in greater detail in the next two chapters. When World War II ended in 1945, a large assortment of capable American composers were practicing their art. Most wrote with at least some degree of accessibility, only a few with hardly any. It was regrettable that Federal support of the arts had disappeared, owing to attacks by conservative legislators against the Federal Music Project program and to the overriding concerns of World War II. Yet, the condition of art music seemed more flourishing than it was at the beginning of the thirties. Some observers were satisfied that backing for the arts had increased more than ever before. They saw financial support coming from wealthy individuals, industry, foundations, museums, and educational institutions. However, they worried, too, that an uncontrolled breeding of new composers was diluting the benefits to be derived from the enlarged sponsorship.[1]

Whether in a personal, national, or international style, new compositions also proliferated. For a brief while, this music found performers willing to air it and audiences to listen to it and frequently approve what they heard. Somehow or other, the total amount of music already written and now being written by musicians as diverse as Copland, Sessions, Cowell, Barber, Moore, and Hanson was adding up to an emerging American musical way of thinking, experiencing, and conceiving artistic works. Upon the foundation now being established, musicians like Copland and Thomson hoped that the next generation could find guidance to build their own musical edifices in distinctive ways. Composers, whether their compositions were easy or difficult to assimilate (Moore or Sessions, for example), believed that what they composed was a normal consequence of their activities as living human beings, if not as Americans, and that it would sooner or later reach a respectably sized audience. However much a few of them might seem to the music public to go awry in their creative results, all the musicians sincerely believed their expressions in sound were the result of an experience in which most other men and women could participate.

The Transformed Musical Environment

Unfortunately, the hopes for the peacetime aftermath of the war soon dwindled to nothing. Various sources of high tension quickly appeared in the postwar years: the Cold War contention with Communism, the persecution of liberals by McCarthyites, the race to build devastating nuclear weapons, the contest over space exploration, wars in Korea and Vietnam, the revolt against racial and gender discrimination, the 100-percent Americanism demanded by political conservatives, and the wooing of anarchy by the young. Topics like mind-stress, unthinking conformity, spiritual malaise, and estrangement from society became commonplace subjects of conversation and concern. Technological discoveries, like robot machinery and computers, were replacing humans in the workplace. The human was turning into a solitary and absurd creature in an absurd universe. He sojourned on earth for a few years, with a constant feeling of aimlessness, bafflement, and loss. Writers like Samuel Beckett and Eugene Ionesco advanced this conclusion.

Music did not remain unaffected. By the 1950s, several musicians were ringing warning bells about the rise of the "absurd" in art. Robert Goeb, recently launched on his career as a composer, lamented that the latest fashion in the arts was the negative one of the "absurd." He urged artists to reaffirm in their work "the basic notion that there is some hope for man and that there are new ways of looking at forms other than purposely seeking the most ungainly or grotesque." He was speaking into the wind. The young composer William Flanagan, for another, was saying that a difficult environment for the arts was forming for musicians of the last generation, who had once been "honored, recognized" and "even successful." He named Barber, Copland, Thomson, and Blitzstein. All sorts of fresh movements were afoot; neoclassicism, post-nationalism, neoromanticism were spearheaded by musicians like Leonard Bernstein, Ned Rorem, Jack Beeson, Peter Mennin, William Bergsma, Hall Overton, Lee Hoiby, and others. Of possible greater consequence to the native music world, the avant-garde was gaining strength, as seen in the serialism of Milton Babbitt and the experimentalism of John Cage and Morton Feldman. To audiences, this music sounded pointless. Flanagan said serious human problems were arising involving these radical departures from prevalent contemporary practices. The industrial civilization of the United States was again being confused with Paris's Left Bank, a trend that would lead American music up a ruinous blind alley and produce "a generation of Ivory Tower misanthropes" as composers. Ominous for the future, he said, the composers prominent in the thirties and forties were being shunted aside.[2]

    A noted composer, writes Paul Turok, was announcing that "tonality is dead. . . . I don't say it . . . history does!" This, though utter nonsense, was "the new thing in criticism." Page after page of the *New York Times* contained composers' discussions of the death of the concerto, the symphony, opera, concerts, tonality, old-style listening. These pronouncements, said Turok, were inhibiting young composers from going in directions congenial to them. Sterility threatened.[3]

    Although their positions were unsupported if not preposterous, the advocates for change and new experimentation insisted on the inevitability of what they promoted. The world was in flux. Outdated and conventional solutions to cultural problems would not do. Not surprisingly, staunch and authentic modernists from the twenties were taken seriously again. Edgard Varèse, no longer in the shadows, found a ready audience among forward looking musicians when he lectured at Columbia University, in 1948, extolling the unknown, untravelled, and intrepid road that he said musical experimenters took. Dare to be revolutionary, he advised. When boldly striking out on their own, musicians were one with science, progress, the other innovative arts, and the future. (These ideas came straight out of the twenties.) He reproved composers influenced by Stravinsky and neoclasssicism. The people criticized would certainly have included several of the major artists of the thirties and forties, including Copland. He said they followed the fashion of the moment and wrote formulaic, insubstantial music. With the illogicalness already in evidence during the twenties, Varèse called such composers lazy or servile syncophants who refused to face the problems of their own day and advised that they get in touch with reality (that is to say, reality as he defined it).[4] American romanticists like Hanson and Barber were not mentioned at all; they were apparently beneath contempt.

Varèse presages the two decades to come, which Alec Wilder characterized as: "An age which has the extremely bad manners and infantile judgment to dismiss as remnants of the past such giants as Hindemith and Prokofief, to name just two, [and] is really not worth the anger of a civilized man."[5] Wilder was, of course, overstating the situation. Nevertheless, enough voices in the music world were raised in opposition to the composers active in the recent past, whether Hindemith or Copland, to make feasible Wilder's accusation.

Again the seed was sprouting of an aesthetic creed fixed on the future. This creed implied that a fresh start had to be constantly made. It acknowledged no antecedents for contemporary art and suggested that each upheaval comprised an important revitalization of music. The disruption might be occasioned by the arbitrary invention of a self-referential series of tones, rhythms, dynamics, etc., which determined the course of a composition; or by the setting forth of a concept to ensure that no two performances of a composition could ever be the same. From either perspective, the most current compositions were not only authentic works expressive of the twentieth century, but the choicest ones available.

The new avant-garde could not accept that innovative works, which they insisted transcended the music of older Americans, had only displaced it. Nor could it accept change as not necessarily denoting progress.[6] On the other hand, Hans Küng pointed out, in 1981, that novel inventiveness could never rule the arts and that a drastic split from the past never give assurance of something superior in the offing. This was especially so in the postwar decades when styles changed with bewildering speed, often induced not by compelling artistic imperatives but the pressures of finding willing performers, competition between composers, the desire to get the media's attention, and the need to meet the requirements of the grant-givers. Once a novel style was around for a short while, many in the vanguard audience were looking around for even fresher styles to champion.[7]

Without question, Varèse was a harbinger of the events that would sweep away the artistic connections with the musicians of the previous generation and install an assertive group of iconoclasts. Their aesthetic imperatives were the opposite of those once true in the years of financial depression and war. It is a historical truism that each artistic movement sooner or later weakens or dies because it does not achieve its ultimate goals and the historical situation changes. With it go the institutions and audiences that sustained it and the esteem accorded it. If lucky, the destruction is mitigated by a few enduring accomplishments and by the remembrance of noble intentions and enjoyable experiences.[8] So it was for the artistry of the immediate past. Whatever else was said of the thirties and forties, these decades had witnessed the creation of musical works that spoke in vital fashion to the music public of their times and continued to affect the public of the postwar decades. Concert repertoires would continue to include them.

The postwar modernists considered such works obsolete and hackneyed. Bellwethers for the new times were the Europeans Pierre Boulez, Karlheinz Stockhausen, and Luciano Berio. In the United States they were Elliott Carter, Milton Babbitt, and John Cage. All of them felt estranged from customary musical procedures and structures, and relegated forthright dealings with the public to secondary place. It was not long before music lovers were once more saying what they were being offered consisted of abstract, unfeeling, and dehumanized sounds that fazed even the most sophisticated among them. A useful delineation of these sounds is given by John Vincent. He writes of the decade of the fifties and its widely influential deviations from established practices. In these years, Milton Babbitt evolved his exhaustive organization of serialism. Elliott Carter concentrated on some distinctive timbre or quality of sound out of which emerged an entire work. John Cage introduced indeterminacy, compositions where no sound is fixed. Earl Brown and Morton Feldman experimented with notation in the shape of graphs and with mobile or open forms. Henry Brant wrote music for ensembles not bunched together but dispersed throughout the concert hall. Significantly,

Vincent says he is describing "music and culture at the close of Western civilization."[9]

Vladimir Ussachevsky and Otto Luening put on their first public concert of tape-recorder music at the Museum of Modern Art, on 28 October 1952, and inaugurated the era of electronic music. Presented then were Ussachevsky's *Sonic Contours* and Luening's *Low Speed*, *Invention*, and *Fantasy in Space*. The effect on the audience was sensational. "Part of the audience thought we had invented music, the rest that we had ruined it," writes Luening. Older musicians were somewhat skeptical; younger ones thought they had uncovered a fresh and fertile sound medium. Then, states Luening, there were "the professional avant-gardists who thought we had invented music only for that week. Now they would move into the fray and show how to do it perfectly." Peggy Glanville Hicks, writing in *Vogue*, says she had a feeling of premonition and vertigo as she listened. The music seemed to come from a primeval age and permeated her subconscious mind with sounds divorced from human feeling.[10]

Both composers were instrumental in establishing the Columbia-Princeton Electronic Music Center. Shortly, several types of electronic music-synthesizer instruments were available to venturesome composers.

Now the composer had the means for registering any sound that he wished, whether from a traditional musical instrument or voice, or from the ordinary noises of home, city street, and countryside. He was able to synthesize any sound he could conceive by operations conducted at an electronic console. He could also exploit sounds obtained from either source, mixing and distorting them as he pleased.

Most of the musical modernisms of the postwar years were extensions of ones that already existed and were not new-minted. The free use of dissonance, discord, noise, and percussive sounds had previously been tried by Cowell, Varse, and Antheil. Constant reiteration of brief note patterns and compact chunks of sound materials, which slowed or stopped the active flow of sound, had occurred in the music of Erik Satie in France, and of Varèse and Antheil. . The juxtaposition of separate musical streams was a practice already evident in the music of Ives and Varèse. Examples of bizarre and inventive instrumentation, including experimentation with sounds produced through electrical means of some sort, had come from the pens of Varèse, Cowell, and Antheil. Interest in the artistic traditions and music of cultures different from those originating in Europe boasted a long history. In short, the post-World War II period was the twenties redux but with a vengeance.

Cultural intolerance was gaining the upper hand among newfound modernists, who were aided and abetted by their cult followers. As was predictable, conservative voices were heard asking for a return to the tried-and-true—here was the only intolerance as modernists saw it. Moderates wondered why compromises could not be reached, after the example of the Roosevelt years—they were thinking in terms of yesterday, claimed up-to-date musicians. Moreover, militants considered compromise a corruption of the artistic drive. To strike out along novel paths entailed dislodging whoever and whatever stood in the way. This was not intolerance to them but radicalism propelled forward by an artistic and moral imperative.

Most composers did consider themselves politically and socially liberal and against the conformity insisted upon by the McCarthyites. At the same time, as innovative musicians subscribed to one or another artistic theory, an aesthetic McCarthyism appeared to grow among them. This is behind John Rockwell's observation about the serialist Columbia-cum-Princeton University axis, which included Milton Babbitt and Charles Wuorinen: "If the polemics of the Columbia-Princeton school had been confined to the championing of its own music, no one could complain. But it is the nature of polemics to be against things as well as for them. . . . Still, the opacity and hostility of the Princeton circle to music it did not understand reached new heights or depths."[11] Even more than had been true in the twenties, composers who considered themselves at the cutting edge of art insisted their direction was the sole direction to go; all other directions were false and not to be countenanced. Thus did authoritarian views gain renewed credence, as if the war against dictatorship meant nothing in the arts.

Coercion in the sphere of music grew as modernism gathered strength. The older composers, who had lived through the painful years of depression and war and painstakingly gestated what they thought was a fresh and viable music, were anxious to maintain the lines of communication with the public, which were being severed one by one. With trepidation, they observed their young colleagues turning to one extreme idiom or other. The dogmas of modernism once more outlawed any music that entertained or proved easy for listeners to assimilate. An unforgiving breed was occupying important university positions, serving on the boards of foundations, advising the people who handed out grants and commissions and made performances possible. Those without a power base dared not cross them.[12]

An ancillary sort of evaluation of recent American music history was taking place in books and articles that purportedly spoke the unvarnished truth about music of the past or evaluated the contemporary scene. The inclusions, exclusions, and comments could not help but influence the views of a new class of au-courant music critic who was arriving on the music scene and a new sort of intellectual who could or would not listen to music but felt that he had to have opinions about it. In the pages on music, older composers like Barber and Hanson might receive short shrift, recent romantics like Lee Hoiby and John La Montaine find scant toleration, ethnic-Americans like Thomas Pastieri and Gian Carlo Menotti discover themselves ignored or subject to vituperation, and once nationally inclined composers like Copland and Moore accused of arriving at a dead end.[13] The music of Charles Ives, from the first two decades of the century, came in for extravagant praise, less for its genuine musical merits, even less for its embodiment of traditional New England values and its freshening of established music practices, and more for its "daring" experimentation and flouting of convention. To merit serious attention the contemporary composer was admonished to write atonally or experimentally or unbeholden to tones of definite pitch.

Ordinary listeners received no invitation to participate in the brave new world of art. In this regard, the modernism of the fifties was far more exclusionary than that of the twenties. Because listeners' minds could not engage imaginatively with an extreme contemporary work, however touted as a momentous cultural contribution, people were now expected to leave it alone, to feel weary or unmoved by it, to find that no provision had been made for their sharing in the composer's creation. "Who Cares If You Listen?"—the title given to the Milton Babbitt article that appeared in *High Fidelity*, in 1958, summarizes this standpoint. Whenever John Cage surveyed an audience pushed into turmoil by one of his pieces, he expressed delight at having stimulated people's reactions and allowed that they could take his work or leave it as they pleased—either response was appropriate for them and acceptable to him.

During the fifties, each of the neomodern composers, having one's self in mind, insisted on the autonomy of the artist and the sovereignty of the artwork. During the sixties the "anti-art" composer like Cage and his unpredictable sounds, which resulted from some "chance" operation or from inferred mental processes, took hold. However seemingly unassertive his claims, the anti-art composer also assumed an overriding significance for what he was originating.

Inescapable, nevertheless, were the contemporary questions stemming from the war just ended and from the collaboration of artists with German Nazism and Italian Fascism: Is the composer, painter, or poet to be held responsible for what he says or does and is any work he produces to be evaluated in its own terms and for itself or in terms prescribed by its creator? The question became especially acute after the poet Ezra Pound won the Bollingen Award for his *Pisan Cantos*, in 1949. Thoughtful men and women objected, refusing to accept the utter independence of art from human activities. They were "sick of the art-adoration" prevalent "among cultured people" and the "art-silliness which condones any moral or intellectual failing on the artist's part." Surely, they said, the origin, configuration, and central idea of an artwork was crucially connected to the external world and the way people other than the artist thought and felt.[14] Thus, a basic footing that gave support to modernism was giving way. Art could no longer enpedestal itself (which it did even when it disavowed such intentions, as with the experimenters of the sixties) and withstand severe criticism.

Ezra Pound was put on trial for collaboration with Fascism and for treason. From 1946 to 1958 the American government removed him to a hospital after a finding of mental incompetency. His "madness of the poet" can stand as the paradigm of the "madness" of postwar avant-garde artists, including composers. These people were driven to the limits of experience, writes Louis A. Sass, in his book *Madness and Modernism*. What they shared with madness was a seriously estranged awareness of oneself, which had parted them from an anchorage in external reality.

They had come upon a language that had a meaning dissociated from anything related to actuality. Sass indicates that another basic footing of modernism was giving way when he says that more and more people were suspecting advanced artists of "cranking out crazy or incomprehensible works," which left audiences "unhappy or confused."[15]

The music public might be wrong, as artists kept on saying, but there was no controverting its verdict once the collective mind was made up. It no longer felt like giving composers the benefit of the doubt, to the extent that it had done so in the twenties. As never before, audiences, except for the small vanguard ones, began to shun concerts of contemporary compositions and to feel less and less responsibility for maintaining composers.

Postwar realities, such as the one just mentioned, could not help but impinge on every composer's life. As advanced musicians tried to regain their footing, the music-publishing predicament grew increasingly bleak. The sale of contemporary-music scores, whether to professionals, amateurs or educators, dropped precipitously. Only the boldest and most prescient of publishers would issue new works and these as reputation-enhancing pieces on which they expected to lose money. For the publication of a contemporary score, a subvention that paid for the expenses involved was usually necessary. Nor did Europeans lend support to contemporary American artists, neither performing the music nor praising the musicians. All the French routinely offered was condescension, the Germans disdain, the English advice, and the Italians indifference.[16] Indeed, we can credit French intellectuals and artists with continuing the views of Americans first voiced in the nineteenth century, kept alive in the early part of the twentieth century, and now proclaimed more vehemently than ever—that the United States harbored a nation of unsophisticated Pollyannas and conformers, revelled in its crass materialism, and smothered every true artistic impulse. Now, as in the earlier part of the century, American composers subscribed to the first two opinions and tried to prove the last accusation did not apply to them.

Established performing ensembles, from symphony to string quartet, and noted soloists reduced their commitment to or severed what tenuous connections they had with contemporary modernism. Extremist composers were forced to form their own performing groups, sponsored usually by museums, universities, or foundations, and to present their music before minuscule audiences under ghetto conditions. The era of the singer and instrumentalist specializing in the performance of modern works had arrived. Relying on private, corporate, and governmental largesse, composers managed to have the expenses for recordings of their music covered. Unfortunately, when these recordings were displayed in retail outlets, scarcely anyone bought them.

For comfort, if teaching positions in universities were unavailable, they gathered mostly in New York City and, to a lesser extent, in Boston, Los Angeles, San Francisco, and Chicago, scraping out livings as best they could. The freedom of expression guaranteed them in the universities, and the false assurance of an urban crowd of like-minded people permitted the insurgents to produce what they wished and masked their growing insignificance to the rest of the world. The larger music public blithely went its own way, enjoying its "obsolete" music, indifferent to the accusations of babbittry.

Postwar Conundrums

"Ask Not 'Is It Art?' Ask 'Did An Artist Make It?' " This rather fatuous admonition was the title of a *New York Times* article on 23 February 1992. It renders the terms "art" and "artist" meaningless. Any composition regarded as inferior in workmanship, tacky, or specious becomes art if the concocter is someone called an "artist", while the question of who is an artist goes begging. Besides, the admonition overlooks the fact that mankind has insisted on judging artworks and has questioned the right of a person to assume the rank of artist, since time beyond memory. It would continue to do so, despite the remonstrances of the insurgents. Around 1967, the conductor Robert Shaw was taking over his new job as music director of the Atlanta Symphony Orchestra. He assured Atlantans that he would foster the classic repertoire, saying that art turns into a classic not because of age but because it remains pertinent (not explaining, pertinent to what or to whom). He then warned that a part of what he would perform would be contemporary music "upon which one has no right or means of exercising a value judgment: the absolutely absurd, experimental, unconventional, uncensored, inconceivable, unbearable anti-music."[17] He abrogates his right to ask "Is it art?" At the same time, Shaw takes what was a serviceable, even prudent, proposition to a doctrinaire extremity. He disavows the possibility of pervasive artistic values, deters thoughtful investigation into their possible existence, and allows nobody the liberty to say anything.

In contrast, the noted theologian and writer Hans Küng dares wonder if postwar modern art has obliterated its centuries-old cultural history and immense capacity to remain meaningful. By challenging all other artistic procedures and standards as they had never been challenged before, it has risked wiping out its own meaning and its importance for others. He concludes: "Is not art too important to be left to artists?"[18]

However experimental were composers of the earlier part of the century, like Cowell and Antheil, they still had connection with tradition or with America's music, whether in the sounds they conjured up or in their rhythms or in their melody. After World War II, composers who saw themselves at the forefront of art eliminated the common American musical language that was still taking shape, only to substitute exclusive concepts and organizations or disorganizations of sound, each of them singular and completely indecipherable to the average music lover. The super-complex and super-rational systems of the new atonalism and serialism seemed as senseless to the ear as the aleatoric practices of the new indeterminacy. Both methods crushed any likelihood of a collective experience, leaving the judgment of even accomplished listeners paralyzed.[19] At least one person, Leonard Meyer, said that the consequence was a crisis in art music. He suggested that universal value and collective experience hinged on the envisioning of a uniformly comprehensive style, which now did not exist. Since stylistic diversity seemed here to stay, he concluded, then the question should not be about art, artists, or values. Rather, one should ask if the particular work listened to is "well-made, challenging, and enjoyable."[20] Yet, one finds three difficulties with Meyer's suggestion. To ask if a composition is well-made is to imply some standard by which to test it; to ask if it is challenging intimates a goad and contentiousness which most music lovers find external to the listening experience; and to rule it unenjoyable is to make a value judgment, which guarantees an assault on the listener's right to say anything at all. During the free fall that characterized postwar art music, even Americans with some listening experience found difficulty in grasping a work built on no recognizable standard, one revealing no appreciable orderliness in design and allowing no telling listening experience, so as to call it well-made. The music spawned seemed a secondary result of a theoretical viewpoint that made considerations of value impossible. It looked as if composers were always wondering what new variant in their ideology to explicate as much as what new music to create. That is not to say that Babbitt, Cage and others did not issue verbal statement after statement to describe and justify what they did. Yet, for listeners, explanation was not enough. Method in conceptualization did not necessarily produce intelligibility in listening. The result was that, because each subsequent work relied on some credo or other, the listener found it valid only if he had faith in the convictions of a specific artist—the mathematical Babbitt and his desire for total serialist control, the uninhibited Cage and his guidance by Far Eastern religious philosophy.

By the end of the fifties, the myths and assumptions that composers had shared with the music public, during the thirties and forties, were completely out of fashion. The public as a whole could no longer imagine the contemporary composer's musical world. The composer was forced to rate first, his vocation, and second, his status amongst those he accepted as his peers, as the decisive criteria of the creative life he chose to lead. On the other hand, however estranged from and in revolt against society, he still expected society's institutions to provide him with a living, a means of performance, and an audience of some sort.[21]

The public reply to the *New York Times* article might easily have been "Ask 'Is It Humbug?' Ask 'Did A Charlatan Make It?'" In the earlier part of the century avant-garde art music had indeed sounded revolutionary and distinctive. The music produced by Varèse, Cowell, Antheil, and Ruggles had emerged as decidedly singular. However, after World War II, the new art appeared "impersonal and interchangeable" to observers like John Lukacs. (In fact many a strictly controlled serial composition could easily be confused with many an uncontrolled indeterminate composition.) Lukacs complained of the "fakery . . . now dominant" both in the generating of publicity for art and artists and in the fabrication of artistic works. To copy or fake another artist's style had been difficult in the past; now the style of most artists "could be reproduced by people with little talent to the point where no one would know the difference."[22] The public suspected a horde of "composers" were writing dreary serial works by the numbers or offering unstructured works, which required no musical training to concoct. Among these musicians were persons who seemed to care more for notoriety than the expression of one's own talents. The public's conjectural response to the conundrum "Is it art?" apparently was "Maybe it's drivel." Undoubtedly such a verdict was upsetting to sincere musicians doing their best to expose some singular vision. It was also a determination too easily reached by slothful listeners for whom listening was an overly passive activity. Nevertheless, the response pointed to the risk run by all artists when each person measures art by his own private yardstick. It allowed for no reasonable dialogue or clear transmission of what the music was intended to convey. Leonard Meyer states that unilateral expression generated only one acceptable reaction: silence. He quotes Tom Lehrer: "If you can't communicate, the least you can do is shut up."[23]

The Shifting Public Scene

Technological advances, incorporated into long-playing records (later, compact disks), cassette tapes, FM radio, television, and motion pictures, made vast quantities of music available to the public beginning with the 1950s. In addition, a great deal of what Americans heard as music was in the form of singing commercials, unrequested background music in supermarkets and offices, and blaring noise from car and portable radios. Advertisers were clothing their messages in whatever sounds would titillate consumers, or at least grip their attention. Furthermore, the immense populace, which had no interest in art music, was asserting its right to hear the music it chose to hear, where and when it chose to hear it. Recordings, movie sound tracks, and the offerings of radio disc jockeys catered to these millions of Americans by tendering them the music they desired—popular music. The pretense that the recording, broadcasting, and motion-picture industries were interested in art succumbed to the drive to maximize profits.

However enthusiastically some optimists spoke of a cultural explosion, there was no gainsaying the potential risk to all serious artistic expression of a strengthening entertainment megabusiness devoted to giving people the commodities that sold best and that allowed the greatest immediate monetary profit.[24] By the end of the century, only a few of the major foreign and American recording companies would be issuing art music by American composers and very few retail outlets would offer it for sale. Magazine after magazine that featured articles on and record reviews of art music ceased to exist one by one, for want of advertisers and subscribers. Newspapers cut back on their concert and opera coverage, even as they increased their reporting on popular music, other entertainments, and "life styles." Indeed, to all effects and purposes, art music was just one of many equal "life styles," and not even one of the more important, that its readers might pursue, as far as newspapers were concerned.

The freedom artists had demanded for themselves was now forcefully exercised by the democratic masses, despite serious musicians' complaints about popular music's babel and shallowness. As Jacques Barzun said, in a democracy, one must "notice the interconnection of phenomena: in this instance, the link between what makes the empty noise and what disseminates the best music; the link between a democratic freedom of choice and the obtruding of popular entertainments on more cultivated ears. We cannot have it both ways . . . ."[25]

A further erosion of interest in art music and tipping of the scale toward different types of popular music, during the fifties and early sixties, was made possible when influential intellectuals like Dwight Macdonald accused the middle class of feigning their devotion to "High Culture"—theirs was a "Midcult" that coarsened it and weakened its vitality. Abetting his attack was Hannah Arendt for whom the "bourgeois" society of educated and cultivated people was a group of snobs who treated culture as a commodity and merely consumed rather than understood cultural works. At least mass society was more forthright when it wanted entertainment rather than culture. Macdonald and Arendt allowed no room for a respected middle-class culture that might act as a balance to the assertions of modernism.[26] Not surprisingly, such criticism discouraged middle-class interest in any art music.

In the face of such assaults on the music public's sensibilities, Harold Schonberg is only superficially plausible in his declaration that postwar audiences were "infinitely more sophisticated" owing, in 1948, to the advent of the LP disk and the subsequent recording of an extensive repertory including works by John Cage and Pierre Boulez. When he adds that "the music lover had a whole world free to explore and many did," one questions just how much exploration of advanced music actually took place.[27] Perhaps he was thinking of the special audiences that formed for early music and the reinvigorated advocacy-coteries for contemporary music, none of them overwhelming in size, leastwise the latter. It is true that the availability of contemporary music on recordings increased tremendously, owing to a small extent to the enlightened policies of one or two people in the recording industry, like Goddard Lieberson of CBS. Nonetheless, since most recordings of contemporary music depended on somebody with money to pay the expenses rather than depend on profits, we would err if we confused availability with widespread interest in musical contemporaneity.

One must also keep in mind that in the fifties and sixties, as always had been true, the main body of art-music lovers was still small when compared with the millions of rank-and-filers habituated to popular entertainment. As in previous years, its members stayed mostly with the classical and romantic repertoires of the eighteenth and nineteenth centuries. These men and women concentrated on the satisfying works composed by reliable standbys like Mozart, Beethoven, Schubert, Chopin, Brahms, Verdi, and Tchaikovsky. If they explored twentieth-century music, they turned to readily understood Europeans like Debussy, Ravel, Mahler, early Stravinsky, late Bartók, Prokofiev, and Shostakovich, and Americans like Gershwin, Barber, the nationalist Copland, and the American-by-adoption Menotti. This music provided palatable melody, invigorating rhythm, and harmony and orchestration constructed with an ear for sound. While quite a few people attended musical performances, most got their music primarily from recordings, tapes, and usually conservative FM radio stations devoted to art music, which reflected listeners' tastes. Listeners would not choose to purchase music they did not know and would not hear much of what was new from radio stations. And if they did, the radio was likely to be turned off. The rising price of concert and theater tickets, the exodus of the middle class to the suburbs (which meant more effort to attend performances and the expense of travel, parking, and dining), and worry over urban crime and safety served to deter men and women from concert and opera attendance. Thus, whatever the new music that managed to get a performance, it was heard only by a fraction of an already small art-music audience when compared to the total population of the United States. Because repeat performances were rare, once heard it was also quickly forgotten.

Why all the serialism, electro-acoustic realizations, tape-distortions of everyday sounds, chance? The middle-class music public of these two decades, far more than in the twenties, was coming to feel not only separated from but plagued by the avant-garde, not just because of what it said but of what it offered as music. Concert- and opera-goers remained adamantly human-oriented and strongly disposed to evocations of sentiment. These Americans now believed that the advanced compositions they chanced to hear were monstrous or remote from their interests. They had little curiosity to explore works that negated the life experienced by the commonality of humans and that scorned the tonal beauty they considered the essence of music. Nor did they accept the admonition that they should care about such works. The chasm separating contemporary composers and audiences, which had grown wide in the fifteen years after World War I and narrowed somewhat during the Roosevelt years, was becoming measureless. It gave rise to Leonard Bernstein's despairing comment, in 1966: "The First World War seemed to mark a full stop: Debussy, Mahler, Strauss, and the early Stravinsky barely made the finish line. . . . From then on it became a hassle: composer versus public. For fifty years now audiences have been primarily interested in music of the past . . . ."[28]

What Bernstein failed to point out was what other important writers were saying—the middle-class culture and music public seemed fragmented, as never before. Even if the contemporary composer wanted to address a public, how could he identify it? This was certainly the opinion of Jacques Barzun.[29] There was no such animal as a monolithic art-music public, a vanguard audience, or a mass audience for popular music. A pluralistic music society was forming comprising many musical alli-

The Resurgence of the Avant-Garde 161

ances, with substantial exchange of participants between them. Most art-music lovers adhered to what was already known and had already proven worthy. But there were other more or less eclectic constituencies, some long in existence, others newly taking shape: those for baroque music and bebop, Italian opera and Broadway musical, classical chamber music and the music-making of the small ensembles splintering from Swing bands, and the compositions of Rachmaninov and Grieg, plus the sounds of Guy Lombardo and Lawrence Welk, to name a few. Each alliance was, of course, quite informal from a cultural viewpoint.

Some musical sectors grew considerably separated from each other. More and more people were solidly inclined to the preservation of their own customs or tended towards distinguishing themselves from the rest of America—African-American groups exploring their musical roots, zoot-suiters with their exclusive musical rituals, the folk-song enthusiasts inhabiting the coffee houses, the subscribers to protest songs and political demonstrations. There were lovers of only medieval music, Josquin and Palestrina, Monteverdi's operas and madrigals, Buxtehude and Bach, Mozart, Beethoven, ballet music, Italian Romantic opera; the list is endless.

In popular music, the branches included Tin Pan Alley, rhythm and blues, rock-and-roll, and country-and-western. There were jazz fans who kept alive New Orleans, Chicago, swing, or other earlier styles, while others subscribed to the more recent bop, cool, and Third-Stream crossover trends. And what of the public for the "semi-classics," from pieces by Johann Strauss to those by Leroy Anderson? The United States was becoming a place of disparate racial, ethnic, and socio-cultural communities each preserving its own special interests, although acting within the margins of a prevalent social framework. People might belong exclusively to one or to two or more of them; an overwhelming number of Americans did. In such a nation the difficulty of maintaining harmony and liberty for all grew enormous. What was one day a slight fellowship, the next day disintegrated into clashing gangs. Yet, each group, however tenuous its existence, clamored for a place in the sun and, as often as not, claimed cultural precedence or preeminence. Beginning at mid-century, the United States had to accommodate many sharply defined cultural parties that were constantly forming and reforming.

When I refer to the convictions of the art-music public, I mean the consensus of opinion, spoken and unspoken, arrived at by most of its members whatever their particular preferences. Even though the contemporary composer failed to identify a large enough public to address, he surely knew by the fifties what sort of music most Americans of his own day, and over the past fifty years, had found unacceptable. If he were an out-and-out modernist, his choice was either to reject and castigate the public's consensual views and rely on his own limited circle of believers, or to create a fiction about an imaginary like-minded public in the present or future.

In modern music, there soon were the divisions, first noted by New York writers, between the more academic and rational "Uptown" and the looser and more intuitive "Downtown" music, and between the subdivisions within these divisions. Each division or subdivision had its zealous supporters. Like the vanguard audiences of the twenties, these similar lay adventurers into the land of the new included persons who responded not always to what they liked but to what they considered they ought to like, not to what they felt but to what they decided they ought to feel, according to the acute art critic Harold Rosenberg. He said further that they saw each new evolution in art as lasting for a finite period before it lost its validity, became a matter of history, and was superseded by another movement.[30]

Here too one finds an agreement, spoken and unspoken, arrived at by most advocates of modernism, however divergent their personal leanings. They endorsed compositions normally in unusual figurations, featuring sounds that unsettled the larger audience and assaulted its most prized views about what constituted music. From the viewpoint of the more conventional music lover, they underwrote works that were intentionally closed off to him, if only to rile anyone with orthodox tastes. Thus, modernism's rebellion against any "prevalent style" and "unyielding rage against the official order," instituted in the twenties, continued with a vengeance. However, after midcentury, it was obvious that it could not "establish a prevalent style of its own; or if it" did, it denied "itself, thereby ceasing to be modern."[31] Stylistic stability was absent.

To conclude and summarize the changes, the major shift in the public scene was the coming into existence of a maladjusted and splintered music public and, concurrently, of an extensive cultural tie-up. This tie-up was also, as far as concerned contemporary art music, the outcome of the composer's need to find people and institutions to reproach for his failure to communicate, plus his refusal to assume accountability for his actions. In addition, this widespread problem in the United States involved the American people's and the modern composers' persuasion that they had a right to every kind of self-fulfillment and indulgence, free of conditions, consequences, and self-denial.

Almost all men and women, whatever their particular partialities, had been unwavering about their negative assessment of atonality and radical experimentation in sound. An unfortunate result was a shortsightedness in post-World War II audiences: They usually refused to listen to all modern works of a highly dissonant, nontonal, and innovative nature. The rejection included imaginative pieces of assured excellence in the estimation of practiced listeners who had no special agendas to advance. Regrettable to say, the public's negative judgment was a given that remained unalterable, however much critics cajoled, criticized, or tried to educate listeners. It served no purpose for the composer, when he failed to reach any sizeable group, to find the inadequacy to lie in the nation's disabilities rather than in his own imperfections or bizarre musical statements. Nor did it cancel his own shortcomings by describing them as really those of society. His conclusions would not get him out of his difficulties. A full reversal of the public's attitude was not in the offing. Thus, the condition of American art music became one of impasse in the fifties and sixties, the public unable and modern composers unwilling to compromise.

The Trials of the Traditional Mainstream

However disparate were personal tastes and however split was the art-music public, the broad outlines of what most listeners found acceptable were in place. The means for an exchange of views between listeners and composers were not in place. The only message the public could send back was a confused one at best, based on its attendance at musical performances and purchase of recordings. When the message turned negative, the explanations for this phenomenon, published in books, magazines, and newspapers, underscored, rightly or wrongly, the dwindling of interest in all art music; the audiences were no longer refreshed by traditional works and no longer willing to be challenged by modern works. Less emphasized were the lack of give-and-take, the disruption of the balance between the imperatives driving composers and listeners, and the urgent need for mutual understanding and reconciliation.

The explanations, nonetheless, often lost sight of the outstanding contemporary compositions esteemed by most members of the public that heard them. Inexorably, audiences had singled out those new works that had kept some faith with the traditional past. In them, the listeners could discern credible diversity in sound and expression. Some pieces drew on folk, jazz, or popular music. Many were recognizably colorful in tone and orchestration. One work might reveal a restrained emotionality; another might appear gutsy in its passion. Nevertheless, there was always variety the listener could apprehend and appreciate. Among the compositions were well-wrought American operas: Vittorio Giannini's The Taming of the Shrew (1950), Gian Carlo Menotti's The Consul (1950) and Amahl and the Night Visitors (1951), Carlisle Floyd's Susannah (1954), Lee Hoiby's The Scarf (1955) and Summer and Smoke (1971), Samuel Barber's Vanessa (1958), Robert Ward's The Crucible (1961), Elie Siegmeister's The Plough and the Stars (1963), Douglas Moore's The Ballad of Baby Doe (1963), and Jack Beeson's Lizzie Borden (1965). Secondly, there were strong instrumental works: Elie Siegmiester's Second Symphony (1950) and Clarinet Concerto (1956), Roger Goeb's Fourth Symphony (1954), Alan Hovhaness's Second Symphony entitled Mysterious Mountain (1955) and And God Created Whales (1970), Vincent Persichetti's Sixth Symphony (1956), John La Montaine's Piano Concerto (1958), Ned Rorem's Third Symphony (1958), William Schuman's Eighth Symphony (1962), Samuel Barber's Piano Concerto (1962), Ray Luke's Second Symphony (1963), Peter Mennin's Seventh Symphony entitled Variations Symphony (1963), Michael Colgrass's As Quite As (1966), and Benjamin Lees' Third Symphony (1968).

Listeners could find in them tonality, functional harmony, clear rhythms, melody they could remember, and expression that addressed them directly. Why, wondered Menotti, must there be "constant and unrelieved use of dissonances." This did not mean that some of the unorthodox changes originating in the twentieth century were not introduced. They were, but judiciously and with an attempt to reconcile them with techniques from the past. None was a reactionary completely embedded in the past. None was interested merely in solving musical problems or seeking out innovation for its own sake as the primary reason for composing. None wrote about himself and about any advanced theory he was expounding in his music.

    Alienation, cynicism, and despair were absent from much of this music. Hope and faith in humanity prevailed. "There must be a virtual euphoria of hope and faith and conviction," said Alec Wilder, a composer whose music the public liked. "All cynicism must be erased from your being."[32] The compositions just cited struck audiences as human-centered and conveying delight, charm, joy, comedy, wit, serenity, bemusement, drama, sadness, or tragedy. For example, in the early sixties, Winthrop Sargeant tried to explain the appeal of Barber's music to the public of the time and wrote of the accessibility of Barber's works to the average educated listener. Barber, he said, "is not afraid of 'charm,' a word that is mistakenly regarded as a devilish one by many of his contemporaries." The music "moves," "conveys emotions and states of mind," "entails an ingredient of suspense, and . . . the listener is drawn into its insistent dramatic flow."[33]

    Whatever else the music did, it also entertained. It did not exist to explicate a theory about some "ism." When Howard Taubman reviewed Rorem's Third Symphony, in 1959, he was not completely sympathetic to the music. Yet, he admitted that Rorem wrote "gracefully, sweetly, and cheerfully. His aim is to divert, and this symphony is a crowd-pleaser. The second movement, with its mild jazz rhythms, evoked a burst of applause." David Amram, whose music showed an awareness of the typical listeners attending performances, described the audience that turned out for a 1960 concert of his music as not from "that uptight world that seems to be so much of the concert scene, especially when contemporary music is concerned. People were coming to hear the music and to enjoy themselves." Nicolas Flagello, another composer of music well-liked by the concert-goers who heard it, said his pieces were intended to be comprehensible to his audience and the composer's greatest task was "to challenge the most sophisticated musician while entertaining the most modest listener."[34]

Charles Ives had long been John the Baptist to modern innovators when Leonard Bernstein and the New York Philharmonic played his Second Symphony, on 22 February 1951. Its idiom reflected the mainstream practices of its own day (1897-1902). In its measures, Ives quoted and contemplated the meaning of nineteenth-century American hymns, popular tunes, dances, and "Columbia, the Gem of the Ocean." Nowhere was the experimentation of his later works in evidence. Majestically, in unpretentious fashion, and without affectation, the symphony's five movements reveal an affection for and a firm belief in the America he knew. Bernstein said it conveyed the real measure of Ives's greatness though it relied on normal procedures, simplicity, and easy listenability. At the work's conclusion, a frenzied and lengthy ovation broke out, which showed how greatly the audience had enjoyed the music.[35]

The symphony disconcerted musical iconoclasts. Some said Ives was kowtowing to his former teacher at Yale, Horatio Parker; others, that he had been forced to write for a public not ready to accept him on his own terms. One detected "primitive quaintness" in the music; another, a complex but hidden modernism. The tendency was to dismiss the symphony. As Paul Lang wrote: "If our performers do not stop at the innocuous Second Symphony but play his great works, we shall discover an American composer compared to whom many of those who were born when Ives quit composing appear as primitives, indeed."[36] Nevertheless, a prevalent respect for the achievements of Ives ("an American original") and his newsworthiness as a cultural sleeper kept the symphony alive in concert and on recordings.

The mid-century composers belonging to the traditional mainstream did not normally fare as well as did Ives. Nobody and nothing focused public attention on them and their works. None was thought an American original or newsworthy. Their music was supposed to speak for itself. When heard, it often pleased. When writing about it, critics pounced on its connections with tradition, finding in every sound an imitation of some past composition or other.

Unfortunately, the music public's regard was divided to

begin with, between composers and performers. The latter tended to be remembered and admired more, especially since they were physically present on the stage. Nor did writers in magazines and newspapers give much notice to the more conservative composers, save for one or two outstanding musicians like Barber and Menotti. The composers neither made noise about themselves nor originated outrageous compositions that created a sensation and thereby commanded the media's notice. What the public did not read about, it did not know about.

As with the moderns, what hearings their music was given came mainly in the form of premiers, with little or no follow-up performances. The composers had to rely on recordings to keep their music alive and in the public eye. On the one hand, the works were unfamiliar to the audience hearing them and not presented more than once; on the other hand, most music lovers stayed home and could not become acquainted with the works directly. Nor would they purchase recordings of any composer who was unfamiliar to them. Both types of listener depended on published reports to help refresh their memories, guide their thinking, and make recommendations on what recordings of contemporary works were worth purchasing.

What was published during the fifties and sixties rarely flattered the music of the traditional mainstream. Invariably, attacks on it by people who had broken with the past, or by writers intimidated by such people, appeared in articles and reviews of concerts and recordings. Anything that sported a triad or a lyric melody, that sounded beautiful in the customary sense of the word, or that evoked strong personal emotion was censured as old hat, clichéd, uninspired, unoriginal, and having nothing new to say.[37] For example, Peter Davis's review of the recording of Giannini's The Taming of the Shrew, in 1971, admits that the opera had been extremely well received wherever it had been performed since its completion in 1953. At the same time, he says it is a poor work, with its "hurry-scurry music," long stretches of sound that are "faceless filler," and musical language "written in a languishing Wagner cum Wolf-Ferrari idiom." I myself attended a Boston performance of the opera in 1960 and witnessed a huge audience of around 9,000 people go wild over its potency, vivid impact, alternating moments of charm and ardor, and luscious sounds—all of this was a secondary consideration for writers of modernist inclination. Local reviewers castigated the composer and abused the work.

Rorem writes that Menotti "single-handedly revitalized the concept of living opera for Americans," but was given the back of the hand by reviewers: "Throughout . . . [the] world his own operas are still played; from the standpoint of ratings he has no complaints. Yet to the Times he recently wailed long and loud about the endlessly derisive tone of his critical reception. Indeed, so discouraged is he with his adopted country that at sixty-three (ca. 1974) he plans to expatriate himself." When the disaster of the premier of Barber's *Anthony and Cleopatra* occurred at the Metropolitan, in 1966, the fault lay principally with Franco Zeffirelli's bloated staging. Nevertheless, caustic review after caustic review maligned the music, calling it weak, deficient in striking ideas, and rickety in construction.[38]

If writers felt free to criticize prominent traditionalists or moderates like Giannini, Menotti and Barber, they had a field day with less known composers of the same persuasion, whom they could denigrate with impunity. Fledgling composers of such inclination were knocked down repeatedly as they took their first steps.[39] Music lovers were discouraged from listening to their works, and performers feared to schedule anything that might win them bad publicity. By the end of the sixties little hope seemed to remain for the continued health of contemporary art music. Few people believed a recovery was in the offing.

Notes to Chapter 6

[1] See, for example, John I. H. Baur, *Revolution and Tradition in Modern American Art* (Cambridge, MA: Harvard University Press, 1966), 134-35.

[2] Goeb is quoted in the jacket notes to the recording CRI SRD 167: *Robert Goeb/Symphony No. 4, Jacob Druckman/Dark Upon the Harp*; Flanagan is quoted in *The American Composer Speaks*, ed. Gilbert Chase (Baton Rouge: Louisiana State University Press, 1966), 264-65.

[3] Paul Turok, "Witchful Thinking and New Music" *Music Journal* (March 1970), 49.

⁴ Fernand Ouellette, *Edgard Varèse*, trans. from the French by Derek Coltman (New York: Orion, 1968), 165-66.

⁵ Alec Wilder, *Letters I Never Sent* (Boston: Little, Brown, 1975), 203.

⁶ Ernst Bacon, *Words on Music* (Syracuse: Syracuse University Press, 1960), 54.

⁷ Hans Küng, *Art and the Question of Meaning*, trans. Edward Quinn (New York: Crossroad, 1981), 43.

⁸ This statement is indebted to Malcolm Cowley, whose comment, in *And I Worked at the Writer's Trade* (New York: Viking, 1978), 16, is paraphrased here.

⁹ John Vinton, *Essays after a Dictionary* (Bucknell University Press, 1977), 119; the quotation forms the subtitle of the book.

¹⁰ Otto Luening, *The Odyssey of an American Composer* (New York: Scribner's Sons, 1980), 16-17.

¹¹ John Rockwell, *All American Music* (New York: Knopf, 1983), 34.

¹² See, for instance, the comments in *William Grant Still and the Fusion of Cultures in American Music*, ed. Robert Bartlett Haas (Los Angeles: Black Sparrow, 1972), 114; Robert Schwarz, "The Met Proposes . . . and Disposes," *New York Times* (2 August 1992), Section 2, p. 1.

¹³ I discuss the views of post-World War II books on American composers, going back to John Knowles Paine, in *The Coming of Age of American Music* (Westport, CT: Greenwood Press, 1991), 191-205; and *A Most Wondrous Babble* (Westport, CT: Greenwood Press, 1987), 39-72.

¹⁴ Irving Howe, *A Margin of Hope* (New York: Harcourt Brace Jovanovich, 1982), 151, 153-54; the words in quotations were said by Clement Greenberg and reproduced in the book.

¹⁵ Michael Vincent Miller, review of Louis A. Sass, *Madness and Modernism*, in the *Boston Globe* (25 October 1993): Section B, p. 14.

[16] On the publishing situation, see Sessions' letter of 1959 to Leon Kirchner, in *The Correspondence of Roger Sessions*, ed. Andrea Olmstead (Boston: Northeastern University Press, 1992), 424; on the attitude of Europe, see Aaron Copland and Vivian Perlis, *Copland Since 1943* (New York: St. Martin's, 1989), 125, 394, 413.

[17] Joseph A. Mussulman, *Dear People . . . Robert Shaw* (Bloomington: Indiana University Press, 1979), 205.

[18] Küng, *Art and the Question of Meaning*, 12-13.

[19] For two commentaries on the new musical modernisms and their effect on listeners, see Wilder, *Letters I Never Mailed*, 203; Christopher Ballantine, *Music and Its Social Meanings* (New York: Gordon & Breach Science Publishers, 1984), 95.

[20] Leonard B. Meyer, *Music, The Arts, and Ideas* (Chicago: University of Chicago Press, 1967), 172.

[21] Harold Rosenberg, *The Tradition of the New* (New York: McGraw-Hill, 1959), 65-66; Suzi Gablik, *Has Modernism Failed?* (New York: Thames & Hudson, 1984), 22.

[22] John Lukacs, *The Passing of the Modern Age* (New York: Harper & Row, 1970), 128.

[23] Leonard B. Meyer, *Explaining Music* (Berkeley: University of California Press, 1973), 5.

[24] In this regard, see Nicholas E. Tawa, *Art Music in the American Society* (Metuchen, NJ: Scarecrow Press, 1987), 13-24, 168, 210.

[25] Jacques Barzun, *Music in American Life* (Bloomington: Indiana University Press, 1965), 65-66.

[26] Daniel Bell, *The Cultural Contradictions of Capitalism* (New York: Basic Books, 1976), 41, 44-45.

[27] Harold C. Schonberg, *Facing the Music* (New York: Summit Books, 1981), 57.

[28] Leonard Bernstein, *The Infinite Variety of Music* (New York: Simon & Schuster, 1966), 9.

[29] See Jacques Barzun, "The Critical Listener," in *Critical Questions*, ed. Bea Friedland (Chicago: University of Chicago, 1982), 31.

[30] Harold Rosenberg, *The Anxious Object* (New York: Horizon, 1964), 237.

[31] See Irving Howe, "The Idea of the Modern," in *Selected Writings, 1950-1990* (New York: Harcourt Brace Jovanovich, 1990), 140-41.

[32] John Gruen, *Menotti* (New York: Macmillan, 1978), 117-18; Wilder, *Letters I Never Mailed*, 133.

[33] See Winthrop Sargeant, "Musical Events," *New Yorker* (14 January 1961): 106; (16 November 1963): 127-28.

[34] John Tasker Howard, *Our American Music*, 4th ed. (New York: Crowell, 1965), 609; David Amram, *Vibrations* (New York: Macmillan, 1968), 357; David Ewen, *American Composers* (New York: Putnam's Sons, 1982), s.v. "Flagello, Nicolas."

[35] See David Johnson's jacket notes for the recording Columbia KS 6155: *Charles Ives: Symphony No. 2*.

[36] Howard, *Our American Music*, 367.

[37] For further discussion of these negative reports, see Nicholas E. Tawa, *A Most Wondrous Babble* (Westport, CT: Greenwood Press, 1987), Chapter 6.

[38] See Peter G. Davis, review of CRI 272: *Vittorio Giannini: The Taming of the Shrew*, in *High Fidelity* (October, 1971): 94; Ned Rorem, *An Absolute Gift* (New York: Simon & Schuster, 1978), 65; Don A. Hennessee, *Samuel Barber: A Bio-Bibliography* (Westport, CT: Greenwood Press, 1985), 172-73; Barbara B. Heyman, *Samuel Barber* (New York: Oxford University Press, 1992), 322-24.

[39] I can personally testify to this, seeing several talented acquaintances leave off composing altogether and, later, hearing from others that they had done the same. My Second String Quartet won the Knight Chamber Music Prize in 1951, but was deleted from a Fromm-Foundation concert because insufficiently atonal. It took me a few years, but I, too, eventually ceased composing music.

Chapter 7

Insular Modernism

The atonal and serial American composers who began appearing in the late forties and early fifties formed the core group that dominated modern music-making for around twenty years after World War II ended. Although their methods of composition had been around since the beginning of the century, they gained a strong hold on American composers only with the fifties. The trend toward increased chromaticism, looser key relationships, and growing complexity in chord structures unrelated to function had been going on throughout the nineteenth century. However, an ear for the actual sound produced and its effect on listeners was also present then. By the century's close, forward-looking musicians were sensing that Richard Wagner, Richard Strauss, and Claude Debussy had pushed the old tonal system about as far as it could go. Therefore, the Viennese composers, Arnold Schoenberg, in his *Three Piano Pieces*, opus 11 (1908-09), and Anton Webern, in his *Five Songs*, opus 3 (1907-09), went one step further. They abandoned tonality for atonality—where no one key was dominant. The focal tonic triad no longer held sway. All twelve tones of the chromatic scale were used without inhibition, and discordant sound prevailed. A free employment of all twelve tones, nonetheless, produced the urgent problem of control, of how to regulate sound. This, Schoenberg first tried to solve in his five *Klavierstücke*, opus 23 (1920-23). The work incorporated, for the first time, the serial organization of all twelve tones of the chromatic scale. A specific order of pitches, which avoided tonal allusions and barred redundancy, decided the entire melodic and harmonic material for the music. Schoenberg, and the composers who later followed his lead, claimed the systems they developed were rational ones and had evolved out of tradition, being a natural consequence of the progression toward greater chromaticism, weakening of tonality, and the blurring of distinctions between consonance and dissonance. Yet, as far as the general music public was concerned, the emphasis seemed more on the explication of a theory, less on the actual sound produced and its effect on listeners. No matter how much Schoenberg insisted that his was a creative act and making music his concern, audiences usually thought otherwise. Fictional stories arose that were detrimental to twelve-tone music. For example, after completing his Fourth String Quartet in 1936, the story was bruited about that a friend stopped him on a Los Angeles street and asked what the work sounded like. Schoenberg allegedly replied: "I don't know, I haven't heard it yet."[1] Although Alban Berg and Anton Webern took up Schoenberg's twelve-tone ideas, very few other composers accepted them.

For about twenty years, innovative American musicians had expressed only a mild interest in the theories emanating from Vienna. Yet during these years, Carl Ruggles and Wallingford Riegger did experiment with atonality and the employment of tone-rows in their music. Aaron Copland made similar gestures during the early thirties. Adolph Weiss, a pupil of Schoenberg, was an American devotee of tone-row composition, starting in 1927. On the other hand, the creative explorations of none of these men made much of an impression on other American musicians and earned hostility from American listeners.

Nevertheless, the twelve-tone system had continued to interest some American composers, especially after the arrival of Schoenberg and other Central-European advocates of the system in the United States. They came from a Germany and, later, an Austria ruled by the Nazis, and from a Europe on the verge of war. In 1947, the American George Perle turned to this method with his Third String Quartet. Three years later Ross Lee Finney completed his Sixth String Quartet, followed the next year by Ben Weber's Symphony in Four Movements, and in 1953 by Roger Sessions' Violin Sonata. All three composers adapted from then on some version of Schoenberg's dodecaphonic procedures for their own use. It must be emphasized that, for all of the American composers named, twelve-tonalism was a means for organizing a composition. It was not the predominant feature or raison d'être of the composition itself. All were sincere musicians, despite the music public's reluctance to accept their music.

Serialism and Atonality

After World War II, several composers began to extend Schoenberg's ideas, especially as interpreted by Anton Webern. Their primary interest was not the public's approval but the formulation of new approaches to music composition. Soon they had evolved the tenets of serialism, the manipulation of a designated set of components fixed in a particular sequence or series. The components, as before, included pitches, but now there was added dynamics, durations of sound, and other musical values. The resultant music required a large percentage of precompositional charting out and, therefore, of artistic determinacy. It evidenced an extremely aware and rational scheme for musical composition, often seemingly the result more of diligent effort than of inspiration. Certainly, Babbitt and his colleagues thought that the devising of theoretical systems was in itself a sort of creativity. Furthermore, because nineteenth-century conventional guidelines were no longer operative, they decided that the composer himself had to give an inclusive organization to his materials, where every element was integrated into a set of determinates.[2]

As never before, voices were raised, including those of advanced thinkers like Sessions, warning that contemporary composers' viewpoints and the musical training of composers-to-be were elevating theoretical concepts and analysis far above craftsmanship and musicality, a direction that could only lead to creative disaster. At the same time, solid musicians like Copland cautioned that this new orientation was having a deleterious effect: "The concentration on analysis of the innards of all works seems rather special to the present period. There was always analysis going on, but not the kind one is familiar with in the pages of *PERSPECTIVES* [the periodical devoted mainly to serialist views]. That's a new manifestation." No interest was shown "in the musical content," only "about the way it's put together."[3]

Theory replaced what actually was heard. Walter Piston tells of a young composer who came to him with a score. Piston asked, "What about the harmony?" and received the reply, "I don't use harmony." "As soon as you put two notes together, you've got harmony . . . somebody will hear this chord over here and think, hmm, G, B, D. . . . How about that?" "You aren't supposed to hear it that way." Piston: "Now, I think that's whistling in the dark to say you're not supposed to. The fact is you do."[4]

Musical composition was more and more considered a question of technical procedure whose devices, routines, and more arcane processes could be gotten from practitioners in the know, recent treatises on the management of music elements, and the esoteric analyses published in *Perspectives of New Music*, the house organ of serialists, founded in 1962. George Rochberg, who was once a member of this movement, later became an apostate from serialism. He then rejected the idea that what happened at any point in a composition had to be largely the product of theory and preconceived organization. Rochberg found himself disturbed because his mind could never anticipate the sounds resulting from the mechanism it had set in motion. He echoes the apocryphal tale about Schoenberg and his Fourth Quartet when he states:

> One suspects that some of the works [serially composed] . . . are not meant so much to be understood, as to be demonstrated. . . . [Yet] we don't understand Beethoven by conceptualizing the scale of the piece and rules of harmony and counterpoint; so why should we 'understand' contemporary music by looking for tone-rows, or rhythmic rows, or dynamic rows, and watching for inversions, retrogrades, and so on? The test for the aesthetic validity of the music . . . has to depend in the end upon its perceptual intelligibility, and not on any demonstration of its underlying organization.[5]

The established structures that had aided listeners' understanding and held their attention were eliminated. Connections with past music were sundered, including the pioneering music of earlier modernists, whether Stravinsky, Bartók, or Berg. The audience could latch on to no identifiable themes, phrases, periods, or developments. No rhythmic pulse was apparent. Harmony served no purpose. Repetition of any sort was avoided. Already, in the early fifties, the realization grew that listeners were feeling thwarted and remembering nothing of what they heard. The music was beginning to strike them as stagnant and motionless, its coloration unchanging.

The new serialism was advanced by three men especially, the German Karlheinz Stockhausen, the Frenchman Pierre Boulez, and the American Milton Babbitt. Both Stockhausen and Boulez had experienced the influence of Olivier Messiaen, whose *Mode de Valeurs et d'Intensités* for piano, of 1949, and *Structures 1a* for two pianos, of 1952, were based on the precompositional selection of a specific set of musical components that determined the music's course. Milton Babbitt, a mathematician and a student of Sessions, proved himself at the forefront of the movement when, in 1947, he wrote *Three Compositions for Piano*, where he serialized not only the twelve tones but also dynamics and rhythms. He followed this with several articles explaining his notions about serialism. These involved the construction of complete musical formats for the compositions still to be written, which in themselves emerged as creative realizations. In 1959, he became a codirector of the Columbia-Princeton Electronic Music Center and shortly produced two works employing electronic means, *Composition for Synthesizer* (1961-63) and *Philomel* (1964).

The majority of American music radicals prominent in the fifties and early sixties exerted a counteracting force against what they interpreted as the isolationism and tight nationalism that followed the war. They also concentrated their attention on the international style of abstract, chromatic, and highly dissonant music sprouting anew in the American ground.[6] Whether Gershwin's *American in Paris*, Barber's First Symphony, Copland's *Appalachian Spring*, or Moore's *The Ballad of Baby Doe*, the likelihood that their tonal-centered attributes would build up into a distinctively American structure collapsed before the sustained onslaught on current music of every description. Nothing native remained, only an international style that had originated in Vienna and, at best, was given an American accent. First, the younger musicians took their cue from the Central-European composers who had come to America just before the outbreak of World War II. Second, they observed the way "Pierre Boulez, Karlheinz, and their aides" had won the "modern-music war between Europe and America for world control over music's advanced positions" during the fifties and found merit in doing the same in the United States.[7] Third, they valued the immediate example of Babbitt and the handful of other Americans experimenting with dodecaphonic procedures.

Aroused by these three influences, the native modernists repudiated all of the recent contemporary music as either crude or superficial: "By the fifties, the combined organization [the League of Composers and the International Society for Contemporary Music] had been seized by Milton Babbitt and others of his views and turned into a forum for uncompromising serialism."[8] Schoenbergian principles, as interpreted and refined by his disciple Anton Webern, and by younger Europeans like Boulez and Americans like Babbitt, had won out.

One or two notable composers who were atonalists did not fit the serialist image. Nevertheless, they too had to exercise some form of control over their musical material. Elliott Carter, for example, decided in 1951 that he would write only to please himself and came out with his First String Quartet. From then on, he would use some specific combination of tones (a *klang*) as an integrating element, from which he derived the ever-varied substance of the work.

Some of the more outstanding and innovatively constructed works of these years are Babbitt's *Philomel* (1964); Rochberg's Chamber Symphony (1953), *Cheltenham Concerto* (1958), and Second String Quartet (1961); Charles Wuorinen's Chamber Concerto for Flute and Ten Players (1964), Duo for Violin and Piano (1967), *Time's Enconium* (1969), and *Contrafactum* (1969); Lucas Foss's *Time Cycle* (1960); Melvin Powell's *Stanzas* (1959) and Piano Quintet (1959); Andrew Imbrie's Third and Fourth String Quartet (1957, 1969); Seymour Shifrin's Serenade (1954), *Satires of Circumstance* (1964), and Third and Fourth String Quartets (1966, 1967); Leon Kirchner's First, Second, and Third String Quartet (1949, 1958, 1966) and Concerto for Violin, Cello, Ten Winds, and Percussion (1960); and Ben Weber's Serenade for Strings (1956) and Piano Concerto (1961).

The Move to Isolation

Several of these Americans had once maintained that no academic institution would preempt them. Now they allowed themselves to inhabit the universities they had earlier considered the mainstay for reactionary musical thinking, giving rise to the phrase academic modernism. They wrote for specialized modern music ensembles sponsored by and "in residence" at universities and traveled from one concert to another, rarely leaving the academic orbit. John Rockwell explained this resorting to the universities as follows:

> Today's composers, in the logical extension of the romantic's demand for freedom ('Who cares . . .'), have alienated not just their public but particularly the wealthier (and thus generally more conservative) members of that public. They are therefore almost forced, apart from peer-dominated pittance grants from governmental agencies, to turn to the academy for sustenance. In the academy, they find sympathy for a linked set of ideas: musical composition as an arena for pure research, an ever more complex musical syntax expanding our perceptual limits, and the long-cherished notion of the inevitable 'lag' between present composition and future appreciation, pushed now almost to infinity.[9]

When asked in 1965 about Stravinsky's advice to composers not to teach at universities, Sessions replied that no problem existed in the United States, since academic composers felt completely free. In contrast, Copland believed, in 1967, that it was unhealthy for all composers to take shelter in universities and thus avoid testing what they did by going "outside, in the big world."[10]

With the year 1966, these academics were sufficiently numerous to form the American Society of University Composers. Among the cofounders were Donald Martino, Peter Westergaard, Henry Weinberg, Charles Wuorinen, James Randall, and Benjamin Boretz—all of their music exhibiting some facet of serial organization in their music. Within twenty years, the membership would grow to around 900. On the whole, these musicians subscribed to the view of Theodore Adorno, an advocate for the serial cause who claimed "there is in every epoch just one advanced stock of [musical] material" (singling out "almost all of current artistic production as worthless"), and that there were "pedagogical virtues" in "academicism."[11]

Enclosed within the walls of higher learning, the composers terminated any show they might have had of communicating with the musical public, satisfied with the prerogatives that came with academic life. Wherever they located, they produced likeminded student composers who, on graduation, needed to find positions within a university, since there was no living for them in the outside world. To cite an example of how these teachers indoctrinated young people with the principles of atonality and tone-rows, Sessions once wrote to Schoenberg that he was making his students analyze and study Schoenberg's Piano Concerto and Fourth String Quartet. One class had spent six weeks on the quartet and listened to it on records for seven hours a week. Sessions said that he also led many discussions on related contemporary-music issues.[12]

For a long while, a self-perpetuating circle of serialists and atonalists prevailed in holding the music-composition posts in higher education and peopling the committees that decided on grants, prizes, and commissions. Thus it was that the Ford Foundation, through the pianist Jacob Lateiner, commissioned Elliott Carter to compose his Piano Concerto. Then, the Martha Baird Rockefeller Fund for Music, the Steinway Foundation, and the National Council on the Arts made possible its performance with the Boston Symphony Orchestra and also the recording of the work. At long last, after looking on from outside the "establishment," the serialists themselves became an influential pressure group and retained positions from which they were difficult to dislodge.[13] "No previous style was nearly so politically adept," the composer William Bolcolm points out, "nor so total in its power to sway and hold the majority of artists as modernism [in the form of this 'post-Webern movement']."[14]

In the role of concerned citizens, these modernists felt repelled by the unscrupulous and reckless political oppression unleashed during the sway of Senator Joseph McCarthy (1950-1954). There was the famous episode, on 22 May 1953, of McCarthy summoning Aaron Copland to appear before his committee and explain his alleged affiliation with Communism. By then, he and Roger Sessions were on the McCarthy list of suspects. An intimidated Passport Office refused to grant Copland a passport for travel abroad, the University of Alabama cancelled its invitation for him to speak at a composer's forum, and the

Hollywood Bowl suspended a scheduled performance of his music. In 1954, the University of Colorado voided his appearance as a Reynolds Lecturer, and both the Borough of Brooklyn and ASCAP, in 1956, took back the formal commendations they had voted to grant him. Chapters of the American Legion vociferously attacked any institution that invited Copland to visit, as they did the University of Buffalo in 1957 and the University of Texas in 1962.[15]

A society that could countenance an enemy to free thought, who was so nasty and infamous, only caused composers to affirm the conviction of their own righteousness, which in any event had usually been a modernist penchant. Modesty about one's artistic accomplishments, we can suspect, was more apt to grow from being appreciated by more than a minuscule audience, which was not in the cards for them. Most modernists had begun with strong beliefs in themselves and this allowed them to continue. They could not accept that what would give them a better and more honest opinion of their music's worth was its ability to touch others in some significant way, not its failure to please. In short, only if the music public had revealed it prized them and thus decided their actual merits, rather than the ones they assumed for themselves, would they have achieved modesty. Since the public neither prized them nor found merit in their music, they remained unhumble and continued their exaggerated estimate of their own importance.

Nobody seized on the occasion to do some examination of his deeper motives and values and to reassess his stance. Musical extremists of the fifties "could now easily throw out the accusation of 'McCarthyism' at any critic."[16] At the same time they formed a protective set within academic walls in order to ward off all adversaries. According to an observation made by Van Wyck Brooks, in 1958, such a circle formed a defensive alliance against what it defined as a Philistine world: "These lonely souls hold hands, as it were, from coast to coast, feeling that they are members of a true élite who are both 'of one's time' and 'in the know.' In their petite chapelle, surrounded by their palisade, they can write [purely] . . . , ignoring the world in which they live . . . ."[17]

Sessions, in 1956, even as he approved the composer's withdrawal into the university, worried about the separation of the new complex music from its human ties. He fretted over the possibility that musical communication was changing from the difficult to the impossible. He held that the problems with winning over listeners were encouraging a counteraction among "the younger of our composers" that amounted to a harmful escape "into self-pity . . . [which was] essentially an act of self-destruction."[18] One of the most influential of the younger composers, Milton Babbitt, did not harbor his mentor's qualms. He admitted to the musical and societal isolation, calling it irreversible, inevitable, yet advantageous to the composer. In 1958, he wrote:

> I dare suggest that the composer would do himself and his music an immediate and eventual service by total, resolute, and voluntary withdrawal from this public world to one of private performance and electronic media, with its very real possibility of complete elimination of the public and social aspects of musical composition. . . . The composer would be free to pursue a private life of professional achievement, as opposed to a public life of unprofessional compromise and exhibitionism. . . . It is only proper that the university, which—significantly—has provided so many contemporary composers with their professional training and general education, should provide a home for the 'complex,' 'difficult,' and 'problematical' in music.[19]

Babbitt then went on to equate composition with research, music with physics, and the composer with the mathematician, claiming they were equivalent to each other. He added that however bored and puzzled an audience was, it had no right to resent and denounce what it could never understand.

A younger and more caustic serialist than Babbitt, Charles Wuorinen, defended the trend toward isolation and at the same time insisted it was society's responsibility to free and provide for its artists. (He advanced no convincing reason about why it was society's responsibility.) He cared not at all about concert audiences, equating them with the mindless and passive listeners addicted to "juke-boxes" in bars. Whether they liked or disliked music was unimportant; their judgment was worthless. They figuratively or literally slept at concerts. His true audience, he said, consisted mostly of other composers, though he hoped that eventually performers and cultivated individuals would be won over.[20]

In part, the stance of Wuorinen and his colleagues was attributable to the unprecedentedly stormy postwar period, with its daunting questions concerning existence in general and one's place in the world scheme in particular. It left unaccepted and exposed young artists trying to live on amidst adverse conditions. They instinctively isolated themselves from the surrounding turbulence and shunned potentially perturbing involvement with others by resorting only to their own intellects and, in their solitude, turning out highly rational and abstract compositions. Moreover, they advised their students to think of music in relation to itself alone in preference to its relation to the rest of humanity, thus increasingly draining it of its essential substance.

Even as American society was turning more and more to popular music, these extremists scorned writing music to entertain, consequently contributing even more to the thinning of the art-music audience. To entertain, they said, made their compositions into marketplace goods and compromised their artistic morality. That master of entertainment George Gershwin, at best only grudgingly accepted into the ranks of creative artists, now received total dismissal. "The Higher Criticism does not permit that name to enter the category of Significant Composers," said an irked Leonard Bernstein in April 1973, and his works were "easily demolished by the Higher Criticism."[21] Alec Wilder, who wrote a series of works deliberately called "Entertainments," did so "to make very certain the audience knew that the purpose of the pieces was specifically to entertain and also specifically not to teach." Predictably, Wilder's music was attacked by a Mr. Long (the pseudonym of Wallingford Riegger) as "unpardonable" because not sufficiently serious, contemporaneous, portentous, and unconventional.[22] Serialists would have read with horror what William Grant Still wrote into his diary, in 1957, after he had surveyed the contemporary-music scene: "There is today a great need for music that reaches beyond the intellect into the listeners' hearts."[23] To them, Still was a sentimentalist.

A younger group of music writers, much more closely identified with the new music, savaged most works that sounded tonal and melodic in the customary sense, especially if they were also popular. Menotti's operas met with vehement ridicule and repudiation as legitimate art compositions: "The insults that most of my operas had to endure . . . would make a booklet as terrifying as Malleus Maleficarum," said the composer.[24] His friend Barber's music offended their ears, though not the public's. They interpreted it as naive, boring, genteel, trashy, too effusively melodic, self-indulgent, showing no talent, in bad taste, and "too shamelessly calculated to appeal to an American audience that . . hated modern music." This music included works like the Cello Concerto (1945), *Medea's Meditation and Dance of Vengeance* (1956), the opera *Vanessa* (1958), and the Piano Concerto (1962). Typical was Alfred Frankenstein's review of the *Medea* music, when played in San Francisco. It impressed him "as unmitigated trash and left a bad taste, although many present obviously like it. They gave Schippers one of the season's warmest ovations when it was over."[25]

Otto Luening, who eventually made a name for himself as a pioneer in electronic-tape experimentation, writes that he composed his *Kentucky Concerto* for the Louisville orchestra in 1951. When it received its initial performance at a "Music in the Making" concert in New York City, in 1952, the audience gave it an enthusiastic reception. Nevertheless, "at the panel discussion, which took place after every forum, one of the panel members thought the piece was too popular and that it really should be called Saturday Night at the Firehouse. A young woman in the audience came to my defense. 'I think what has been insinuated about Mr. Luening's piece is all wrong,' she said. 'When I arrived here I felt somewhat depressed, and his *Kentucky Concerto* gave me unadulterated pleasure the first note to the last. I feel as if I could fly.' She flapped her elbows a bit. The audience cheered, and I blushed. I have not forgotten that perceptive young woman."[26]

The atonal camp of composers found no nourishment in the rapprochements between composer and public hammered out during the late thirties and forties, and evidently questioned the devotion to laissez-faire that sparked contemporary American culture. In the 1950s, Copland's style in *Rodeo* and *Appalachian Spring* was found dated, suspect, and lacking integrity because well-liked. Only Copland's works whose style yielded to the serialists, like *Connotations* (1962) and *Inscape* (1967), had hope for advocacy among the younger set. In 1968, Copland admitted that musicians like Babbitt and Carter had replaced him as leaders of American music, because they did not bear the stigma of having composed successful music, which made one "automatically suspect."[27]

If a young contemporary composer dared to write in a tonal style, he courted ostracism. This assuredly came true for William Flanagan. Ned Rorem claims that though Flanagan excelled as a song composer, he was "indifferent to innovation for its own sake." The great demands he made of himself and the ceaseless condemnation he experienced from the powerful serialist camp produced unbearable tensions—"the increasing stress of being an unappreciated conservative in a time of artistic upheaval, was partly responsible for his suicide," in 1969. Another young composer, Lee Hoiby, quickly realized that contemporary modernists would move to deny him performances and credibility as an artist, despite warm approval of his music by audiences: "I thought I would have a pretty easy time of it. My music was accessible. Audiences loved it. But I had a rude awakening. Critics did not like it. I was definitely out of step with the 1950s."[28] As a contrast, these same critics commended music like that of Easley Blackwood's First Symphony (1958) for the consistent use of dissonant, rigorous, and difficult language, for adhering to an exceptional "gravity of utterance," and for an "absolute refusal to indulge in the kind of instrumental or expressive monkeyshines that is said to curry favor with audiences and make for easy listening." Hardly any major commentator was willing to expose himself to censure with no likelihood of retreat as was Winthrop Sargent, who said the Blackwood symphony was nothing but "foundation music" meant to win the approval of influential colleagues and to find grant money, despite its lack of meaning for audiences.[29]

The radicals of the twenties and early thirties had attempted to address a group of supporters from the larger musical world who supported them and allowed them to represent its taste in music. However, in the post-World War II period, it was soon apparent that the new radicals had lost the regard and allegiance of any weighty body of music lovers, however restricted in size, outside their own ranks and the university. Nor were the revolutionary European composers willing to support them. One notes, for example, Boulez's caustic remarks about *Perspective of New*

Music and its serialist writer-composers, entrenched in American universities, who thought they were "great scientists", but were merely academic pedants: "I know great scientists and they possess invention and imagination. Composers who publish in this journal never discuss important questions of choice and decision. They write only about putting different things together. This is not an esthetic point of view. It's what I call a 'cashier's point of view'." Predictably, these remarks, infuriated only the university composers. The music public took no interest in the controversy.[30]

Whatever power their militancy had during the fifties would dissipate in the sixties. By the seventies the severe serial and atonal movement that dominated the fifties was virtually extinct. One recalls Montaigne's essay on "Moderation," where he warned that grasping any idea or principle too fervently can make us venomous, hostile to discourse with others, hostile to pleasure, and unable to benefit ourselves let alone others.

The Resurrection of the Autonomous Artist

"We must insist, above all, on the autonomy of the artist, and resist with the greatest energy all those who, whether incited by totalitarian movements or by the pressure of large-scale economy, would press for limitations of that autonomy." These words of Sessions, uttered just after the end of World War II, failed to foresee that the composers, once granted their complete freedom and not forced to follow "the law of the lowest common denominator, in providing the public with 'what it wants'," would themselves exhibit totalitarian cultural traits. In addition, they would write a great deal of music that offered less than the "vital experience" he valued. Here, he was embodying the views of the older modernists from the twenties and of the younger serialists and atonalists of the fifties and sixties. The same was true when Sessions, perhaps disingenuously, spoke of the aims of contemporary American composers being no different from those of any other time or place. These aims, he claimed, focused on using one's assets, whatever they might be, to compose artistic works significant for their creator and in relation to his surroundings, "just as artists have done in other times and places."[31] He left out the bothersome idea that the most illustrious composers of 100 or more years before had the attitudes and the pleasuring of their patrons and audiences also in mind. For example, on the one hand, eighteenth-century music lovers throughout Europe appreciated the sensuous appeal of contemporary Italian music; on the other, Sessions, from his mid-twentieth century perspective, did not care for it: ". . . in the eighteenth century Handel and Mozart went to study in Italy. Bach studied the music of Vivaldi (God knows why)."[32]

The renewed distortion of the past and reinstatement of the values of the twenties appeared in the writings of Richard Goldman, fourteen years younger than Sessions. In the year 1954, he wrote that in order to achieve excellence, music that constituted "high art" had to demand effort for its perception. Its composers had to consciously avoid evoking the "cheap response" from the mass of Americans who were, after all, "mediocre and . . witless." Then he made another distorted antidemocratic comment, which would appall any believer in what America stands for: "Prince Esterhazy at least listened to Haydn's music and, from what we are told, appeared to enjoy it. He did not, it may also be noted, feel obliged to share his enjoyment with those who could not hear, or to convince the entire population of Hungary that listening outside the windows would make them 'cultured'."[33]

To any American concerned with the preoccupations, needs, and well-being of their fellow men and women, such a dismissal of people is unacceptable. He would have asked why composers, through serial and atonal compositions, had to mirror the anxieties and turmoil of their time? Why not show through music the confidence and trust in those human principles that have endured over the centuries, the humanist would reply. Art should offer a promise of better things than just desolation.[34] It was also highly doubtful that a contemporary Prince Esterhazy would have enjoyed such music as the serialists wrote. Indeed, members of the former aristocracy were certainly not provided at birth with musical insight and the gift for listening. Moreover, the generality of music lovers, in the late-twentieth century, were more apt to be discerning, tolerant, and willing to give the composer a chance to have his say. In Prince Esterhazy's time, the highborn audience was habitually orthodox, suspicious of artistic individuality, and insistent on having amiable rather than consequential music from their servant-composers.

All this said, the staunch modernist of the fifties and sixties held that the general music public had no legitimate claims on the artist. To create a valid musical composition required absolute freedom and personal honesty. A commitment to artistry exonerated the insistence on a self-reliant way of life. The creation of a work of art was, among other things, a demonstration of supreme emancipation that displaced the unavoidable competition with other composers, the corrupting drive for success, and the financial trafficking that went with earning a living. For example, Mario Davidovsky, active in the Columbia-Princeton academic orbit from the late-fifties on, whose music combined mathematics and electronics, said that he thought of the audience as an abstraction and not as a part of the creative process. He relied on himself alone. Yes, he did wish for success, for recognition of his abilities, but such considerations did not affect the choices a composer elected to make, as opposed to the compulsory acts of those music writers who demonstrated mere proficiency and aimed at commercial success: "My success is measured by the success of the piece itself, not by the success of the piece in terms of the critical or the audience reception."[35] What he meant by the success of the piece itself, he failed to explain. Apparently, Davidovsky means that he himself was satisfied with what he had wrought, that alone mattered—certainly a curious interpretation of success.

In the same way, Elliott Carter said that in the early fifties he decided it was not his professional and social responsibility to write interesting and understandable music for others, much as others might want him to. His interests did not lie in this direction. Rather, he wished to concentrate on what had always been his main concern, the writing of "advanced" works whose complexity demanded considerable exertion for musicians to perform and listeners to understand. He would always rely on his own "private judgment," without worry about his music's reception by an audience. Popularity was of no importance to him.[36]

Countering Goldman, Davidovsky and Carter's claim of disinterest in public acceptance was John Gruen's statement: "I have always considered anyone who denied wanting to be a star a barefaced liar. As for me, I want to be a star." By this he meant, among other things: "A composer of unrivalled genius and untrammeled invention whose awesome creativity has made him the undisputed king of the concert hall—and tin-pan alley?"[37] By the time he wrote this, around 1967, Gruen had interviewed many composers and written about them, their attitudes, and their music.

Whether in the mind of Sessions, Goldman, Davidovsky, or Carter, there was an element of faulty reasoning in being indifferent, if not pleased, because one's music was "advanced" and required so much effort to comprehend that scarcely anyone is won over by it. Without doubt, they wanted their music performed and heard by someone, no matter their disclaimers. They surely did not want to hide their works in a drawer. Therefore, their rejection of the public, which was abrim with possible listeners, showed disdain for what was most worthwhile in their vocation. As they persisted in saying they wrote only to express themselves, they should not have felt surprised because it became an actuality. Few music lovers would experience the desire to listen. Indeed, the music existed for the composer alone, and the audience felt no inclination to encroach on his subjective contemplations. Many a sincere music lover would have preferred that the artist try to grasp and assimilate, to the best of his ability, everything that was happening within him and within all human beings, so that his music could reveal the heights of human experience, whatever the abnormalities of the times in which he lives.

A common charge was that the serial and atonal composers took themselves too seriously; most, though not all, found the depiction of happiness to be a trivial occupation. They seemed to specialize in the representation of anxiety, complaint, and affliction through fidgety and ephemeral instrumental sounds and through austere or psychotic declamation if the voice was used. They failed, critics said, to see that constant somberness too often proved tiresome, because every somber composer evidenced earnestness about something that nobody else cared about.[38] When they elevated a work into the masterpiece class, they justified their act as did Richard Goldman of Wallingford Riegger's Third Symphony, at the time that it won the New York Music Critics Circles Award, in 1948: "It is forceful, original, serious, terse, moving, and skillful. It will, of course, find no easy road to popularity, for while skill impresses and originality sometimes amuses, passion frightens and independence offends many frequenters of concert halls. In unpopular virtues, Riegger's work abounds. . . . He is too sincere a musician to coin musical small change for the machines of mass distribution."[39]

In constancy to seriousness and originality, the modernist, like his older colleagues from the twenties, detected sincerity and integrity. For example, when Ives's music of fifty years before was rehabilitated in the postwar decades, it was not because of its debts to the past, nor for its many instances of humor. Witness Carter's romantic and fictional interpretation of the musician he admired: Ives, to him, was an eminent composer. The eminence stemmed from Ives's musical presentations, which were vigorous and incorporated the conflict between a highly original and visionary artist and the American public. This conflict produced anger and exhaustion in Ives and forced him to withdraw into a subjective world.[40]

It was plain that the views of the modern composers of the earlier post-World War I years were resurrected with a vengeance at mid-century.

The Public Response

What sort of music lover did the innovative composers hope to win over? Wuorinen's "cultivated individual" was echoed in Carter's "ideal listener" and both recalled Sessions's "intelligent listener" and Copland's "gifted listener." A person of this description, they agreed, had a natural aptitude for listening and did so alertly and frequently, until he became so familiar with a difficult work that he enjoyed it and could remember it whenever he wished. What he had knowledge of was the total structure, the musical details, and the expressive intent of the piece.[41]

Nevertheless, it was preposterous thus to assume the possible existence of such a listener even in small numbers. Scarcely anybody could be the appropriate type of auditor for music of this sort. When confronting a severely serial composition, how many people could be receptive, informed, enthusiastic, and capable of consuming all the discordant sounds without indigestion? Some admonitions to do this, coming from composers and their advocates, suggest illusion, a patrician assumption that one can be simultaneously relaxed with and thoroughly informed about posttriadic music that followed no common-practice guidelines.

It was not just the technical aspects of serial music that bothered many Americans but also a suspected expressive dishonesty. The minimalist composer Steve Reich observed some years (1987) after the heyday of serialism, that he respected Schoenberg but resisted writing like him. He also had some regard for Stockhausen, Berio, and Boulez, who had been trying "to pick up the pieces" after World War II, but not for the American composers of like persuasion. "In the real context of tailfins, Chuck Berry, and millions of burgers sold—to pretend that instead we're really going to have the dark-brown Angst of Vienna is a lie, a musical lie, and I think these people are musical liars and their work isn't worth . . . (snaps fingers) that!"[42]

The unhappy realization that an audience for his music was almost nonexistent prompted Babbitt to say, in 1958, that composers like him were anachronisms. However much time and energy went into composing a piece, the music had no value to either the performer or the general public. It received one or two performances at poorly attended concerts, whose attendees were mostly other professionals. "At best," he said, "the music would appear to be for, of, and by specialists."[43]

Neither composer, performer, conductor, nor music critic could be taken as models for enlightened listening, wrote Jacques Barzun in 1965. No audience with the competency the composers had in mind existed in actuality. What they had to deal with was a heterogeneous constituency that felt it possessed intelligence and that corresponded with the social diversity of American society.[44] It also accepted no obligation to devote its spare time to repeatedly listen to a new work that more often than not proved upsetting.

Elliott Carter, when explaining his Double Concerto for Harpsichord and Piano with Two Chamber Orchestras and his Duo for Violin and Piano (1961 and 1974, respectively), put his finger on an element that disturbed the music public extremely about the new music: "The music gives the impression of being continuous, of evolving constantly from beginning to end. . . . While this earlier music [that he wrote before the fifties] was based on themes and their development, here the musical ideas are not themes or melodies but rather groupings of sound materials. . . . . There is no repetition, but a constant invention of new things."[45] The off-putting methods to listeners that Carter employed were the constant evolvement of new sounds, the absence of recognizable theme or melody, and the complete rejection of repetition.

The passion for an imposed order that the eye could detect but the ear could never hear also dissuaded people from listening. In the 1920s, when Varèse and Antheil were evolving novel structures, their music sounded as if it was developing organically. It had a sense of mystery and a definite personality about it. Often it seemed that creative vision, not invariably commanded by intellect alone, was acting on the material. There was always at least a tacit acceptance of the unavoidable connections between inspiration, musical design, and artistic mastery. They allowed recognizable repetition to occur. Acceptance of their music may not have been as wide as the composers had hoped, but at least people listened to, got excited over, and discussed it.

As a contrast, the works of the post-World War II years too often appeared interchangeable one with another, all conforming to the same mold. The music was uncompromisingly experimental, originating from a narrow range of assumptions. Each composition resulted from a singular combination of postulates. The audience heard few passages memorable enough to distinguish one piece from the other. Getting to know even one piece took a tremendous amount of listening time and did not make it easier to get to know additional works by the same composer. No wonder only extremely small numbers of Americans turned out willingly to hear it. Beyond the circle of the composers, their few followers, and writers specializing in modernity, hardly anyone mentioned the music, let alone got excited over it.

Serialism struck the music public as exaggerated adherence to a singular and artificial manner of composing. Like Van Wyck Brooks, many of its members suspected such mannerism to be "the sign of a second-rate mind; pride in mannerism is the sign of a third-rate mind."[46] Moreover, several of the more talented modernists, like Elliott Carter, did worry about the promotion of rigid musical systems that froze into place the ideas of composers like Schoenberg, Berg, and Messiaen. He saw this as leading into a blind alley.[47] Or, as the composer Roger Goeb said, "serialization and other similar techniques" were becoming sterile mannerisms because they were "so useful to the academically minded and the non-musical composer[s]," who were flooding the market with "superficial and totally unsatisfactory examples of this kind of music."[48]

Intricate discussions about the new music emerged from the modernist camps and took the form of radio and pre-concert lectures, in articles appearing in music and, to a lesser degree, general periodicals and newspapers, and in books entirely devoted to the subject. These sometimes were helpful to pedagogues. But the elaborate arguments for specific artistic doctrines and the endless explanations of creative techniques perplexed the nonprofessional. Only a few writers provided guidance to the music while omitting ideological rambles. Only a few commentators exercised the gentler art of persuasion and made a lucid investigation of topics that might engage the amateur. Though no amount of persuasion would have penetrated to torpid auditors wanting merely to soak up tones sensuously, this approach might have proved valuable in winning over at least some alert music lovers who wished to get more out of listening to new works.

Under the best of circumstances, the music was hard to sell. When Boulez took over the musical directorship of the New York Philharmonic, in 1971, he desired to focus on the serial-atonal repertoire in order to learn whether this music, if it appealed at all, did so only to the eye, or to the ear as well. He hoped to lure an audience by arousing the interest of the New York pretenders to superior knowledge and taste, as he had done previously in Paris: "To start, you always find two hundred fanatics. They are very easy to find, too easy sometimes. What is important is to raise the number. If you have a few, people will think, 'I must go there. I should go there. I should know about it. . . . I don't want to seem backward'." If the music struck listeners as impressive and somehow stirring, then serialism might supplant tonality. Eventually, he would learn that however much exposed to this music, most listeners felt alienated by it.[49]

As a case in point, in the same year that he assumed the leadership of the New York orchestra, Boulez initiated a four-concert series, entitled Prospective Encounters, which he anticipated would narrow the gap between modernists and listeners.

An audience of 350, all presumably interested in contemporary music, attended the initial concert of 17 October. Although he had considerable reservations about contemporary American composers and their music, Boulez presented Mario Davidovsky's *Synchronism No. 6*, for piano and synthesized tape, and Charles Wuorinen's *The Politics of Harmony*, for a chamber ensemble, three singers, mime, and actors. Paul Jacob and Boulez lectured the audience about the music's technical meaning. On the other hand, the attendees asked questions mostly about its emotional characteristics and received the reply from Jacob: "I don't think of music in those terms." According to Harold Schonberg, neither piece went over at all. For example, listeners found Wuorinen's music amounted to forty minutes of dreary, repulsive, nonmelodic sounds during which the singers abused the English language. Indeed by the time the piece ended, three-quarters of the audience had fled. From this and other like events, Schonberg concluded: "The decades of serialism did nothing but alienate the public, creating a chasm between composer and audience."[50]

Yet, in the face of these events establishing the contrary, advocates for the new persisted in superimposing their own fictional gloss on what was happening. To cite one instance, Alfred Mayer saw fit, in the pages of the *Music Journal*, to criticize Schoenberg's reports about the negative effect of serialism and electronically synthesized music on the general audience. He feared that the views of the "arch-conservatives" might prevail and warned that one such, Peter Mennin [!], whom he regarded as a reactionary composer and administrator of the Juilliard School of Music, was even then attempting to gain control of the Metropolitan Opera. In contrast, Mayer stated, Pierre Boulez was creating a new audience for modern music and restructuring the New York Philharmonic in an unprecedentedly different direction. He ended by insisting that Americans had to face up to the unusual discoveries in music and the radical changes they were bringing about. Americans had no choice about it.[51]

Yet, after all the attempts by Boulez to advance the new music, listeners increasingly refused to attend and of those that did, scarcely a person remained until the close of a concert. It is true that his experiment with "Rug Concerts" saw the hall filled with young people, but the attraction was more the fame of Boulez, the chance to make a "revolutionary" statement, and the fun of sitting on the floor. At other concerts of advanced music attended by a supposedly erudite audience made up of intellectuals, avant-garde musicians, composers, and others in the know, the performances might be an utter disaster of wrongly played notes and distorted interpretations. Yet, these "experts" could be heard giving an ovation to the music and glorifying the composers. Not understanding but a political demonstration by the partisans of the new was the result.[52] With incidents like these in mind, one can understand the outspoken Ralph Shapey's remarks about his "neurotic compulsion" to compose music. He said:

> It's neurotic because this world has no use whatsoever for us, let's face it! Beethoven, Mozart, etc., the old masters, were part of their society. You might say it was a special society, and it was: It was the elite of their day. But we don't have any elite today. Unless you want to call the intellectuals the elite. But intellectuals, if they are the elite, are just as bad as the rest of the human race, because they have to have their rear ends tickled all the time. They're so sophisticated. . . . I'd rather jam a hat rod into them![53]

What Shapey failed to state was that neither instrumentalist nor listener was always certain he knew what the music was all about, for example, in Shapey's orchestral trilogy, *Ontogeny*, *Invocation*, and *Rituals*, of 1958-59. The music sounded post-Webern, atonal, fanciful, and with motives so constantly varied no passage seemed to relate to any other. Nor were his explanations helpful, when he spoke of "Art transcending the moment, into "Infinity;" of art's "inevitability," "Oneness," and expressing "the unfathomable."[54] When performance errors occurred, even sincere listeners might believe their ears were absorbing the composer's thoughts.

Serious listeners, other than the zealots, soon were opting to stay home when threatened with new music. Comments I have heard at concerts of serial and atonal music, like: "I don't know what's going on from one second to the next," "The subject matter and expression are too limited and the style never varies," "From now on count me out. Listening to that stuff is like living in a constant nightmare," and "Why should I pay to suffer?" indicate the nature of their complaints. By 1970, Paul Turok was reporting that the audience for serious modern music had become "infinitesimally small." The composers themselves felt compelled to attend, however uninterested in the music they might be, and to react favorably to what they heard, so that the colleague being performed would reciprocate by attending and praising concerts of their own music. Turok interpreted this as an "enforced pretense of equality as damaging as the constant company of other composers to the individual's desire to create only as he sees fit."[55]

One cannot indifferently discard the complaints of the thoughtful music lovers who deplored these new styles. They heard in the music a denial of the circumstances and predicaments of existence as they experienced it. They criticized the composers for retreating into abstractions, confining themselves to private expression, and employing special figures and forms that puzzled the general listener. Furthermore, Americans found it difficult to relate to compositions that relied so much on what sounded like undigested Central-European influences.[56]

One listener, a musician and a Ph.D. candidate at the University of Massachusetts at Amherst, said that serial works were like "rubber and cement" meatballs to him. He heard only "nauseous sounds," even though the composer fanatically insisted the music was profoundly serious and that he laid "claim to personal and all-exclusive communication with the Muses." This listener refused to feel intimidated by the assertion that only educated and sensitive men and women could understand the avant-garde and that the remaining listeners were "inferior" beings. The obsession with originality was opening the door to all manner of anti-art. People longed for music that "sounded good," that comforted, inspired, and charmed them, that gave them the "inexplicable sensation of delight that past music is so able to bring forth." To insist that cacophony was "music of our times" was blather. Other eras had witnessed civic catastrophes and devestating wars that encouraged all sorts of anxieties. They did not feel impelled to produce ugliness. Why should we?[57]

Aaron Copland remarked that he found listeners left with "a chaotic impression" of contemporary music. Nobody could discern whatever the underlying structure was: "The control was entirely behind the scenes." The music "seemed atomized in its texture" and "completely athematic." He heard no continuity or flow, and could not guess what would come next. Many people complained about the static quality of serialism, a sameness of color, an overuse of glassy. Indispensable were the vibraphone, the celesta, the harp, the glockenspiel, the piano, and the percussion. "The new music, moreover, made extreme demands on the technical abilities of even the best interpreters."[58]

In 1970, Wuorinen completed his *Ringing Changes for Percussion Ensemble*. For about seventeen minutes the listener heard pitched and nonpitched sounds organized around a twelve-tone set. One Bostonian, sincere in his love for music, said to the author that he had listened several times to a recording of the music,[59] trying to get something out of it. Yet, all he heard was an opening battery of percussion, then a quieter pinging of single tones. The more he listened, the more he thought it was a "waiting" music, waiting for something of substance to happen. Soon the succession of sounds slowed considerably and his attention drifted. This happened to him at every session, however much he tried to be fully sensitive to the work.

After being told this, the author had a group of mostly younger people[60] listen thrice to Wuorinen's *Percussion Symphony* of 1976, thinking it might be more meaningful because between the three atonal movements were two entr'actes that used Guillaume Dufay's fifteenth-century setting of Petrarch's "Vergine bella." Wuorinen explained that no direct link tied the entr'actes to the other movements and that he was not practicing "collage in the fashionable present-day manner. . . . the most compelling motive was, literally, to provide the relief afforded by light-textured and simple (but sophisticated) diatonicism, as a contrast amd foil to the denser, louder contrapuntalities of the main movements."[61] The group listened, filled with a sense of obligation, but reported they could in no way reconcile the Dufay with the Wuorinen music. Absolutely opposite styles seemed incongruously juxtaposed. The row-generated sounds seemed mere gibberish next to the meaningful tonal music.

Faring a little better with this group was Milton Babbitt's *Philomel* (1964), for soprano, recorded soprano, and synthesized sound. They could make sense of the John Hollander poem centered around the Philomel myth, as told by Ovid: Raped by King Tereus and with her tongue torn out to silence her, Philomel flees into the forest, keening, attempting to form words. She gradually is transformed into a nightingale and as a bird rediscovers her voice. This audience said they heard an expressionist monodrama involving a tortured being never free of pain, an afflicted creature in a haunted soundscape. The text helped to orient them in the music. However, hearing the wildly leaping-about sounds was an ordeal that they were not sure they wished to reexperience. No, they all admitted, they would not voluntarily listen to the composition again.

Similar trials were conducted with works like Elliott Carter's Piano Concerto and Ralph Shapey's *Rituals for Symphony Orchestra*.[62] Nothing succeeded in gaining the group's favorable regard.

To what has been said one should add that when composers loosened their reliance on rigid musical constructs they did begin reaching a bit more of the audience. The experienced conductor and composer Leonard Bernstein had observed that those atonal, twelve-tone, and serial works best received by audiences were ones "richest in tonal implications," citing examples by Schoenberg, Berg, Stravinsky, and Webern.[63] In America, Leon Kirchner's First Piano Concerto (1956) was one such work, more approachable than Carter's Double Concerto, though not so conservative to please a very large audience. While writing it, the composer did not follow the strict precepts of "the new aesthetic engineers," as the composer put it. It showed some affinity with customary musical practices and let "imaginative invention" relieve the baffling mass of graphs, prepared tapes, electronic manipulation, and theoretical stylistic details beloved to the contemporary avant-gardist. Another such work was Tobias Picker's Rhapsody for Violin and Piano (1978). Picker did accept the idea of the twelve pitch classes but allowed himself the liberty of altering the music until it sounded right to him. He even permitted melody as it was commonly understood to enter.[64] To be mentioned in this context is the engaging chamber opera *Mr. and Mrs. Discobbolos* (1966), a depiction of an ludicrous couple leading a pointless existence, described through tart, entertaining, and strikingly clever music—rare qualities in atonal compositions. The atonal core is not overly assertive, and harmony more sonorous than not.

Yet, avant-garde purists would have looked askance at

either composition. Only music that smacked of revolution, not reconciliation, would have pleased them. One is reminded of Otto Luening's consternation when his pioneering electronic-tape music, premiered at the Museum of Modern Art, in 1952, set New Yorkers buzzing. He was astonished when this event instantly propelled him into the ranks of the avant-garde and won him modernist friends. However, none of these friends knew or cared to know about his other, more conventional, works.[65]

By the end of the sixties, thoughtful critics of all persuasions were concluding that serial and atonal music had arrived at an impasse. They found most of its practitioners too one-sided in their views and too preoccupied with aesthetic theories and artistic practices of slight interest to the music world. Whatever would gather strength in the artistic world, it would not be an extension of the dominant avant-garde styles. The ground lay fertile for the revolt against rationalism to seed itself and grow rapidly.

Notes to Chapter 7

[1] I first heard this story at Harvard, in 1950, told by a music-faculty member. It cropped up again at Boston University some five years later, related by a student majoring in music composition. Almost twenty years later, I heard a member of the audience at Tanglewood tell it to a companion during the intermission at a summer concert of the Boston Symphony.

[2] Benjamin Boretz, *Dictionary of Contemporary Music*, ed. John Vinton (New York: Dutton, 1974), s.v. "Babbitt, Milton."

[3] Edward T. Cone, "Conversations with Roger Sessions," *Perspectives on American Composers*, eds. Benjamin Boretz and Edward T. Cone (New York: Norton, 1971), 99; Cone, "Conversations with Aaron Copland," *Perspectives on American Composers*, 143-44.

[4] Peter Westergaard, "Conversation with Walter Piston," *Perspectives on American Composers*, eds. Boretz and Cone, 166.

[5] Christopher Butler, *After the Wake* (New York: Oxford University Press, 1980), 34-35.

[6] John I. H. Baur, *Revolution and Tradition in Modern American Art* (Cambridge, MA: Harvard University Press, 1966), 22.

[7] Nathan Broder, "The Evolution of the American Composer," in *One Hundred Years of Music in America*, ed. Paul Henry Lang (New York: Schirmer, 1961), 34-35. The quotations are from Virgil Thomson, *Virgil Thomson* (New York: Knopf, 1966), 419.

[8] John Rockwell, *All American Music* (New York: Knopf, 1983), 18.

[9] John Rockwell, *All American Music*, 32-33. See also Robert Starer, *Continuo: A Life in Music* (New York: Random House, 1987), 87-88.

[10] Cone, "Conversations with Roger Sessions," *Perspectives on American Composers*, 98; Edward T. Cone, "Conversations with Aaron Copland," *Perspectives on American Composers*, 143.

[11] Peter Bürger, *The Decline of Modernism*, trans. Nicholas Walker (University Park, PA: Pennsylvania State University Press, 1992), 42, 44.

[12] Roger Sessions, *The Correspondence of Roger Sessions*, ed. Andrea Olmstead (Boston: Northeastern University Press, 1992), 349.

[13] Virgil Thomson, *Virgil Thomson* (New York: Knopf, 1966), 422.

[14] William Bolcolm, "Introduction," to George Rochberg, *The Aesthetics of Survival*, ed. William Bolcolm (Ann Arbor: University of Michigan, 1984), viii.

[15] Aaron Copland and Vivian Perlis, *Copland Since 1943* (New York: St. Martin's, 1989), 190-201.

[16] William Barrett, *The Truants, Adventures Among the Intellectuals* (Garden City, NY: Doubleday, 1982), 95.

[17] Van Wyck Brooks, *From a Writer's Notebook* (New York: Dutton, 1958), 164-65.

[18] Roger Sessions, *Roger Sessions on Music: Collected Essays*, ed. Edward T. Cone (Princeton, NJ: Princeton University Press, 1979), 66.

[19] Milton Babbitt, "Who Cares If You Listen," *High Fidelity* (February 1958), reprinted in *Contemporary Composers on Contemporary Music*, eds. Elliott Schwartz and Barney Childs (New York: Holt, Rinehart & Winston, 1967), 244, 249.

[20] *Contemporary Composers on Contemporary Music*, 368-69.

[21] Leonard Bernstein, *Findings* (New York: Simon & Schuster, 1982), 305.

[22] Alec Wilder, *Letters I Never Mailed* (Boston: Little, Brown, 1975), 123-24.

[23] Verna Arvey, *In One Lifetime* (Fayetteville: University of Arkansas Press, 1984), 175-76.

[24] John Gruen, *Menotti* (New York: Macmillan, 1978), 189, 194.

[25] The criticisms are excerpted in Don A. Hennessee, *Samuel Barber: A Bio-Bibliography* (Westport, CT: Greenwood, 1985), see especially 188, 193, 271, 275, 280, 287, 323. Frankenstein's comments are reproduced on page 287.

[26] Otto Luening, *The Odysssey of an American Composer* (New York: Scribner's Sons, 1980), 545.

[27] Ned Rorem, *Settling the Score* (New York: Harcourt Brace Jovanovich, 1988), 264.

[28] Walter Cavalieri, "Lee Hoiby, A Summer of Success," *Music Journal* (January/February 1980), 10.

[29] The remarks on Copland were made by Israel Citkowitz, in the *Musical Quarterly* for July 1954; the praise of the Blackwood symphony came from Jay S. Harrison, in the *New York Herald Tribune* for 13 November 1958; Sargent's assertion appeared in the *New Yorker* of 22 November 1958. All three statements are reprinted in John Tasker Howard, *Our American Music*, 4th ed. (New York: Crowell, 1965), 482, 605. Ned Rorem's comment comes from his brief article, "Flanagan, William (Jr.)" in *The New Grove Dictionary of American Music*, eds. H. Wiley Hitchcock and Stanley Sadie (London; Macmillan, 1986).

[30] Joan Peyser, *Boulez* (New York: Schirmer, 1976), 181-84.

[31] Roger Sessions, *The Musical Experience of Composer, Performer, Listener* (Princeton, NJ: Princeton University Press, 1950), 126. The last quotation comes from a lecture given at Brandeis University in January 1954, see *Roger Sessions on Music*, 179.

[32] *Roger Sessions on Music*, 218.

[33] Richard Franko Goldman, *Selected Essays and Reviews, 1948-1968*, ed. Dorothy Klotzman; I.S.A.M. Monograph No. 13 (New York: I.S.A.M., Brooklyn College, 1980), 1, 3.

[34] Indeed, this is precisely what the humanist-musician Pablo Casals said. For an informative commentary on this view, see Van Wyck Brooks, *An Autobiography* (New York: Dutton, 1965), 461-62.

[35] Cole Gagne and Tracy Caras, *Soundpieces: Interviews with American Composers*, (Metuchen, NJ: Scarecrow, 1982), 138.

[36] Liner notes to the recording, *Elliott Carter: String Quartets Nos. 1 and 2*, Nonesuch H-71249.

[37] John Gruen, *Close-Up* (New York: Viking, 1968), viii-ix.

[38] This sentence borrows from Anthony Trollope, who makes an almost identical commentary about members of the British Parliament, in *The Duke's Children* (1880, republished, London: Oxford University Press, 1973), 282. The association of modernism with seriousness is discussed by Richard Poirier, in *Images and Ideas in American Culture*, ed. Arthur Edelstein (Waltham, MA: Brandeis University Press, 1979), 125; and by Diana Trilling, in *Reviewing the Forties* (New York: Harcourt Brace Jovanovich, 1978), 114-15.

[39] This appeared in the *Musical Quarterly* of October 1948 and was reprinted in Goldman, *Selected Essays*, 48.

[40] Elliott Carter, "Shop Talk by an American Composer," in *Problems of Modern Music*, ed. Paul Henry Lang, published as the *Musical Quarterly*, 46, no. 2 (New York: Schirmer, April 1960): 200-201.

[41] Rockwell, *All American Music*, 42; Roger Sessions, *The Musical Experience of Composer, Performer, Listener* (Princeton, NJ: Prince-

ton University Press, 1950), 87; Sessions, *Questions About Music* (New York: Norton, 1971), 18; Copland, *Music and Imagination* (New York: Mentor, 1959), 18.

[42] Edward Strickland, "Downtown: An Interview with Steve Reich" *Fanfare* (March-April 1987), 49.

[43] Babbit, "Who Cares if You Listen?", 244.

[44] Jaques Barzun, *Music in American Life* (Bloomington, IN: Indiana University Press, 1965), 97.

[45] Liner notes to the recording *Elliott Carter: Double Concerto for Harpsichord and Piano with Two Chamber Orchestras, Duo for Violin and Piano*, Nonesuch H-71314.

[46] Brooks, *From a Writer's Notebook*, 19.

[47] Carter, "Shop Talk by an American Composer," 190.

[48] Liner notes to the recording *Roger Goeb / Symphony No. 4, Jacob Druckman / Dark Upon the Harp*, CRI SRD 167.

[49] Peyser, *Boulez*, 2, 255, 264.

[50] Harold C. Schonberg, *Facing the Music* (New York: Summit Books, 1981), 57, 207-08. Peyser, *Boulez*, 188-200, gives a similar description of this concert, two-thirds of whose audience, Teresa Sterne of Nonesuch Records claimed, consisted of professional musicians.

[51] Alfred Mayer, "Electronic Music: Like It or Not" *Music Journal* (April 1973), 17.

[52] Peyser, *Boulez*, 227, 245.

[53] Gagne and Caras, *Soundpieces*, 375. Shapey said this during an interview, on 18 February 1980.

[54] Notes to the recording CRI SD 275, *Rituals for Symphony Orchestra*.

[55] Paul Turok, "Witchful Thinking and New Music" *Music Journal* (March 1970), 49.

[56] I am indebted to John Baur for these conclusions; see *Revolution and Tradition in Modern American Art*, 137-38.

[57] Robert Scott Kellner, "Avant-Garde Meatballs: Are They Edible?" *Music Journal* (March 1973), 16, 51-52.

[58] Aaron Copland, *The New Music, 1900-1960*, revised and enlarged edition (New York: Norton, 1968), 175.

[59] Nonesuch H-71263, an LP recording. The listener was in his thirties, worked in a record store, and regularly attended concerts.

[60] These were twelve men and women, aged eighteen to thirty and enrolled in my twentieth-century American music class. All had had experience in music listening and said they liked several compositions by composers like Stravinsky, Bartók, Barber, and Copland.

[61] Jacket notes to the recording Nonesuch H-71353.

[62] Recordings RCA Victor LSC-3001 and CRI SD 275, respectively.

[63] Leonard Bernstein, *The Infinite Variety of Music* (New York: Simon & Schuster, 1966), 13.

[64] Liner notes to the recording *Walter Piston: Symphony No. 6 / Leon Kirchner: Piano Concerto No. 1*, New World NW286; liner notes to the recording *Music of Tobias Picker*, CRI SD427.

[65] Otto Luening, *The Odyssey of an American Composer* (New York: Scribner's Sons, 1980), "Preamble."

Chapter 8

Iconoclastic Modernism

By the sixties, perceptive Americans had reached a point of unease and disillusionment concerning their country's cultural history. This dissatisfaction was a part of a general questioning of the direction American society was heading. More and more, composers who were inclined toward innovation found themselves defiantly challenging the music public as they rarely had in the past. For many of these musicians, the confrontation arose because some profound mental and emotional pressure urged them on. They had not made up their minds to be cantankerous, nor did caprice motivate them. Several of them acted from deepseated principles. Others were oblivious to the fact that they were questioning the significant premises advanced by their society. Whatever the cause for their actions might have been, the effect was unprecedented. As soon as favorably disposed commentators impressed the minds of the vanguard audience with what was happening, the new musical revolutionaries surfaced as a contentious band acutely aware of itself and its self-appointed role in American culture.

American music lovers had witnessed one wave of modernism after another. From the beginning of the century, each newly conspicuous innovator had viewed what had gone before him, however revolutionary, as an obstruction to be eliminated and replaced. Each radical change had meant a fresh start. The penchant was to rate our cultural predicament as without antecedents and former times as beside the point. Inevitably, this induced confusion in the minds of the music public. It also encouraged a spurious antagonism between people-oriented and self-oriented musical deviations from established custom. Unfortunately, this meant, too, that most convictions about music would have little staying power. They lingered for a short while only to be discarded in favor of what seemed superior ones. Then, these also were dismissed as useless. Notions of this sort about avant-garde music, with no one idea or style able to win the abiding support of more than a minuscule audience or even of the next generation of composers, ensured that each succeeding type of contemporary music had no foundation to build upon. It guaranteed impermanence. One cannot wonder why the comment was made: "America struck foreigners as a society that canceled tradition . . . where children stood up to and often walked all over their parents."[1]

By the sixties, brand-new disillusionment set in among modernists. Confidence in a sensible and serene tomorrow started to appear misplaced. The prevalent Western culture was no longer worthy of endorsement, what with absurd colonialist wars, the palpably mealy-mouthed insincerity of spokespeople for church and state, civil rights violations, and the acute perception of the "haves" exploiting the "have nots." Its eradication became a commendable cause. The urge to badger society with mindless and preposterous sights and sounds increased. It required only a small step to maintain that in our bankrupt society no criteria remained with which to assess an artwork and no terminology for challenging it. Composers joined in the effort to insinuate disintegrative compositions into society in order to shatter its present features and cumulative standards, however compelling and imposing. Old guides for shaping convictions were no longer operative. The imminent emptiness and the ultimate perception of a barren void that such activities portended went unheeded at that time.

Frank Kermode points out, in his *Modern Essays*, that these ways of thinking were bolstered by potent interpreters of the contemporary age like Marshall McLuhan and others, who spoke of "a cultural mutation" that had rendered "the old 'humanism' powerless to judge or communicate" because it had given way to mutants who spoke "an anti-language and aim at anti-art . . . and instead of merely revising the concept of form—as the Romantics . . . did—have abolished it." He includes John Cage with Marcel Duchamp, Jean Tinguely, and Robert Rauschenberg, saying that all four had interests in common. To all of them, art was less interesting than life and should correspond to it. Impersonality was favored; impermanence in art objects was advocated. Chance was an adventure ripe for experimentation. All four rejoiced when working "on the borders of farce." They made "random and unpredictable things in a world consisting of random and unpredictable things, an activity that is anyway absurd. . . ." Theirs was an extremism whose "disparagement and nihilist rejection of the past" were founded "partly on ignorance."[2]

Adventuring Into the Unthinkable

The tendency toward iconoclasm in the arts was already evident at the beginning of the century. Calculated senselessness, the denial of standards of beauty, and the rejection of established principles of order had permeated several modern artistic circles in Europe by the time of World War I. They continued to do so into the twenties. Witness the poetry of Tristan Tzara, the art of Marcel Duchamp, and several musical works by Erik Satie—much of this activity coming under the heading of "Dada." As pointed out in the first two chapters of this book, the attitudes and music of Leo Ornstein, George Antheil, Edgard Varèse, and Henry Cowell, all of them creatively employed in this period, also shared in this apostasy from tradition and this disinterest in the absolute rationality of strict serialism.

Other American composers, too, were exploring avenues that deviated from commonly understood Western practices. Charles Griffes (1884-1920) had, around 1917, already shown an interest in Far-Eastern musical cultures. His *Five Poems of Ancient China and Japan* and *Sho-Jo*, a dance-pantomime, utilized Japanese melodies and approximated the rhythms, "harmonic" import, and instrumental effects of the Far East. Alternatives to Western musical tradition were further manifested when Colin McPhee (1901-1964), who had studied with Varèse, went to live in Bali, in 1933. There, he took instruction from Balinese music teachers, and grew fascinated with the percussive sounds of the Balinese gamelan, the indigenous type of instrumental ensemble. The orchestral *Tabuh-Tabuhan* (1936) resulted from his interest in exotica and received performances in many American cities. McPhee would live his last years in California and have more than a little influence on composers there.

Born in California, Harry Partch (1901-1976) pursued his own idiosyncratic ideas: discarding Western tradition, taking an interest in the customs of the Amerindian and East Asian civilizations, devising his own aesthetic out of them, and inventing his own musical instruments and musical speech. For approximately eight years, beginning in 1935, he lived as a hobo, a homeless, indigent drifter who hitchhiked the American highways and railroads. Then, in 1941, he wrote *Barstow*, a recitation of hitchhikers' graffiti, heard against an instrumental background peculiarly his own. In 1943 Partch came out with *U.S. Highball*, this time with the vocal intoned by a tramp-character named Mac. Twelve years later he wrote *The Bewitched*, whose sections received subtitles like "A Soul Tortured by Contemporary Music" and "The Cognoscenti Are Plunged into a Demonic Descent with Cocktails." The influence of the Noh play, from the Japanese Kabuki theater, is readily found in it. Of import to the course that modern music was taking in the late sixties, he emerged from comparative obscurity in 1968. It was then that the Whitney Museum, in New York City, sponsored a concert of his compositions and put on an exhibit of his extraordinary instruments.

In some respects Partch was a musical counterpart to the American "Beats," who began appearing in the late forties.[3] His interest in the ritualistic cultures of ordinary people and the experiences of his own riffraff life set him apart from the typical academic modernist, who often harbored an indifference to or a contempt for the Philistine masses. What direction Partch's elitism took, if such it was, centered on a fascination for the customs, rituals, and music-making of people other than common Americans. However, this propensity usually revealed itself alongside a responsiveness to mundane reality and the American people who had to endure it, a responsiveness that occasionally turned into a musical commemoration of vulgar taste. Thus, Partch could serve as an example to a younger generation not aristocratically inclined to scorn "inferior" cultures, nor intent on escaping the uncouth rabble.

Nevertheless, a depreciation of music with symbolic meaning for the general music public, and for those in the serial and atonal camp, took hold swiftly during the sixties. By the end of the sixties, serialism was no longer at the forefront of modernism. Morton Feldman, a leading exponent of change in the sixties, told his confederate Robert Ashley, in August 1964, that in his opinion art always involved politics. In addition, composers of each new generation inevitably became revisionists, discarding what had seemed seminal to the older group. As far as he could see, Pierre Boulez did not know what he wanted to be. Milton Babbitt was too "mechanistic" and, like Karlheinz Stockhausen, "had created nothing new." He and his colleagues, Cage, Brown, and Wolff, did not exchange intellectual ideas, which was akin to taking opium, as did the serialists. They wished instead "to explore their own sensibilities."[4]

By the sixties, many people involved with contemporary music, were also concluding that the rational serialist and atonal compositions belonged to yesterday's art and were not pertinent to today. When Andrew DeRhen heard a string quartet by Stefan Wolpe performed in October 1969, he said that serialism as represented in this work now sounded dated to New York's concertgoers. Fresh ways of using it had to be found, which the Wolpe piece failed to do. Only the very beginning and the conclusion struck him as interesting; the remainder paraded the same tired effects beloved by serialists, like abrupt pizzicato passages interrupted by sections calling for swift bowed passages.[5]

In the same month, another reviewer wrote of hearing Charles Wuorinen's serialist *Making Ends Meet* for piano. He also spoke of its datedness and found it "a total dud." Indeed, to him: "The materials were so drab, the phrases so remorselessly hammered-out, that I felt as if I were witnessing a sordid domestic squabble where wit lies low and passion peters out."[6]

Of that month's offerings of serial and atonal compositions in New York, only Leon Kirchner's *Music for Orchestra* found favor. Philip Hall approved the way it did not fall into lockstep with the other music in this style. During the thirteen minutes of playing time, he heard an outstandingly wide range of orchestral resonances and dramatic moments. These arose from a sincere creative impulse and were employed for the sake of expression. What is more, recognizable repetition occurred. Although here and there similar to the music of Sessions or Webern, the piece had individuality and could be enjoyed. The *Music for Orchestra* was anything but dull and passé.[7]

Despite what Hall said of the Kirchner composition, the unremitting demolition of the more communicative musical cultures and the musical signs through which they were understood reached a culmination during the sixties and early seventies. We should expect, next, that a few composers on the cutting edge might pursue their own, fundamentally different, interpretation of what constituted creative, if not psychic, genuineness. This would include the pursuit of alternatives to extant musical signifiers, whether of the traditional or serialist sort. They would spurn music whose parameters were all defined and search for sounds free of inherited meanings and, frequently, of precisely pitched tones. Thus "liberated," they insisted, sounds might well epitomize a human's immediate or innermost spiritual perceptions, or embody intuition or comparable subjective experience. The iconoclastic musicians would contend that they had to smash the everyday sameness of matter, including that of music, in order to obliterate the limitations they claimed people imposed on all facets of their experience. To apprehend the seemingly ineffable, composers had to overthrow entrenched musical philosophies, idioms, and structures. An impulse lived in several of them to reclaim, at the least, a few suggestions of transcendent significance for a civilization now in bondage.

All of the lines just described converged in the mind and methods of John Cage (1912-1992). Quickly siding with his viewpoint in the early postwar years were the composers Lou Harrison, Morton Feldman, Earle Brown, Christian Wolff, and David Tudor. As the movement gathered strength in the sixties, Lejaren Hiller, Ben Johnston, Alvin Lucier, Robert Ashley, Gordon Mumma, and Nam June Paik came aboard. Cage more than any of the others would help undermine the reign of rational modernism, despite the fact that among his teachers was Schoenberg and that he was a serial composer for a short while. He would be the most important trendsetter toward startlingly unique ways of thinking about the arts in general and music in particular. The ultramodern dancer Merce Cunningham and the freewheeling painters Robert Rauschenberg and Jasper John became his allies. Following in Cage's footsteps, Earle Brown would claim an affinity to the "mobile"-sculptor Alexander Calder, and Morton Feldman to the quiescent transcendental-expressionist painter Mark Rothko.

Not surprisingly, important support for the musical insurgents came during the sixties from the radical artists and museums dedicated to contemporary art. Soon, Virgil Thomson could say that "Dada has won" and even in the universities, "Cage and Boulez are gods." At the same time, he warned that this did not mean they had achieved prominence throughout America. Thomson cited "cities, all too common West and South, where Mozart and Brahms are still a rarity and Beethoven's Ninth Symphony has not been heard."[8] During the next decade, more than a few musicians favoring drastic reforms won consequential faculty positions. By the end of the seventies, when an increasing number of them assumed consultative roles to private and public funding institutions, a substantial flow of money surged in the direction of the iconoclasts.

Born in California, John Cage had another Californian, the boldly innovative Henry Cowell, as one of his teachers, and soon, as a friend. In addition, he felt the influence of Varèse, and developed an admiration for Duchamp, Satie, and Ives. Surely, the work of Griffes, McPhee, and Partch formed a part of his awareness.

In the postwar years Cage came out for musical activities that were spontaneous and unpredictable. On the one hand, he embraced "camp," in the shape of purely ornamental, lighthearted, impertinent, and blithely unconcerned offerings, whose sharp edge of wit sliced through the overly solemn and learned artistry of his academic colleagues. On the other, he invoked the principles of Zen Buddhism and its admonition to attain spiritual insight through self-validating and nonlogical truths. In accord with Zen, he saw music as a process rather than a finished score that had resulted from artistic and egoistic thinking. However, as Gunther Schuller noted, Cage barely ever occupied himself with Asian musical traditions in themselves.[9]

To Cage, a score was an invitation to engage in a series of loosely specified actions, which flowed onward timelessly; or, to put it differently, a score was an outline of a set of circumstances that, when followed, were rendered throughout as a course of unpredictable exchanges continuously succeeding each other. Indeterminacy and the play of chance, he found preferable to the composer's control of his material. For example, throws of the dice, then a consultation of the *I Ching*, the ancient *Chinese Book of Changes*, removed egotistic generation of a score. Cage's aim was to contrive "free" performances of a conceptualized "work," none sounding like another.

This random selection of material could only be made tolerable if one assumed that people wanted to live in utter disorder and enjoyed formless matter or that they considered boredom, which resulted from the defeat of understanding, a legitimate component in art. If they did not accept any of this, then they could easily accuse Cage of a deliberate and conscious neglect of his artistic obligations and of alleging deep significance for something that was nonsensical.

For his followers, however, Cage could do no wrong. Richard Kostelanetz, to name one, certainly tried to intimidate detractors when he wrote that Cage was a rare figure who, if he did not exist, "the Philistines" would have needed "to invent." Cage's was "the sort of eccentricity that unenlightened minds can smugly dismiss without a glimmer of revelation."[10] About the same time, David Cope was insisting that indeterminacy was not a diversion or fleeting conceit; it was the fundamental confrontation of aesthetics, art, and history as they had been understood. The musical world had to come to grips with its very concept, not its musical results. If its philosophy was not considered and rebutted, it would obliterate, if it had not already done so, "the structure, terms, and aesthetics of music and art as contemporary Western civilization has come to know them."[11]

Nonsense, replied Terence J. O'Grady. None of what Cope said was true. Nobody was obliged to accept indeterminacy as an aesthetic philosophy, nor the compositions that resulted from its cultivation. The real test was in the experiencing of the musical results. And paramount here were "the evaluative capabilities which, presumably, the musical audience has always exercised." He called Cope's statement a list of "cosmological platitudes" that arose from an exceedingly vague and poorly explained philosophy, whose details had not been set forth and examined.[12]

Another critic would have countered that it was evident in Cage that obliteration of identity replaced self-consciousness, and a kind of extraneous and arbitrary command replaced artistic emancipation. Throughout history, mankind had uttered bitter complaints against the contrariness of fate; now Cage preferred it to the discomfort of expanding his self-awareness. In its own way, his capitulation to indeterminacy and the rule of chance was a bondage cloaked as enfranchisement.[13]

Gunther Schuller surmises that the turning to chance and other like procedures was owing to a deficiency in training and perhaps talent: "The problem for me with John Cage—and we were very close friends—was that he just was not a very good composer in the sense of a skilled craftsman clearly in control of his craft." Schuller implies that what Cage did was rid himself of the possibility of comparison to a standard.[14]

Unaffected by inhibition or censure, Cage's remarkable mental abilities devised continually shifting innovative procedures.. The aim was to make sure that whatever the results, they amounted to aimless operations. "Well, the grand thing about the human mind is that it can turn its own tables and see meaninglessness as ultimate meaning," he said.[15] Any sound, including noise, was acceptable save those conventional tones produced in traditional ways. Tunes, he said, imprisoned the senses through personal emotive expression. They had to be supplanted by refreshing percussive clatter. He did not want people frequenting concert halls in order to sense that music was doing something to them. Affective eloquence and listeners' reactions induced through the relationship of sounds were abhorrent to him. Audiences should be interested in the sounds themselves. Why bulldoze the composer's ideas and feelings into the heads of the audience? Such coercion served to bolster the composer's ego and made the listener become insensitive to "very interesting sound." Surely he was just teasing when he said: "Giving up Beethoven, the emotional climaxes and all, is fairly simple for an American." Yet, in a passing moment of reality, he also admitted that he had no hope for changing listeners' attitudes.[16]

Rhythm, Cage thought, suggested the imprisoning regulation of tempo and pulse. Preferable was the freeing of soundflow to proceed without the suffocation of preplanning. The simultaneous combination of tones into chords implied a systematic arrangement of some sort. This had to disappear to be supplanted by a continuum, no moment of which could be distinguished from neighboring moments except by arbitrary division.

For the reasons just cited, he and his composer friends inveighed strongly against the customary composer's control over the music on the page and the manner of performance on the concert platform. On one occasion, Cage abruptly exited from a Stockhausen concert because he said the German composer was "controlling" the musicians.[17] He overlooked the fact that somebody must "control" the performance by setting down a description of the composition that performers will comply with, by giving directions about how the music is to be produced, by planning for the concert event, and by putting it on at a stated location and hour.

John Cage: Music from a Singular Perspective

Earlier Cage compositions, such as *the Sonatas and Interludes for Prepared Piano* (1946-48), which evoked the tinkling percussive sounds of the Balinese gamelan, and the ballet *The Seasons* (1947) were meant to voice the immutable sensibilities esteemed by India's sages. Both works, whatever their purported meanings, displayed a composure of feeling so cool that it verged on expressive and musical stagnation. The pieces for prepared piano required a lengthy preparation of the piano, consisting of the careful introduction of various intrusive materials into its insides. The organization and interrelation of sections were realized as manifestations of mathematical proportions, a framework difficult to actually hear. His goal was to realize a non-Western ideal, an externalization of sensibility, rather than any strong inward preoccupation.

In the music just named, Cage does not stray far from conventional notation. This was not true for *Music of Changes*, which he wrote for piano, in 1951. Again, his aim is to externalize sensibility, to achieve complete objectivity. He makes use of coin flips and next studied a ready tabulation of possibilities in order to arrive at a loosely-defined pitch, sound duration, pace, etc. The book of *I Ching* was consulted in random fashion to help select these possibilities. Note values and rests are abandoned. The fixing of musical events was to be decided by the pianist.

This was also not true for the utter silence of *4' 33"* (1952), the experimentation with wind sounds and city noises of *Williams Mix* (1952), the mingling and reshaping of the babel from ordinary life of *Fontana Mix* (1958). These works suggested a more insurgent approach to composition. Finally, there was the highly irritating effect on the public of the cacophonous *Imaginary Landscape No. 4* (1952) for twelve radios, the orchestral *Atlas Eclipticalis* (1964), a computer-spawned work allowing autonomous and uncoordinated players' improvisation that insured disorder and confusion in performance, the insane *HPSCHD*, which Cage wrote in collaboration with Lejaren Hiller (1969), where a bedlam of sight, sound, and dance was unleashed on those present, and the senseless simultaneous playing of *Regna with Apartment House 1776* by the Boston Symphony, in 1976. In these last works, he carries out his belief in anarchy and abolition of rules: "I'm all for multiplicity, unfocused attention, decentralization; and so I would be on the side of individual anarchy with minimal government," he once said.[18]

To describe one of these compositions further, *HPSCHD* was conceived through chance-selection and was intended basically for several harpsichords and for recorded tapes created by a computer. These tapes contained an immense variety of soundscapes. Large areas of choice were left to the performers. When first put on, in May 1969, at the University of Illinois at Urbana, light beams and flashes, photographic slides, movie films, and dancing accompanied the five hours of deafening pandemonium. Listeners, bewildered and lost in a sound-jungle, were expected to ge22t what they wished out of the experience. As might be expected, many wanted to get out of the hall as quickly as possible. They gained only insanity in the confrontation.

Regarding *Imaginary Landscape No. 4* and works like it, Cage has commented:

> It is thus possible to make a musical composition the continuation of which is free of individual taste and memory (psychology) and also for the literature and 'traditions' of art. . . . Value judgments are not in the nature of this work as regards either composition, performance, or listening. The idea of relation . . .being absent, anything . . . may happen. A 'mistake' is beside the point, for once anything happens it authentically is.[19]

To what he seems blind is the fact that the conception of any work is never free of individual taste; also for him to say that mistakes are beside the point is a way of deflecting, even disabling, criticism. Cage insures that the music has neither social relevance nor communal accountability. What remains is a singular concept, realized in consistently unalike performances. About this consequence, Suzi Gablik observes: "No longer compelled to direct art toward the collective ends of society, he [the artist] must —if he can—distinguish himself through outstanding uniqueness. But this emphasis on uniqueness has hindered the development of any collective style—in the face of such continuous questioning of all aesthetic modes and norms, modernism has never established a style of its own."[20] Moreover, it is illogical for Cage to say that value judgments are out. For him to say so is in itself a value judgment; to put together a musical concept necessitates a value judgment; to realize the concept in performance may involve choice, therefore a value judgment, by performers; to listen involves a value judgment if any understanding is to result—otherwise, a vacuum of meaninglessness results, and the listener asks why he should endure an experience that is without meaning.

The last works named above promoted chaos. Yet, Cage maintained in his consequential book *Silence* that chaos affirmed life. People read a bid to reevaluate their lives, to explore, to enter any course they preferred. His intention was to awaken the individual to the life he was living, "which is so excellent once one gets one's mind and one's desires out of the way and lets it act of its own accord."[21] Music historians have frequently reproduced this admonition without considering its possible foolishness. When examined alongside the unavoidable demands on every person's life, pain is inevitable and little is allowed to act of its own accord. In the face of loved ones unhappy, suffering, hungry, and dying, what is excellent about living seems absent. It is more than doubtful that men and women really want to "integrate" their daily lives after the Cageian musical examples. They assuredly are not ready to reject the "artificial" artistic works by Michelangelo, Shakespeare, and Beethoven that warm their spirit and let them aspire to be more than brutish savages.

Moreover, not a few thoughtful readers worried that Cage's invitation to alter one's personal life had parallels in the violent radicalism, the rampant taking of drugs, and the harum-scarum advocacy of unusual and impracticably ideal schemes for living that characterized the sixties and early seventies. He and the activists of the sixties went over the limit in spurning sensible reasoning, accountability, orthodox employment, and improvements in the world of living things and the outdoors. The immature defiance of any control of the young and their offensive behavior toward society went hand in hand with the musical iconoclast's desire to thoroughly discompose audiences. The outrageous utterances of the student revolutionists revealed the same rejection of reason and intellect as those of the composers. One recalls Robert Ashley's advice to Gordon Mumma, in 1968, about giving a concert in Los Angeles: "They'll probably invite you to play there eventually. When they do, do something outrageous." When asked twelve years later if he had actually said that, Ashley replied: "Oh, I always say that. Oh, God—I mean, it's only interesting to do something outrageous. I only hope I haven't lost the touch!"[22]

The contemptuous young people, like Cage and his musical colleagues, looked Eastward to get their bearings. As John Patrick Diggins pointed out, many young people in California "aspired to higher truths . . . [and] enrolled at Berkeley to study Chinese and Japanese and later went to the Orient to practice Buddhism."[23]

To some critical readers of Cage's words, the composer seems to promote the indifference to the human condition of the East over the humanitarianism of the West. Several people have pointed out Cage's approval of the Shah of Iran's patronage. He participated in the mounting of novel public displays while, nearby, political prisoners were tortured and died. They have also condemned Cage's admiration of Mao Zedung and the Chinese "Cultural Revolution" that caused so much suffering and destruction of human life. Marshall Berman, who mentions these defects in Cage, grants that the composer "breathed fresh air and playfulness into a cultural ambiance which in the 1950s had become unbearably solemn, rigid, and closed." However, he also underlines Cage's "failure of moral imagination" and "critical perspective." Berman concludes that Cage's is a "seriously flawed" modernism.[24]

Further evidence of Cage's flawed political judgment is furnished by Stephen Montague. During an interview in 1985, Cage told Montague that he had no interest in American popular music, nor in America's governmental institutions. He wanted to leave the United States and go to live in Bolivia, because "no one there is interested in modern music." Montagne then pointed out that Bolivia was quite a politically nasty nation, but Cage replied with: "It's not very good here in the United States either."[25] Interestingly, he did not rush to live in Bolivia.

The vote on Cage was clear. Except for the handful of devotees and a cult following, both the instrumentalists who had to perform the music and the general audience who had to sit through the performances totally rejected what he offered. To listeners, the silent pianist of *4' 33"* was an amusing gimmick when first encountered but otherwise of no interest, no matter what Cage's followers might say about it. The bedlam generated by *Atlas Eclipticalis* was not amusing at all. Most of those present expressed outrage. Musicians protested and auditoriums emptied.

Yet, Cage, like Babbitt, showed unconcern about cultivating the general music public. Communicating with it in commonly understood ways was not his goal. He wanted a music that was "attractively disinteresting" to the public; not one that provided "distraction, entertainment, or acquisition of 'culture'."[26] Discernment was what he was after. Cage's approach to music-making, like Babbitt's, was highly internalized. Both musicians wanted men and women to purify their listening capacities so as to be receptive to a presumptively more enlightened view of musical meaning. Differing from Babbitt, Cage wished to command the attention of more than a few people whatever the necessary means, including affronting them. Affront them, he did. They in turn refused him recognition as a bona fide composer. That recognition came only from like-minded avant-gardists, institutions anxious to be perceived as at the forefront of contemporary artistic movements, the predictable cultists and fashion-followers, and those anti-the-status-quo Americans who found they could make a political, if not trendy, statement by attending performances of his music. He did open wide the door to new possibilities in the arts. At the same time, however, he made room for less talented musicians, among them sensationalists, who promoted their own musical grotesqueries, knowing no standards existed to prove them wrong. Thus, Morris Dickstein can describe the sixties as "a topsy-turvy age that often turned trash into art and art into trash, that gaily pursued topical fascinations and ephemeral performances and showed real genius for self-consuming artifacts." The decade, he said, showed composers putting little value on art because they preferred "raw life."[27]

Alan Rich, a writer normally very receptive to modern works, comments on how easily the aims of the serious innovators could be perverted. In 1970, the performance of what he thought was an inferior concoction by John Fischer highly disturbed him. Yes, he knew he was living in a time that proliferated new musical devices and concepts. Some of these attained success; most failed to catch on. What really bothered him was "the constant perversion of strong and interesting ideas as they progress toward becoming household words," as witnessed in the Fischer work. "The danger . . . is that the sort of thing Fischer tried to do at NYU can easily come to represent to the public the genuine article. . . ."[28] Rich was perhaps fortunate to think he knew the difference; the public never felt it did know.

Whatever idealism these modernists professed, it emerged from a romantic stance that assumed the exhaustion of traditional musical culture and the insolvency of the rational methodology of the atonalists. They supposed that they were bound to take over cultural leadership, after which the erection of an undefiled musical edifice might commence. None thought it possible that they would play into the hands of conservatives and that the "control" they spurned would revolve to the diehards who wanted it for themselves. Reactionaries were soon scoffing or snickering at the whimsy that after old-line values were destroyed, the next concern would be the inauguration of fresh ideologies that could and would rehabilitate the musical life of society.

First, owing to the isolative rationalists, then to the iconoclasts, the public's abandonment of contemporary music grew well advanced by the end of the sixties. No longer did any semblance of a unified musical society with a shared musical language exist. Artistic institutions seemed to fall over themselves to condone the most fatuous notions and theories. In fact, the emphasis upon conceptualization so typical of advanced artistic thinking, rather than upon skilled artistry as it was commonly understood, seemed "to have made it difficult to distinguish between art and non-art, artist and non-artists, between simply doing your own thing and the production of an enduring object."[29] Because everything done in the name of music was equally exemplary, an ominous propensity arose to disapprove nothing, to neglect making careful distinctions concerning aesthetic worthiness. For this reason the up-to-date manner of producing sounds often gave warning of turning into a banal concomitant to run-of-the-mill living.

Leonard Meyer, who rejected Cage's idea of "mindless innocence," said it was impossible to wipe out psychological predispositions or cultural preconceptions. Whether Cage liked it or not, men and women, including music lovers, did select from, categorize and examine their experience. There was an urge to distinguish from some viewpoint "the essential from the accidental." He casts in doubt the tenets of musical indeterminacy and the like, when he asserts: "A meaningful, a humanly viable world must be ordered and patterned into relationships of some sort. This is the case not only in everyday existence, but in the arts and sciences as well."[30]

Radically Different Musical Approaches

No longer did the composers who, in one way or another, agreed with Cage desire to function within the parameters of the completely rational, nor to produce works whose every detail was defined. This did not mean they were all replicas of Cage. The gamut of approaches to composition could go from one extreme to another. There was the stentorian chatter and deafeningly loud electronic clatter of an Ashley piece, where the rhythmic pulsations of popular rock music took over. In contrast, there was the absolute emotional zero of a Feldman piece, where usually the random motion of the constituent sounds was at a minimum and the degree of audibility at a whisper.

Few other composers wanted to eliminate the composer altogether in the delineation of a musical score. Unlike the complete indeterminacy of Cage's *Music of Changes*, Feldman often practised a more circumscribed indeterminacy indicated through graphic notation, that is to say the use of visual signs to suggest the limits or circumstances within which a performance may result. One finds this in *Ixion* (1958) for chamber ensemble, where the composer's written directions outline the primary concept of what the composer has in mind and a few indications of the course of action needed for realizing his intentions. His *The King of Denmark* (1964), for solo percussionist, presents graphically only broad indications of pitch and rhythm. Playing is done with fingers and open hands, though other parts of the arm can be employed. The composer asks for a hushed rendition from beginning to end. This composition is typical of Feldman's output, with its placid veneer, frozen expression, comprehensive lack of motion, and tones seemingly coming from a distant and strange world. Otto Luening has given a description of a Cooper Union concert where Feldman's *Marginal Intersection No. 1* (1951) was played twice, first as the composer intended, second as a distortion of the composer's intentions—a hazard inherent in any work that built in a degree of indeterminacy:

> The musicians were given indications as to whether they were to play in the high, medium, or low register of their instruments; within that register they could play any note they liked. This was the first time an orchestral work by Feldman had been performed. It was beautiful, exciting, and hypnotic. A member of the audience insisted on having the piece repeated. The naughty orchestra players stuck to the indicated registers but selected as notes within the register their favorite solos from classical and romantic music. A great time was had by all.[31]

Earl Brown's scores, often written in a most nebulous "open form," allow for some selection. To cite one instance, his *Available Forms* (1961) allows the leader of a chamber group to choose when to shift from one episode to another. Lukas Foss was attracted to the possibilities of instrumental improvisation within a composer-defined context, especially as realized by his own Chamber Music Ensemble, which he organized in 1957. Such improvisation is a central idea in *Time Cycles* (1960), where the composer provided the ensemble with interludes during which players could extemporize.

Further divergence from Cage occurred with composers' interest in and wish to emulate not only in the philosophies of the East, but also the music. Griffes, McPhee, and Partch have already been mentioned in this regard. After World War II, Henry Cowell came forward to spark greater interest in Asia's musical traditions. He had heard some of this music while growing up in California. He called attention to it, in the 1930s, by bringing its performers into his music classroom at New York's New School for Social Research. Then, in the postwar years, he traveled to Asia in order to study its various musical systems. As creative results of his studies, he offered the music world his *Persian Set* (1957) for chamber orchestra, his Symphony No.13, *Madras* (1958), and his two Concertos for Koto and Orchestra (1962, 1965). In 1961, during a discussion of his *Madras Symphony*, Cowell asserted:

> Music must look ahead to new forms and methods of expression. That is why I am fascinated by the music of India in particular and other Oriental countries in general. I believe that through combining the technical structure of Oriental music with the harmonic and melodic patterns of our culture, we can produce something that will give a new direction to musical art.[32]

Several composers, mainly those born or residing in California, took his advice seriously. Lou Harrison, for one, had studied with Cowell. He made a journey to the Far East at the beginning of the sixties, where he investigated Korean, Chinese, and Javanese music, musical instruments, and musical performance. The aftermath of his experience was heard in works like *Moogunkwha* (1961) for Korean court orchestra, *Pacifika* (1963) for Eastern and Western instruments, and *Serenade for Betty Freeman and Franco Asseto* (1978) for Sundanese gamelan, degung, and suling. Alan Hovhaness, though born in Watertown, Massachusetts, also discovered an interest in Eastern music and traveled to Asia. In a handful of pieces, he dabbled in Korean-, Japanese-, and Indian-inspired sounds. But his main interest focused on the music of his own Armenian heritage, in compositions like the fascinating Symphony No. 9, *St. Vartan* (1950) and No. 24, *Majnun* (1973). Other composers would come along and write a work or two based on Eastern precepts, but not too many remained very long in this area.

Because the several compositions named were deeply involved in some traditional musical expression, they did not exhibit the intimidating singularity of Cage works from the sixties on.

However exotic the music was, tunes and rhythms were discernible. The sounds were often pleasing, especially to listeners who had experienced in some degree the disintegration of their own culture. Yet, because a great deal of what was Western in music had been removed rather than modified, the effect could be considered ultimately iconoclastic.

The attention given to the cultures of the East, as just mentioned, was laudable when it led to intellectual or spiritual understanding, imparted knowledge, enlightened the mind, and freed people from ignorance, prejudice, and false beliefs. There was much to be said for the enlargement of vision and for the understanding of people different from one's self. However, it also made room for adepts ready to exploit the curiosity aroused by the non-Western arts. Their involvement with exotic civilizations was hardly bona fide. Indeed, it showed them to be scarcely above the level of watchful opportunists. One might also wonder if their pursuits were an outgrowth of an uninformed indifference to or ignorance of their own culture.

For all of the colleagues and followers of Cage, make it new was their dominant guide for sound production in their nonconformist pieces. By 1966, Donald Erb could say that music had undergone drastic changes, with many time-honored concepts, and those of the previous generation of modernists, cast aside. Today, he continued, "Music is, in its broadest sense, sound. Sound is endlessly fascinating in its own right."[33] Tom Johnson, around ten years later, observed that: "Sound has become almost an obsession for contemporary composers. As if the emphasis shifted to sound itself, the palette provided by traditional voices and instruments sometimes seemed too limited, and composers began looking for new colors. Gradually they admitted more and more sounds into the vocabulary of music, often to the extreme distaste of audiences." Sounds now tended to replace melody, harmony, and rhythm: "And in the best contemporary music," he baldly claims, "these sounds are as vital as any melodies, harmonies, or rhythms have ever been."[34]

Some sounds had clear links to Cageian precedents; other sounds extended even further the Cageian mind-set and musical inclinations. As with Cage's prepared piano, any traditional instrument might undergo "preparation" of some sort, which would radically alter its tones, or it could be played in a most unconventional manner. A variety of freshly invented musical instruments or instruments from a fundamentally different culture sometimes substituted for the established Western instruments. The vocalist no longer just sang tones. One heard snorts, halloos, whinnies, shrieks, whimpers, tongue clicks and clucks, noises resulting from the finger-manipulation of lips, throat, or cheeks and from objects placed before or in the mouth. If these were not sufficiently inventive, there was always the unlimited assortment of sounds produced through the taping of ordinary noises, generated by nature, animals, or humans. To cite one composer, La Monte Young in one piece might be fascinated by the whir of insects and in another by the hum of a high-tension line step-down transformer. Skirting the flagrantly preposterous was the electronic amplification of heart beats, blood running in the veins, stomach gurgles, brain waves, and the like. Alvin Lucier, in a work called *Music for Solo Performer* (1965), tried attaching electrodes to his scalp and sent the amplified brainwaves out through loudspeakers, to the consternation and, eventually, the booing of the audience.

Clearly, an unlimited source for new sounds was through the use of electronic devices. Some innovators used electronic synthesizers and other like apparatus as adjuncts to chance selection and to musique concrète, taped versions of natural sounds. Others preferred to exercise some measure of control over the finished product. Richard Maxfield, who usually took his cue from both Cage and Feldman, was one of a handful of iconoclasts whose views about electronic composition were similar to Babbitt's and contradictory to Cage's. He said that he liked the fact that electronicism allowed the composer to produce his own definitive musical performance, free of mistakes and misinterpretation. It was an alternative to indeterminacy and to allowing choice to performers. At the least, it allowed one definitive realization of the artist's intentions and would serve as a guide to others who performed the work. Additionally, electronicism enabled the composer to remain independent, his integrity intact, without need to compromise.[35] The pseudo-scientific gobbledygook used to explain electronic music like this was typified by remarks Maxfield made concerning his *Night Music* (1960). The sound of the piece, he said, resulted from an interchange between an oscilloscope and a tape recorder. "The supersonic bias of the tape recorder was mixed during the recording process with a supersonic sawtooth waveform from the oscilloscope." He explains that the oscilloscope's generator received two external signals: "a second supersonic sawtooth wave and a variable frequency sub-audio pulse." The "sub-audio pulse" continually put the oscilloscope output through "multiples and submultiples of the locking signal." Moreover, the "bias frequency" of the tape recorder worked with the oscilloscope "signal" to generate "inverted reflections throughout and beyond the audio frequency range."[36]

Did a listener really want or need to know this?

Taking Maxfield's view one step further, Morton Subotnick created several compositions by electronic means whose complete realization by the composer was made into recordings, with no provision for other performances. In some, the input of one or more regular music instruments was required, but a "ghost score" activated within an electronic synthesizer succeeded in completely manipulating the sounds so that they were completely metamorphosed. A few of his better known compositions conceived entirely on a synthesizer are *Silver Apples of the Moon* (1967), *The Wild Bull* (1968), and *Sidewinder*. Employing musical instruments whose tones were transformed electronically are *The Wild Beasts* (1978) and *After the Butterfly* (1979).

When musicians performed a piece, they were not always confined to a stage. They sometimes were scattered throughout the concert hall or were asked to move about as they performed. They were called upon to speak, required to wear masks or costumes, and asked to do a bit of acting. Brant was one supporter of compositions featuring what he described as "directional sound." In 1958, his *Mythical Beasts* was done in New York. A bassoonist and cellist were placed in different aisles. In the back of the hall was a trombone; in a corner, a percussionist; in the balcony, a singer; on the stage were a violinist and string-bass player. As Jay Harrison describes the episode: "The conductor raised his hand, dropped it slowly, and the whole bewildered pack of musicians began to play one after another in a fashion describable only as desultory. . . . The result was disaster."[37] George Crumb was another devotee of this sort of theatrics. In the orchestral suite *Echoes of Time and the River* (1968), he makes the percussionists and wind players march about the stage as they perform. Three enigmatic apothegms are whispered or shouted by the players: one, the motto of his state,

West Virginia, about mountaineers living free; another from a verse in a Federico Garcia Lorca poem about suffering time; and the last, a nonsense word, "krek-tu-dai," a concoction of the composer. In his *Vox Balaenae (Voice of the Whale)* (1971), prompted by the vocalizing of the humpback whale, he electrifies his instruments, casts a dark and vivid blue glow over the stage, and has his instrumentalists wear face coverings.

Every now and again, a composition was created that required the active participation of the audience. Sometimes the audience was taken out of the concert hall and onto elevators, into swimming pools, or onto the streets. Creative imagination ran rampant. Make it new was apparently leading to anything goes! One example is provided by David Jones, whose *Exits and Entrances* was performed in December 1969. It was, for that year, a voguish presentation in which musicians were situated in precise locations throughout the hall. Shortly after the performance began, a woman playing a bassoon put aside her instrument and began to recite from the writings of the Austrian-born philosopher Ludwig Wittgenstein. One by one, the other performers did likewise. Next, the audience was asked to participate, after scraps of paper printed with Wittgenstein's profoundly vague words were passed around. Absolute confusion resulted, which the loud wail of a siren halted. Everybody returned to their former positions as a solitary trombone intoned the tune to "When the Saints Go Marching In." The piece then closed as it had begun, leaving no conviction that anything of substance had taken place.[38]

Audience participation is expected in Gordon Mumma's *Cybersonic Cantilevers* (1975). Monitor stations with microphones and earphones allowed people to suggest the sound materials from their seats. They could submit anything they pleased—recordings brought from home, their own voices, their own noise making. The various sounds were then processed and sent back to the audience over loudspeakers and through the earphones. Pauline Oliveros, in *Horse Sings from a Cloud (Rose Mountain* (1977) allowed any musician and any member of the audience to sustain any sound they wished until the urge to change it ceased to exist. At that moment they could exchange it for another sound. Her aim was spur-of-the-moment give-and-take between all the men and women present.

This last could be taken as purely hypothetical "music," as could also her *Sonic Meditations* (1971-72), where she advises the taking of a nighttime stroll, to be done as soundlessly as one can, so the soles of the feet can be converted into substitutes for the ears.

The reign of anything goes encouraged the production of nominally musical compositions containing little or no actual music but designed to make a political statement. Steve Reich's *Come Out* (1966) is obsessed by the words "come out to show them," repeated endlessly in overlapping waves, in order to protest a beating that took place in Harlem. Salvatore Martirano's *L's G.A.* (1968) denounced the Vietnam War with tapes, movies, and music hazardous to the eardrums. Or they might capture a frightening vision, as in David Del Tredici's *I Hear an Army* (1964), for soprano and string quartet. The composer calls it "a description of a nightmare, growing steadily more terrifying as it progresses." The sleeper finally frightened into wakefulness feels, not relief but "only the despair and loneliness of a love lost."[39] A nightmarish quality also invests George Crumb's *Black Angels (Thirteen Images from the Dark Land)* (1970), for electrified string quartet. The piece is intended to oppose the symbols of innocence and corruption, faith and cynicism, God and the Devil. The instrumentalists count ritualistically in several languages. Schubert's melody to the song "Death and the Maiden," Tartini's trillo di diavolo sounds, and the tritone (historically designated as the diabolus in musica) are heard as enhancements to the eerie amplified sounds of the strings. Aiding the surrealistic effect are the unusual bowings on the "wrong" side of the strings, the trills produced by fingers wearing thimbles, and the performers putting down their normal instruments to tap tam-tams and run a bow over water-tuned glasses.

Anything goes also heralded in the uninhibited use of obscene and lurid images. An example was Ashley's discourse on oral sex, *Purposeful Lady Slow Afternoon* (1968), described as electronic music theater. Another was one of Kenneth Gaburo's *Lingua* series (composed between 1965 and 1970), the *Lingua II: Maledetto*. Seven speakers allude first to the screw as a metal fastener, then rave lewdly on about "screwing" as a sexual act. Was obscenity purveyed in musical compositions to become a part of the artistic tradition? Was it to resemble a prolonged discord to compensate for the pleasing tones of traditional music and the perceived prudery of American society?[40] Van Wyck Brooks wondered "how long does this kind of reaction perform a real function?—and does one not feel a kind of monotonous adolescence in our use of the cloacal word and the scene it evokes?"[41]

The Audience Gives Its Answer

Although the composer decided what was to constitute the basic idea of a work, however generally outlined, he felt no compulsion to apprehend the work's actual effect on an audience. As a result, he needed the listener to be friendly disposed in order to have his music well received.[42] Usually, such a listener had to suspend both reason and belief: entirely for a completely disordered Cageian work like *HPSCHD*, less for a Feldman work where tones are heard, as in Feldman's *Rothko Chapel*, and least for a work harking back to some intelligible music tradition, as in Hovhaness's *St. Vartan* Symphony. This is what Bernard Holland meant when he described Lukas Foss's *Baroque Variations* (1967) as "an acid trip of sorts."[43]

When composers like Pauline Oliveros, La Monte Young, and Terry Riley wrote music under the influence of Zen Buddhism, it was the listener seeking slow-but-steady spiritual understanding who was most sympathetic to their offerings. During the late sixties and early seventies, many a young person was willing to sit, as did the Zen musicians, cross-legged, slowly inhaling and exhaling to achieve complete relaxation, and putting himself in a state of mystical participation with the players and the music. Listening to Terry Riley's *Shri Camel* (1976), for electronic organ with tape delay, empathetic listeners said they gained knowledge of "the ultimate for a meditative mind-expanding experience." It was "music for hypnotic trance," "psychedelic," "illusionistic," "hallucinatory," "ecstatic." The constant repetitions created "an aura of infinitude and timelessness." One felt "the wisdom" of the "inner body."[44]

These were years, according to Frank Kermode, when much that was done in music purporting to favor drastic reforms, like living by the precepts of Zen, was based on hypothetical postures that were later found questionable. He thought that there was "a certain prestige to be had in minorities [small, special audiences] by professing to concur with what appear to be revolutionary advances in thinking about the arts, so that to find an audience claiming proficiency in a 'new' language is at present [ca. 1970] by no means difficult."[45]

What the musician who dissented from Western traditions hoped for was a listener able to garner positive emotional reactions from most sensations that he encountered. These sensations might come from tones, but they also might come from any vibrations that accosted the ears. The receiver of these sounds had to create a musical framework on his own. Hardly anyone can abide anarchy. If the composer would not do it for him, the listener had to lay on some pattern—a gestalt that configured and integrated his experience so as to make it comprehensible. A few could be thusly gratified.

The great majority, however, could not and indeed did not want to remember what it heard. Often, a question arose about the technical competency of the composer. Did he do what he did because he could do no better? As Suzi Gablik said, modern at to the public suggests "a loss of craft, a fall from grace, a fraud, or a hoax." There is a temptation for people to think, "when confronted with a work they do not like and cannot understand, that it was done especially to insult them." Inevitably, modernism gives off "a sense of fraudulence," which has, from the beginning, "hung round its neck like an albatross."[46]

Occasionally an unexpected gimmick would amuse people. Most of the time, they were convinced that their ears were enduring subjective caprice and torment. This was certainly the case for the men and women who heard the premier of Cage's *Renga with Apartment House 1776* with me. It is amusing and untrue, therefore, to find their reaction described as "vicious," during an interview of Cage. Cage himself is way off the mark when he explains that "people became annoyed, I think, simply because I superimposed the spiritual songs of four different peoples."[47]

In 1986, Paul Hartley, of San Francisco, in a letter that appeared in *Fanfare*, spoke of Cage's music. His letter suggests that he held no bias against contemporary music as such. Yet, he writes that he found "Cage's compositions usually unbearable, even when it may be up to something that I'm interested in following." In the same way that chance-based compositions allowed the performers to choose the kinds of sounds that correspond to Cage's outline, audiences and himself in particular had the choice of opting not to hear the music at all. "Cage puts up a professional front of a sort" by claiming he composes music, but "he does this without actually carrying out the (former) chief duty of the composer: To supply a planned experience, with whatever technical ingenuity may be required to make it convincing and vivid, and to give you a signal when this aesthetic episode is over."[48]

What would Mr. Hartley have thought of one performance of Young's *Poem for Chairs, Tables, Benches, Etc.* that lasted only a quarter of a second, the time it took to move a bench ever so slightly; or of Young's conceptual composition "Build a fire in front of the audience," where the composer elected to burn a violin? When asked how many times such a work could be performed, Young replied: "It has maximum effect the first time somebody becomes aware of it."[49] Did anyone ever want to repeat the "musical performance?" Did anyone consider it "music?"

After such representations in the name of music, the music public found it difficult to envisage additional extremism or toppling of standard practices. To music lovers, if any thingumajig whatever could be regarded as music, drastic change and the breaking of precedent looked out of the question and not worth having. In an important sense, these two works of Young were sounding the death rattle of modernism. However open music lovers, and even professional musicians, tried to keep their minds, they were wearied by the overkill in provocations passing as music and by the burgeoning of conflicting artistic beliefs. They were disgusted with the ostensible leaders in culture who showered honors on a work like Cage's *Atlas Eclipticalis*, at whose performances they had walked out. They could not abide the lack of system and craved some united, orderly and aesthetically consistent rationale for modern music. To them, most iconoclastic compositions represented a digression, not a step forward along the path of civilization.

Performances that demanded their participation did not mollify audiences. As Ben Johnston once confessed, in most such circumstances men and women became intractable, since they had never agreed to be manipulated.[50] Even when they sat quietly in their seats, as they did for Cage's *4' 33"*, they still felt they were used. Cage made his point about silence. So what?[51] When Richard Maxfield, and so many other modern composers like him, compared people to Pavlov's dogs and sneered at their "conditioned responses"[52] in the concert hall, they refused to be maneuvered into meekly accepting his strictures. Certainly, they were tired of statements like those of Lukas Foss, about never thinking of the concert audience when he wrote, about his wanting listeners "willing to follow me into my world, into my dilemma, into what I'm seeking. When something interests me, I take it for granted that it will interest somebody else, somebody like me."[53]

Finally, more than one iconoclastic composer, like the serialist composer, suggested that the music public consisted of self-satisfied persons who conformed to humdrum middle-class ideals, wallowed in the conventional, and wanted only already known musical amusement. Such Americans should stay away from contemporary concerts. "Only those who are receptive to the extraordinary" should come. "The majority who mainly seek familiar entertainment will help by staying away until they become properly curious as to what the informed are talking about."[54]

The majority never did become that curious. What is more, by the end of the seventies, if asked who Maxfield, Young, Riley, Lucier, and Feldman were, few Americans would know or would care to know. If asked who Cage was, a small number might recall him as an eccentric, more as a kind of clown, and most as perhaps a gadfly. When an occasional concert-goer named a Cage piece that was found interesting, chances were overwhelming that it would be either a prepared-piano composition, *The Seasons*, or the String Quartet—all early works and not determinedly indeterminate. People did come to see and hear him during his later life, but mostly because he was an oddity. He had not changed the direction of their tastes by one iota.

Notes to Chapter 8

[1] Edmund Fawcett and Tony Thomas, *The American Condition* (New York: Harper & Row, 1982), 2.

[2] Frank Kermode, *Modern Essays* (London: Collins Sons, 1971), 47, 52, 60-61.

[3] See Russell Jacoby, *The Last Intellectuals: American Culture in the Age of Academe* (New York: Basic Books, 1987), 68.

[4] *Contemporary Composers on Contemporary Music*, eds. Elliott Schwartz and Barney Childs (New York: Holt, Rinehart & Winston, 1967), 363-64.

[5] Andrew DeRhen, "Juilliard Quartet: Wolpe Premiere," *Musical Quarterly* (in *High Fidelity/Musical Quarterly*) (January 1970): 13.

[6] "Jean, Kenneth Wentworth, piano 4-hands," by "J.H.", *Musical America* (in *High Fidelity/Musical America*) (January 1970): 20.

[7] Philip Hart, "Kirchner's Music for Orchestra," *Musical America* (in *High Fidelity/Musical America*) (January 1970): 13.

[8] Virgil Thomson, *Virgil Thomson* (New York: Knopf, 1966), 422.

[9] William Wians, "The Complete Musician: A Conversation with Gunther Schuller," *Fanfare* 16 (1993): 76.

[10] *John Cage*, ed. Richard Kostelanetz (London: Alan Lane, the Penguin Press, 1971), 193.

[11] David H. Cope, *New Directions in Music*, 2nd ed. (Dubuque, IA: Brown, 1976), 169.

[12] Terence J. O'Grady, "Aesthetic Value in Indeterminate Music," *Musical Quarterly* 67 (1981): 369.

[13] For the ideas expressed in this paragraph, I am indebted to Christopher Lasch, *The Culture of Narcissism* (New York: Warner, 1979), 178-79.

[14] Wians, "The Complete Musician, A Conversation with Gunther Schuller," 76.

[15] Cage, *Silence*, (Middletown, CT: Wesleyan University Press, 1966), 195.

[16] Cole Gagne and Tracy Caras, *Soundpieces: Interviews with American Composers* (Metuchen, NJ: Scarecrow, 1982), 78-80. The quotation is from John Cage, *Silence*, 262.

[17] Trevor Wishart, in *Whose Music?* by John Shepherd, Phil Vereden, Graham Vulliamy, and Trevor Wishart (New Brunswick, NJ: Transaction, 1977), 247.

[18] *John Cage*, ed. Richard Kostelanetz (London: Alan Lane, the Penguin Press, 1971), 7-8.

[19] John Cage, *Silence*, 59.

[20] Suzi Gablik, *Has Modernism Failed?* (New York: Thames & Hudson, 1984), 24.

[21] John Cage, *Silence*, 12.

[22] Gagne and Caras, *Soundpieces*, 22-23.

[23] John Patrick Diggins, *The Rise and Fall of the American Left* (New York: Norton, 1992), 208.

[24] Marshall Berman, *All That Is Solid Melts into the Air* (New York: Simon & Schuster, 1982), 31-33.

[25] Stephen Montagne, "John Cage at Seventy: An Interview," *American Music* 3 (1985): 208-09. The two men met on 18 March and 29 May 1982.

[26] Cage, *Silence*, 64.

[27] Morris Dickstein, *Gates of Eden* (New York: Basic Books, 1977), 91-92.

[28] Alan Rich, "On the Off-Beat," *Musical America* (in *High Fidelity/Musical America* (June 1970): 7.

[29] Christopher Butler, *After the Wake* (New York: Oxford University Press, 1980), 119.

[30] Leonard B. Meyer, *Explaining Music* (Berkeley, CA: University of California Press, 1973), 3-4.

[31] Otto Luening, *The Odyssey of an American Composer* (New York: Scribner's Sons, 1980), 544-45.

[32] Martha L. Manion, *Writings About Henry Cowell* (New York: Institute for Studies in American Music, Brooklyn College, 1982), 47.

[33] Donald Erb, jacket notes to Vox Turnabout TV-S34433: *Donald Erb: Symphony of Overtures, The Seventh Trumpet, Concerto for Solo Percussionist.*

[34] Tom Johnson, jacket notes to the recording New World NW 237: *Paul Chihara: Ceremony II (Incantations)/ Chou Wen-Chung: Suite for Harp and Wind Quintet/ Roger Reynolds: From Behind the Unreasoning Mask.*

[35] *Contemporary Composers on Contemporary Music*, eds. Elliott Schwartz and Barney Childs, 352.

[36] Richard Maxfield, in the jacket notes to the recording Odyssey 32160160: *New Sounds in Electronic Music.*

[37] Jay S. Harrison, in the *New York Herald Tribune* of 2 November 1958, as quoted in John Tasker Howard, *Our American Music*, 4th ed. (New York: Crowell, 1965), 575.

[38] Andrew DeRhen, "Evenings for New Music," *Musical America* (in *High Fidelity/Musical America*) (March 1970): 19.

[39] Del Tredici is quoted in the jacket notes to the recording CRI SD294: *David Diamond: Nonet, String Quartet No. 9/ David Del Tredici: I Hear an Army, Scherzo.*

[40] As early as 1958, Van Wyck Brooks was commenting on obscenity as an American literary phenomenon, see *From a Writer's Notebook* (New York: Dutton, 1958), 31.

[41] Ibid, 32.

[42] See Christopher Butler's comments on Cage's *HPSCHD*, in *After the Wake*, 108.

[43] Bernard Holland, "Brooklyn Philharmonic," *New York Times* (27 October 1992), Section C, 14.

[44] Hugh Gardner, jacket notes to the recording CBS M35164: *Terry Riley: Shri Camel*.

[45] Kermode, *Modern Essays*, 60.

[46] Gablik, *Has Modernism Failed?*, 13.

[47] Gagne and Caras, *Soundpieces*, 75.

[48] Paul Hartley, letter published in *Fanfare* (January/February 1986): 24-25.

[49] Edward Strickland, "The Well-Tuned Piano: An Interview with La Monte Young," *Fanfare* (September/October 1987): 87-88.

[50] Gagne and Caras, *Soundpieces*, 71.

[51] Butler, *After the Wake*, 68.

[52] *Contemporary Composers on Contemporary Music*, eds. Schwartz and Childs, 354.

[53] Gagne and Caras, *Soundpieces*, 203-04.

[54] *Contemporary Composers on Contemporary Music*, ed. Schwartz and Childs, 353.

Chapter 9

The Second Wave of Conciliatory Composers

Ned Rorem had made a comment in 1958 that seemed to have become an actuality around fifteen years later: "I am clear about the only trouble with Milton Babbitt being that he still takes music seriously. As though it mattered!"[1] The observation underlines the fact that, save for a few people, among them "advanced" thinkers of academic affiliation or inclination, music lovers had not come to regard him of particular importance to them. In 1969, Andy Warhol declared during a television program: "The day will come when everyone will be famous for fifteen minutes." A corollary to this statement was the notion that after the fifteen minutes were up, oblivion would replace fame. The brief fame came to the serialists right after the war. When their "fifteen minutes" were up, the iconoclasts took over for "fifteen minutes." Then, though Cage preserved his reputation as an eccentric character, these musicians, too, sank from public view to be replaced by composers seeking a way back to audiences, who no longer gave thought to contemporary music. Surmises like those of Rorem and Warhol were on the minds of a growing number of musicians from the seventies on.

Prominent composers, during the twenty-five years after World War II, had advocated drastic change in musical styles and perceptions. By the mid-seventies, they were realizing that, whatever the innovations, whatever the efforts of the artist, whatever the merits of a composition, and whatever the accolades of the moment, these innovations, efforts, merits, and accolades quickly became a part of yesterday's scene. More than ever, impermanence predominated as an artistic reality.

Especially with the arrival of the eighties, many composers were wondering how to expend their artistic efforts less needlessly, with results more beneficial to themselves and the music public. They knew they had pushed themselves to the fringes of society. They also knew that their avant-gardism had gone on the defensive, and their self-sufficiency (whether economic, social, or artistic) was a fiction. The eventual rescue of art through radical means no longer seemed realizable, at least not in the terms once set forth. Hardly anyone was accepting the idea that forward-looking composers measured out creditable or sensible "truths," and that their music expanded the listener's imaginative powers and perceptions. Observations like that of William Phillips, from 1957, were now accepted among influential members of the artistic world: "The idea that art is the dispenser of moral and philosophical truths is only a myth, though a prevailing one in our culture." The result is that "art has become an easy prey . . . to all kinds of theories and causes that claim to have discovered some . . . truth."[2]

In several important respects, we will find, that rehabilitated modernists and an upcoming batch of younger composers would parallel the thinking and modifications of musical style that had taken place in the late thirties. However, they would not often reinstate the musical Americanisms so important to the earlier compatriotic composers.

Changing Viewpoints and Approaches to Composition

Several prominent modernists had advanced the necessity for, and virtue of, difficulty in musical performance and in understanding as a concomitant of twentieth-century cultural life. To be sure, a handful of stalwarts continued to defend their position throughout the twentieth century. On the other hand, the growing view was that unidiomatic writing and incomprehensibility were faults in contemporary music, erroneous notions that were components of "the central mythology behind the modernist cult" that many composers were ceasing to believe.[3] To cite one composer, by 1978, Gunther Schuller was saying he no longer agreed that "it was shameful to write music somebody could remember, could immediately understand, or find accessible."[4] Even the declaration that ultimate aims of the artist were to achieve originality and sincerity was found questionable. W. Jackson Bates, Harvard Professor of Humanities, rightly pointed out that these were doubtful ideals, since no one would ever dare say he wanted to be unoriginal or insincere.[5]

The composer concerned with reestablishing the line of communication with an audience confronted a dilemma for which he had no ready answers. On the one hand, he felt that an artist who used dated modes of musical communication could not generate a rousing aesthetic encounter in the listener. A musician of this kind did not produce something from his imagination; he merely replicated the expression of others. At the same time, the composer understood he was no longer at liberty to do anything he wished. It led to anarchy and its attendant confusion and disorder. He could no longer accept Cage's assumption that anarchy provided everyone with the greatest chance to realize his latent creative nature. Yes, the composer had to discover what was natural to him. However, he had to accept the fact that the decades when art was thought to progress, and to evolve from one new method to another, were over. Innovative possibilities were exhausted. It was time to restructure and assimilate the possibilities already uncovered. "In the arts . . . we no longer look to the avant-garde pushing its vector into the unknown," wrote Sven Birkerts. "We no longer think of art as discovery. Instead, we have the aesthetics of combination, the presentation of old materials."[6]

Gail Kubik confirmed the dilemma facing composers when he spoke about "reaching out" to an audience "with a music that is intelligible and which 'communicates' but which involves no compromise in the basic creativity of his idiom." A great deal could be said in defense of writing "with complete freedom [so] that you have the widest possible range of emotional expression." However, one could also write honest music that made sense to the majority of the music public. While so doing, whatever the restrictions felt by the composer, they were "essentially technical in nature and need not involve the slightest esthetic compromise. Instead of using a musical language which involves 'long words,' it seems to me possible to express the same idea with 'short words.' It is the idea which is expressed that is important, and as long as the idea is expressed with no watering down of the composer's style, I see no reason why it must be necessarily concluded that a simplified musical speech is, a priori, routine, banal, and uncreative."[7]

Once numbered among the modernists, David Del Tredici set forth his position succinctly when he said around 1980: "Composers now are beginning to realize that if a piece excites an audience, that doesn't mean it's terrible. For my generation, it is considered vulgar to have an audience really, really like a piece on a first hearing. But why are we writing music except to move people and to be expressive."[8]

Cage and Feldman had exalted boredom and had talked some people into believing them. However, as experimenters pushed on to preposterous extremes, dissenting voices were heard as never before. After a Feldman concert, in 1971, where the attendees numbered less than a hundred people, Andrew DeRhen had the courage to write: "Nothing can rouse the moribund muse of Morton Feldman. At any other time in musical history, it is doubtful that someone of Feldman's nontalents could have ever attracted notice. But during an age when nihilism has thrived in music—particularly the avant-garde—there is obviously a place for a composer who has plumbed new depths of boredom, uneventfulness, and navel contemplation."[9]

To be sure there were listeners who continued to find genuine merit in the works of a Babbitt, Cage, or Feldman. At the same time, the overwhelming majority of music lovers were convinced, as they had always been convinced since the close of World War II, of their worthlessness. Most significantly, several well-known composers, formerly occupying the most advanced positions in contemporary music, were now finding for the public.

What is more, artists who had been pushed aside were returning to the limelight. A manifestation of this occurred in 1979, when Copland was asked to conduct the National Symphony, of Washington, D.C. Audiences had loved and continued to love his Americanist works written over two decades, beginning in the mid-thirties. However, intense postwar pressure from the serialist camp had influenced him to turn away from communicative writing. With the rise of the iconoclasts, Copland found he no longer could countenance what was happening to music and said so. Of significance is the nature of the program he selected for the Washington concert: "I chose works that were serious but approachable: Ives' *Decoration Day* was an obvious choice; Gershwin's *An American in Paris* supplied the infectious bounce of our popular music; and Samuel Barber's *Overture to the*

School for Scandal provided the lively opening. Of my own, I chose *Fanfare for the Common Man*, the Clarinet Concerto, and *Lincoln Portrait*. . . ."[10]

About the time of this concert, we find former trendsetting composers, conductors, and other musicians again finding good things to say about the music of European Romantics, like Brahms and Rachmaninov, and well-liked contemporary European composers like Shostakovich and Britten. They reinstated Barber into the ranks of major American artists and, on occasion, even had kind words for Menotti. In a sudden shift, one or two expressed curiosity about the works of much older composers like John Knowles Paine, George Chadwick, and Edward MacDowell. Contemporary composers who happened to be women took up the cause of Amy Beach. A little more interest, but not nearly enough, surrounded younger contemporary composers belonging to the more traditional mainstream, like Lee Hoiby, Leonard Bernstein, Peter Mennin, Ned Rorem, and Robert Ward.[11]

One way or another, creative people wished to ease their feeling of cultural discontinuity between previous and present times. Michael Kammen states that this was a feeling experienced by most Americans, after the wholesale discarding of tradition that took place in the sixties and early seventies. In reaction, nostalgia began to affect "much of the populace as a whole during the seventies and eighties."[12] Composers, who at one time espoused one or another posttriadic style, now looked nostalgically back to eras where order, lucidity, and certitude had prevailed, and looked back enviously to composers who had not felt creatively ill at ease, nor fragmented in their concept of what was right, worthwhile, or desirable to write. To hear snatches of sound that could belong to Beethoven, Schubert, Bach, or even as far back as to Machaut, in new American works signaled this nostalgia.

No longer was it fashionable to ceaselessly criticize the assimilable composers of traditional bent for writing music that was too "easy" to listen to or for producing compositions that had experienced a measure of popular acclaim from contemporary audiences, which was formerly taken as a sure sign of superficiality. These well-received musicians had not called themselves unappreciated foreseers of things to come, whose rewards lay in the future. They had been acutely aware of the here and now.

Some composers who had cultivated the modernist ground now suspected that these more traditional musicians might have been right after all. In 1978, Gunther Schuller reminisced:

> I am a composer, and . . . I have also been a fighter and activist for new music for many decades. . . . Perhaps naïvely, I used to take comfort in the notion that almost all new art . . . is at first rejected or greeted with apathy, and that it takes a generation or two for the audience to catch up with the front runners. . . . I resigned myself to the notion that the complexities of Schoenberg, Webern, and Ives would have to wait their thirty- to forty-year turn to be received and understood. The problem is that it is no longer thirty years; it's getting to be sixty years [in 1978]. And my earlier optimism has long ago been replaced by a growing discomfort that that old axiom really never had much substance.[13]

It was a healthier sign when composers found it unnecessary to denigrate composers whose music was stylistically different and able to attract a sizable following. They were learning that the acceptance of a work by the American public would not come after an obliteration of its customary beliefs, but rather after Americans integrated into their beliefs a contemporary music that conveyed meaning in comprehensibly human ways. If musicians allowed themselves to be also sustained by these beliefs, they in due time might succeed in hitting upon a joint meaning that satisfied both composer and audience.

It is obvious from what was just said that the restoration of cultural meaning in artworks was becoming a prime concern. It seemed more obvious that whatever freedoms artists allocated to themselves, they should also try to create within a shared, even traditional, milieu that contributed a structure of concepts, values, and customs. Within this setting, they, as members of the community, could make independent artistic offerings that complied with the exigencies of the music public. This, several composers recognized although what they might do about it was less clear. Jacob Druckman, for one, found it uphill work to shape works to reach a large public. Yet, as early as 1972, he was saying: "There is a tremendous grass-roots reaching out on the part of contemporary composers—not necessarily pandering to wider audiences but to reaffirm a sense of communication. I think we are getting over being unembarrassed by certain nineteenth-century concepts like 'morality' in music, or, 'uplift,' or 'spirituality.' A few years ago nobody would have breathed such words."[14] By 1983, when he became the director of the Horizons '83 festival, sponsored by the New York Philharmonic, he was announcing the birth of a "New Romanticism," although he forgot that a number of traditionally romantic composers had been around for a long time. In all probability, his point of reference was the wave of defections from the several modernist camps then taking place, in favor of the sounds, rhetoric, and expressiveness of the nineteenth-century composers. Regrettably, the works that he presented still had firm connections to previous modernisms and fell flat with audiences.

To have no key to value and no modes of evaluation had proved almost disastrous to modern music. At a luncheon attended by several younger composers and myself, around 1985, Elie Siegmeister said that when Cage shrank musical worth to anything that could be conjured up by his unbridled imagination or that resulted from chance, he took a big stride toward the disorder that came close to suffocating music. One young man responded by saying that persons like Cage, with an internal resistance to accepting any sort of evaluative process, can convince you that two plus two add up to ten or nothing. For a while, he himself was so convinced. Cage, he said, can argue, sometimes convincingly, from postulate to judgment, and make no mistake about it, there were judgments made. Yet when he declined to affix plus and minus attributes to his conduct, Cage also allowed that whatever he did was good. The young man, with unusual frankness, said he had learned to find fault with tradition, to find corruption in people and circumstances that contravened his whims and impeded his private plans. These were failings he was trying to overcome. Siegmeister then spoke about the folly of several modern composers, sometimes obvious, sometimes concealed, who reacted negatively to what they interpreted as a dying civilization not knowing how to heal itself. He finally said something about getting an absent human element back into music. To this, the others agreed.[15]

The musicians present at that luncheon granted that the independence to freely express one's self had corroded the criteria for aesthetic comparison. Under such conditions, nobody could determine what was qualitatively excellent, and they as composers were suffering because of it. For too long, musicians had up-ended the balance between their creative freedom and their responsibility for reaching out to listeners. Needed was a restoration of this balance, where composers abated their unilateral demands to the degree where they might coexist with the music public in an adequate equilibrium.[16]

What has been said above reinforces what I have maintained several times in this book, that all creative effort of consequence depends basically on the adjustment and balancing of contrasting positions, doing what needs to be done to reach an audience and maintaining one's independence, the honoring of tradition and the right to resolutely venture into the unknown, to keep faith with the past and to work to transform it. Only with system, coupled to an uninterrupted succession of creative events, would there be enough stability in any newly introduced musical procedure to provide the means of perceiving to what exactly it amounted. One could then find the way to evaluating it as praiseworthy or blameworthy, as advancing or constricting the experiences of humanity. Music had no means by which its presence, quality, or genuineness was determined external to itself. For this reason, the act of creating it and receiving it with approval had to rest on the composer's discernment as he engaged with both common usage and the capacities and expectation of listeners.[17]

Again, we can see that balance is needed; otherwise, obsessional manias can take over whose final legacy to the composer is a lifetime spent in the purposeless production of music. David Keane once said: "If the only audience he [the composer] requires is himself, that is his privilege of course, but he must not complain about the audience that fails to appreciate his music."[18]

Emotional expression as the general public understood it was making a comeback among contemporary composers intent on rebuilding their bridges to the listener. George Rochberg, an apostate from serialism, spoke, in 1972, of music needing to "convey eloquently and elegantly the passions of the human heart," a consideration never forgotten by Beethoven, Chopin, and

Bartók. He spoke, too, in favor of reinstating the primacy of the ear over the eye and brain when it came to musical creation.[19]

Twenty years later, sentiments such as those of Rochberg had grown even stronger among the younger set of composers. For example, Stephen Albert began his career in the sixties as an atonal and electronic composer. When the seventies arrived, he began a changeover to tonal, melodic, and orchestrally colorful music into which he injected a great deal of emotion.[20] In a eulogy over Albert's untimely death in 1992, Edward Siegel quotes the conductor Gerald Schwarz as saying of Albert:

> He believed his music was music that was full of melody, full of passion, full of drama. It was music that was harmonically based, clearly based on a set of chords to ground it in a way that we all could feel, harmonically and melodically, where he was going with music. What was always clear was the incredible depth of the music. It was never superficial or superficially sentimental. He tried to write music that was powerful, meaningful and at the same time listenable. He talked about inevitability, and I for one feel that he succeeded miraculously.[21]

As the seventies turned into the eighties, it became clear that the convictions of the avant-garde composers no longer agreed with the actuality of America's cultural life. Indeed, even the term "avant-garde," which implied unorthodoxy and experimentation, was proving rather meaningless and was now being replaced by another term, "cutting-edge," meaning simply that one was at the forefront of the artistic movement wherever it might be heading. Pertinent is the remark by the composer Roger Starer, who accepted the necessity for musical experimentation, but wondered why "every musical experiment" had to be "exposed to the public." Experimental works should receive tryouts before small limited groups. Only if the results proved successful were they to be "offered to the wide public." Who was to make the judgment concerning an experimental work's success? Starer here is pessimistic: "There is a modern music establishment, which runs concert series, gives prizes and controls the committees that dispense grants. Unfortunately, this establishment is run by the very people whose music has driven audiences away from concerts of new music. They are the ones who wrote articles like 'Who Cares If You Listen?' "[22]

Starer shows sympathy for what he defines as the ordeal of listeners who have to experience novel approaches to music that are at best half-digested. The thought of the original creator contending with the Philistines was held by fewer and fewer people, including composers. Radical Left; radical Right? A pox on both your houses: this was the new thought entering the minds of reformist musicians.

A few composers, among them Christopher Rouse, were rejecting the notion of the public as dim-witted and brutish. The contemporary individual, Rouse said, was performing "a heroic act" by merely living. "Losing a parent or spouse or child, being rejected in love, the destruction of one's ideals—these things unite us all. Yet, because they're so common, we tend not to notice those who can't get over these blows."[23] This is a statement, made around the beginning of 1993, that could just as easily have been uttered by a compatriotic composer in 1935.

A concise comment on the reformist bent of composers in the decades after the mid-seventies was given in a letter that William Kraft sent to the *Boston Globe*, in February 1993, in response to Stephen Albert's death and the obituary mentioned earlier that Edward Siegel had written. Kraft, who for a long while had built his reputation upon music featuring the percussion section, said:

> Siegel not only wrote a brilliant essay on Steve but, by explaining Steve's aesthetics so well and revealing his innermost thoughts and opinions, clarified the aesthetic of an entire group of composers that are not heralded as a group because they don't have names like minimalism or experimentalism or serialism. Rather, they (and I consider myself to be one of them) belong to what must be considered the mainstream composers allied to the long tradition of composition that was detoured by the many splits that occurred after World War II.[24]

Trying to Find an Appropriate Music

From the mid-seventies on, art composers took an indisputable step away from serial, atonal, experimental, and other types of radical writing. It was a decade when their colleagues overseas were taking similar steps. Their music affirmed a new freedom, the freedom not to write in one or another of the modernistic styles of the past three decades if they so wished; the freedom to jettison rigid credos, musical theories, and what was currently in vogue among extremists; and the freedom to write works whose sounds might prove understandable and please a large music public, rather than confounding and acceptable to just a few other composers, professional reviewers, and to listeners tolerant of unusual sounds. The music also would incorporate style choices drawn from broad areas of interest, including time-honored art music of the Western world, popular music, jazz, traditional song and dance, and an array of musics from various ethnic groups and non-Western cultures -- not merely to experiment unilaterally but to see if something unhackeneyed yet potentially viable might ensue.

The danger the composers had to keep clear of was that this selection of musical elements from various sources could sometimes suggest an artistic agnosticism that avoided a strong belief in any one course of action. Such music might entertain for a while, but could have no lasting power. It might seem to have no clearly defined or serious purpose for being, and no connection with any deep convictions held by the American music public or with any solid traditional base. Eclecticism in this instance was a cloak that the composer hid behind.

The same was true of the new romanticism that grew in the eighties. With it came another hazard. The emotion that Barber portrayed naturally and imaginatively in his music, in works like *Knoxville: Summer of 1915* (1943), might, in the hands of a latter-day composer, serve as a varnish for superficially, even cynically conceived compositions, "a sound and fury, signifying nothing." The composer had to be a genuine believer in what he was doing.

There was also the stumbling block of negativism to be avoided—the assumption of a course of action mainly because it was not what had gone before. I reacted uncomfortably to William Bolcolm's assertion: "We are in the 1980s, and it is generally accepted among most artists that modernism is on the wane. What is happening now is less a new movement—although critics have been quick to name it postmodernism—than it is a movement away from movements, those schools and 'isms' that have bedeviled art and led toward its current sclerotic self-consciousness."[25] Negative reaction is not enough. Bolcolm should also say toward what the movement is headed.

Another peril hid in the desire to build a special, albeit a good sized, audience for one's music. Potentially, it could prove condescending, demean large numbers of listeners, and promote its own sort of exclusiveness. Philip Glass maintained, in 1989, that he wrote for the theater audience, not for concert-goers. He offered no hard evidence to prove the following: "The audience that comes to the theater, in my opinion, has a broader interest in the arts. They may know something about the visual arts or something about dance, and I find it a more interesting audience, generally speaking. Whereas the audience that confines itself to the concert hall may not be very much in touch with the rest of the artistic community."[26] At the end, the "theater" audience could leave him as high and dry as any concert audience could.

Be that as it may, the renewed interest in tonality, diatonicism, consonance, distinct rhythms, recognizable melodies, and harmonic even triadic sonorities was welcome to most of the music world. There was also the precedent of composers who had never deviated from a traditional approach: John La Montaine, Lee Hoiby, Ned Rorem, Jack Beeson, Leonard Bernstein, Peter Mennin, Benjamin Lees, to name seven of them. All had written exemplary works, expertly structured, ingratiating to the ear, and conveying a host of expressions. La Montaine's *Wilderness Journal* (1972), for baritone, organ, and orchestra, Hoiby's opera *Summer and Smoke* (1971), Rorem's more recent songs and *Sunday Morning* orchestral suite (1977), Beeson's chamber opera *Dr. Heidigger's Fountain of Youth* (1978), Bernstein's Divertimento for Orchestra (1980), Mennin's Eighth Symphony (1973), and Lees' Passacaglia for Orchestra (1975) demonstrated an unequivocable interest in commanding listeners' attention with music that remained true to the composer's principles. None completely subscribed to a nineteenth-century style; all utilized one or more twentieth-century devices, though prudently.

Compositions demonstrating this same interest soon appeared, written by musicians who had been modernists. Like the "prodigal son" who had led a life of self-indulgence then returned home, the reformed modernist received a great deal of the media's attention. Like the "good son" who had remained home, the consistently tonal composer was neglected. Nevertheless, former modernists did try to make amends for their past excesses. Typical of their new attitude—after Michael Colgrass, who was formerly a complete atonalist, won the Pulitzer Prize in 1978 for *Déjà Vu*, he said:

> I'm very concerned with the rhythmic structure and substructure of a piece, and the melodic and lyric shaping of it, even if that lyric shaping is very abstract. I'm very interested in the harmonic underpinning, because you can't have a lyric shape without a harmonic structure. It will collapse after a while if you don't have that scaffolding. I guess... I'm interested in harmony, rhythm, and melody. All the music I know that is strong, is strong in all three of those areas.[27]

Typical as well was the rebellion of Jon Deak against his modernist teachers. In 1981, when his recording *Musical Tales*, consisting of "The Ugly Duckling" and "Lucy and the Count," came out, he commented: "My composition teachers had been telling me to avoid traditional classical harmonies. I, however, have always found them clean, strong, and to the point. The fact is, I just don't like harmony any other way."[28]

Typical also was the decision of Frederic Rzewski, in 1975, to persuade people to join him in the repudiation of Chile's recently installed dictatorship by writing a brilliantly virtuosic, warmly romantic, and enticingly melodious set of variations on the Chilean song "The People United Will Never Be Defeated." In every way, it was a sure crowd pleaser.

Into the conciliatory camp came other musicians, among them John Harbison, Joseph Schwantner, David Del Tredici, Domenick Argento, and Ellen Taaffe Zwilich. Artists like these had a deep rooted desire to communicate meaningfully once again. They realized that if they reckoned on the public's trust they had to prove themselves through what they composed and not what they said. Expression had to come across as genuine, as indisputable human feeling felt by a real human being. The sound had to have recognizable elements of what had been and still was considered beautiful.

Tilson Street's Adagio for Oboe and String Orchestra (1977), Ellen Taaffe Zwilich's First Symphony (1983), and Stephen Albert's symphonic *Riverrun* (1984) all seemed to exhibit this kind of feeling and beauty. All three works gained the esteem of audiences. As a sign of the changes taking place in cultural attitudes, all three works won Pulitzer Prizes. To these should be added Harbison's *Marabai Songs* (1983), glowing with ardor and replete with infectious rhythms. Argento's serious opera *Postcard from Morocco* (1971) and comic *Casanova's Homecoming* (1984) also try to reach audiences.

Theatrical gestures and dramatic performance that might interest concert-goers were concomitants of several prominent composers' works, some more successful with audiences than others. John Corigliano's Oboe Concerto (1975) incorporates both the tuning and untuning of the orchestra into its fabric. The oboe resembles an actor on stage. At one moment the oboe sings lyrically, at another moment it raucously reels off one note after another. Now it engages in intense drama; next it wails out a Saharan-desert tune. His *Pied Piper Fantasy* (1982), a flute concerto, is even more obviously theatrical, depicting the arrival of dawn, the piper's melodious song, his cacophonous battle with the rats, and his leaving with the children to catchy march music. Costumes and special lighting enhanced the vivid mise-en-scène. Spectacle and music do entertain. What was of utmost importance: in both pieces, there was music to which audiences could relate. Whether the two compositions would live on through the ages could be safely left to the future to decide.

In contrast, audiences found Jacob Druckman's *Brangle* (1989), commissioned by the Chicago Symphony, more difficult to accept. Theatricality was at the center of the coloristic orchestration and assorted sound effects. Not much else was there that proved attractive to the general public. The first movement, "Macho," consisted of rude chords clanging solitarily or in collision with each other. Was the music assertively virile or a meaningless jangle of sounds, and did anybody care? The middle movement purported to be "Languorous." It did induce listlessness and then stagnation. The last movement, "Driven," appeared not driven at all, instead sounding strained, overly drawn-out, and inert. Where was the "grass-roots reaching out" and the reaffirmation of "a sense of communication" he was quoted earlier as approving?

Dramatic coloration and evocative atmosphere are also found in Joseph Schwantner's *Aftertones of Infinity*, which won the 1979 Pulitzer Prize. There was a smoother mix of contemporary and traditional practices. Ecstatic release was tempered by formal clarity, and up-to-date dissonance by consonance. The piece occupied a level of accessibility between the Corigliano *Pied Piper* and Druckman's *Brangle*.

Extramusical allusions abounded. Composers liked to take their cue from the literary works of a single author—Stephen Albert from James Joyce, David Del Tredici from Lewis Carroll, George Crumb from Federico Garcia Lorca. For example, Del Tredici's *Final Alice* (1976) was one of several compositions that centered on the Alice of *Adventures in Wonderland* (1865) and *Through the Looking Glass* (1872), and the real-life Alice Liddell. The references were readily recognized by concert-goers. The opera-like story that unfolds in recitatives, arias, and dramatic scenes proved delightful. Tonality, simple songs (one of them as if a nineteenth-century sentimental ditty), and diatonic writing contrast with exuberant, rough and noisy passages illustrative of the manic moments in Carroll's tale. The "Apotheosis" at the end is deeply moving in its expression of artless sincerity. Audiences immediately took to the piece. Like Corigliano, Del Tredici did not stop to worry about what future generations might think. He was addressing the present day.

Going back to the style or even the actual music of a earlier composer became commonplace. Easley Blackwood, cited in Chapter 7 for his problematical atonal writing of the sixties, had changed over into a tonal composer in the eighties. Robert McColley, in a 1993 article in honor of Blackwood's sixtieth birthday, states that in a recent cello sonata he tried to write what Schubert might have written if he had lived another fifteen years, and in a symphony, what Sibelius might have written in 1915. The music demonstrated Blackwood's return "from the outer edge of atonal and polyrhythmic complexities to lucid, comprehensible tonal works."[29]

George Rochberg was the composer who received perhaps the greatest publicity when he renounced serialism, in the seventies, as an overly exclusive approach to composition and took renewed interest in older styles. He demoted the value of egocentric writing that was intent on originality at any cost. He was after the variety and subtlety of expression denied him when he adopted a stringently atonal style. The Third String Quartet (1972) contains allusions to Beethoven, Bartók, and Mahler. Its sound swings back and forth between the grand and the simple. Not the least of the work's virtues are recognizable themes and communicable emotionality. His Violin Concerto of 1975, though still containing noteworthy dissonances, also boasts appealingly lucid sonorities with triadic references. At times, the music invokes the pungent expressiveness of Bartók; at other times, the sumptuous sensuousness of Mahler; and once or twice the capricious whimsy of Prokofiev. His *Concord Quartets* (the Fourth, Fifth, and Sixth), premiered in 1979, cover similar ground. The last of these quartets incorporates a second and fifth movement resembling Beethoven and a third movement based on Pachelbel's Canon. These compositions received much greater acceptance than compositions he had written previously. Not surprisingly, Rochberg spoke in praise of concert-goers, saying he could depend on them to give him a perceptive hearing. No composer, he said, had "the right to demand of audiences that they spend a lifetime listening to or studying a handful of pieces because you say they're good."[30]

The problem for Rochberg and other musicians reassessing the past was the integration of the welter of styles to which they had recourse so that their works did not sound only like hodgepodge. Whatever their momentary successes, they eventually had to impress listeners as being more than actors who had donned costumes for the interim and, once the play was over, would doff them and return to their real selves. Such a consideration was on the mind of Allan Kozinn when, in 1991, he reviewed a concert given by the American Composers Orchestra. The composer Michael Torke, who was then twenty nine years of age and receiving a great deal of notice in New York, had appeared as piano soloist with the orchestra in his own piece, *Bronze*. Kozinn writes that in *Bronze*, Torke "had abandoned the search for his own voice in favor of 19th-century pastiche." He heard "well-chewed but not quite digested bits of" Tchaikovsky, Brahms, and Beethoven, as well as "a variety of Romantic poses—from sweet lyricism to jangly bluster." Kozinn ends by praising the Barber First Symphony of 1936, heard directly after, because Barber the composer was authentically present in the music.[31] However, we should keep in mind that comparable accusations were levied at Barber when his symphony was first heard. The passage of time alone would tell if Torke had something vital to say.

Several attempts were made to reassess the viewpoints of the compatriotic composers of the later thirties and forties in the hope of finding an American musical tradition of more than momentary significance. One instance that comes to mind was the "Highbrow/Lowbrow" concert that took place in New York's Merkin Concert Hall, in January 1991. Pieces by Ives, Gershwin, Copland, Carter, Bernstein, Rochberg, and Rzewski were offered for reappraisal. The music employed ragtime, folk melody, popular song and dance, and jazz and blues. The audience found the music engaging and exciting. Was what was heard "America's musical tradition in transformation," as the concert's backers claimed? Donal Henahan, critic for the *New York Times*, thought not.[32] Nevertheless, the concert did demonstrate an ongoing interest in Americana by composers and a readiness to take pleasure in it by listeners.

When musical orientation of this sort was combined with American subject matter, then native opera did catch the attention of Americans. This was certainly so for George Gershwin's *Porgy and Bess* (1935), Marc Blitzstein's *Regina* (1949), Carlisle Floyd's *Susannah* (1955), Douglas Moore's *The Ballad of Baby Doe* (1956), and Robert Ward's *The Crucible* (1961)—all of them representing the prevalent sensibilities and values of American society; all of them successes, some more than others. All five operas reveal the marks of a professional opera composer, wrote Conrad Osborne. The composers knew how to create a vocal line that set forth action and character and sent its message out into the theater against an orchestra that was not pulling its punches. They used music to dramatize the inner thoughts, desires, and conflicts of the characters. Scenes received appropriate musical structures that defined the events taking place. And entire works were clothed in an attractive musical idiom.[33]

According to Osborne, the operas named, shared a conservative melodic and harmonic language, and a simplicity of musical utterance and theatrical effect, which contributed "to a clarity and directness that audiences tend to appreciate." What is more, he said, their vocal settings were "still the leading element in the scoring." They carried "the drama through" and allowed voices to "open up and create living moments that hold emotional potential." This, he said, was opera's "most basic pleasure, the thing that draws most of us to it in the first place." If it was not present a work could not lead "the sort of life outside the opera house that enables it to penetrate our more general culture."[34]

Henry Mollicone was the kind of professional that Osborne could admire, when he wrote *The Face on the Barroom Floor*. The locale was a barroom in Central City, Colorado. The first performance took place in 1978, and the opera quickly went from Central City (where it is done every year), to Boston, Omaha, St. Louis, and Kansas City. Everywhere, it had an enthusiastic reception. The drama was fascinating; the music, whether honky-tonk or otherwise, completely disarming.

A last compositional movement, which stood out beyond all others in the eighties, was minimalism, a mode of musical expression that was spare, often impersonal in tone, and exceedingly repetitive. It was anticipated at the beginning of the century by Erik Satie, whose *Vexations* for piano was a thirty-two bar strain to be played quietly and slowly 840 times in succession. In the sixties, La Monte Young and Terry Riley were writing compositions that made maximum use of a minimal amount of material. It was also a decade when electronic-music studios sprang up and musical instruments dedicated to electronic sound production came into use by jazz and rock musicians. Into prominence, too, came Cage's ideas about non-purposeful but continuous action and Feldman's about simple music of indeterminate duration. These several directions came together in the music of Steve Reich, Philip Glass, and, later, John Adams. Theirs, however, was music that was distinct from any of these antecedents. When, in the fall of 1965, Steve Reich came to New York, he found himself at that time "very much out of place. Downtown it was basically works by or in imitation of John Cage, Morton Feldman,

Christian Wolff, and Earle Brown. Uptown it was pieces in imitation of Stockhausen, Boulez, and Berio."[35]

The minimal music of Reich and Glass had a tonal focus and machine pulse. Commonplace jejune stuff, given a rudimentary triadic format and played by an ensemble that mirrored popular-music instrumentation, produced a situation of maximum predictability. Mechanically pulsating rhythms, animated and confident in nature, helped alleviate the incipient tedium. A "crossover" audience made up of artists disenchanted with the avant-garde and young people who had grown up with the sound of rock or jazz in their ears found the Reich and Glass compositions easy to approach and attended the concerts in growing numbers. They wanted, and now found easy to deal with, more attainable music that nevertheless moved along unique routes. It was once pointed out to Reich that he had a young audience that went for the persistent pulse and the reiterated patterns. He was asked if he had an interest in rock. "No," Reich replied, "but I had a tremendous interest in jazz when I was younger. . . . My music has a beat, and, perhaps you can dance to it, so in that sense it's closer to jazz or rock and roll than it is to the music of Boulez, Stockhausen, Berio, Carter, Cage, and Crumb. And I would add that most of the music we know and love has always stayed in touch with popular, folk, and dance sources whether it's Bach, Bartók, and Stravinsky, or Ives, Gershwin, and Copland." Glass, who worked with rock musicians, had an ensemble that often played in rock clubs. "The music has a very visceral effect," he said. "It's disarming for many people, too, partly because of the amplification, but mainly because of the directness of it."[36] Both men achieved prominence in 1976, when Reich's *Music for 18 Musicians* and Glass's opera *Einstein on the Beach* received premiers.

Reich continued to gain a reputation as an accessible composer and win over a sizable clientele, as slowly he expanded his style to adopt mainstream ideas and to avail himself of more orthodox instrumentation. His music was especially agreeable when exemplified by exultant works like *Tehillim* (1981), for four sopranos and orchestra. The title means "praises"; the text is from the Book of Psalms. The ecstatic organum of the Notre Dame school, of the Middle Ages, is brought to mind.

Glass's *Einstein on the Beach* called for a more devoted assemblage, one ready to savor some five hours of performance where nothing much happens on stage. Although the audience saw the Philip Glass Ensemble, solo singers, choruses, and actors assembled before it, the absence of a plot and lack of dramatic variety meant that appreciation could come only through the mind's responding with sympathetic vibrations to the character of Alfred Einstein, his person, the attributes that identified him (mathematics, the violin), and his political and social impact. The audience also had to be willing to accept the excessive amplification of workday triadic chord sequences, brief melodic designs based on a scale, and phrases recurring unremittingly for extended time lengths. It could easily fail to hear the transformations in the music achieved through the addition or subtraction of notes but done so imperceptibly as to be difficult to detect.

Several minimalist operas followed which started off sounding as if mystical fervor and devout meditation were behind them. Yet, as the repetitions piled up on each other, what the ordinary music lover soon felt was emptiness and ennui. Ten minutes after the opening of his operas *Satyagraha* (1980) and *Akhnaten* (1983), considered two of his best, and one's senses could become mummified. To be sure, Glass had his devotees and opera houses were often filled with them. However, many people who attended the performances admitted they did so because they wanted to participate in an unusual undertaking and what was publicized as a momentous occurrence. Whether they enjoyed the music was beside the point. Richard Dyer attended a presentation of Glass's ninth opera, *Voyage*, in 1992, ostensibly based on Columbus's sea journey to America. He decided that Glass's music had become dully routine and that "Glass's reputation" stood "highest among people who don't know much about music, while his work bores or irritates those who do." *Voyage* was impressive visually but lacked substance. "There was very little reaction from the audience during the performance; afterward a bit of jeering cut through all the cheering, but probably neither was a response to the work or the performance—people had their minds made up beforehand."[37]

The habitual attendees of opera and concerts that Glass said he spurned in favor of artists, young people crossing over from rock, and "theater" people, however narrow Glass found their taste to be, were the backbone of art music. Others came and went. They were always there, if anyone was. Scarcely any of the "crossover" auditors were crossing over to accept other forms of art music. Their tastes were mercurial, frequently immature or ill-formed. One suspected that they would bestow their allegiances elsewhere at a later date.

Presumably, Glass's music put on its best face when the composer led his own ensemble. Even then, the mainstream listener might be put off. In 1987, Aaron Shatzman attended a concert by the Philip Glass Ensemble, with his wife Vicky and her friend Karen. Works by Glass, written during the past few years were performed. The first half of the concert was devoted to the most minimal of minimalistic, played at a painfully loud sound level. He was unable to keep his attention on the music. His wife Vicky said she was bored. And Karen's thoughts had wandered "to the final exam she was preparing for her pediatrics students."[38]

Shatzman was pained by the earsplitting amplification. The endless repetitions numbed his mind. On the other hand, he did concede that Glass's special audience probably found the music fascinating and entertaining. Like Dyer, he thought that Glass's music attracted individuals who shared "few musical or cultural attachments."[39]

Whatever Dyer and Shatzman thought about the music, Glass's style was changing. Whether the change was sufficient to attract more of the customary audience was another matter. He may have perceived that *Einstein on the Beach*, appropriate for the sentiments of the seventies, no longer fitted the standpoints at the century's end. The theoretical understructure and the musical style by means of which Glass perceived and regulated his compositions was a little less prized. Held a little more in esteem was a coming together of heretofore separate Western practices. In several ways his music still remained disconnected from what was going on elsewhere and, as the years went by, was in danger of being left behind. He began to write for traditional Western instruments. Harmony grew richer; melody longer; rhythms more varied; repetition less incessant. A reconciliation of popular with art music was on the way. This was evidenced in the *Low Symphony* of 1992, written for symphony orchestra. Here, he turned out a somewhat zesty and at intervals a pleasing composite of sound. The tunes came from the [low] rock music of David Bowie and Brian Eno. They were outfitted in "high" artistic apparel that here and there suggested Ives, Antheil, Weil, Gershwin, Copland, and Bernstein. As Edward Rothstein commented: "It almost seems as if Mr. Glass is now engaged in a personal recapitulation of musical evolution." He also noted that Glass's "easygoing simplicity" often projected "an overly precious satisfaction." At times, as in the third movement, the music seemed "almost too elementary."[40]

John Adams was a minimalist who, on balance, showed a greater flexibility than Reich or Glass. The listener can hear some expressive variation and gradation in the volume of musical sound. There were also smidgens of emotional phrasing, and tries at dissonance for dramatic purposes in his music. He won some notice in 1977, with *Phrygian Gates* for piano; more in 1978 and 1980, with *Shaker Loops* for string septet (later for string orchestra) and *Harmonium* for chorus and orchestra, respectively; and even more in 1982, with *Grand Pianola Music* for soprano, winds, and two pianos. As with so much other minimalist music, the staying power of Adams's compositions has not been strong. For example, Howard Kornblum was quite enthusiastic about *Harmonielehre*, when he first heard it eight or nine times on a recording, in 1986. He found it "expressive, meaningful, and an encouraging sign of the future." However, a year later and after further listening, his enthusiasm had dampened: "The piece hasn't worn well, after all. Hearing it now, I find my attention wandering; the repetitiveness has become irksome; the substance offers me nothing to 'hang my ears' on; I can't get intimate with it."[41]

A bigger effort than these came in 1987, with his opera *Nixon in China*. Despite the few conventional operatic approaches that he employed, and some strong critical acclaim notwithstanding, the generality of opera-goers did not take to it. Possibly, Conrad Osborne put his finger on the problem when he said that the minimalism of Reich, Glass, and Adams had achieved a certain "penetration into more general culture. But since the effect of their writing depends either on pure reduction (of pitch range, dynamic range, color span, sexual identity—as in Philip Glass) or on retention of some of these qualities under a ritualistic, affectless discipline (as in John Adams's 'Nixon in China'), for a lover of operatic singing to confront it is to encounter a stranger on the road who is hurrying eagerly toward the small town you've just fled in boredom-induced delirium."[42] Unless minimalism changed into something quite different, it was bound to date.

Reading the Listener's Mind

The National Endowment for the Arts made a decision in 1992 to decrease its grants to cities and to states, in particular New York and California, which was ominous for contemporary music. The Endowment interpreted cities like New York City as restrictively concentrated on particular musical activities rather than a place whose activities were of consequence to the larger musical world. Listeners, including composers, were tending more and more to do their listening at home, via recordings and the broadcasts of F.M. radio and T.V. stations. In short, the audience for contemporary music had little connection to any city's concerts and more to the recordings it chose to purchase at the local music store.[43]

Even in the few localities where contemporary compositions were regularly heard, the music remained ghettoized. The music public had learned that certain performing groups devoted themselves to serial and atonal music, others to iconoclastic and experimental music, and avoided both. When recordings of this music were made by these groups, they had scarcely any takers. The rule was that even in New York City, the usual turnout for new music numbered less than 200 people and threatened to shrink even more. A shortage of funds was endemic, even more so at the century's close, and the search for donations was hectic indeed. Those universities which once gave support to new music, found much less surplus money at their command in the nineties, and less faculty and student interest in the contemporary music scene. Music was a logical area in which to economize. At the same time, traditional performing groups rarely presented anything from either camp. It was this state of affairs that the conciliatory composers were hoping to change.

Whatever the failings of the music public, one had to accept the fact that it contained members who were both well-informed and perceptive. Composers had failed in their endeavor to "educate" them into appreciating posttriadic styles. The attempts at intimidation had not helped, either. No human was ready to devote all leisure time to giving attention to a smattering of musical items, which some "authorities" put forth as excellent. Nor had anybody the patience or the necessary freedom from the demands of work and home.

All of this, the conciliatory composers recognized and had tried to compose music in line with this understanding. Yet, even when a composition of theirs caught the public fancy, it was not easy to turn things around. Alan Hovhaness had composed several works over the years that appealed greatly to listeners. These compositions usually drew inspiration from Hovhaness's Armenian background and from Renaissance music. Immediately coming to mind are his early *St. Vartan* Symphony (1950); later, the *Mysterious Mountain* Symphony (1955); and still later, *And God Created Whales* (1969). He continued to write appealingly evocative music throughout the seventies and eighties. Yet, he was criticized for his ethnicity, his adherence to tonality, and his pleasuring of listeners. Musicians drew a veil over his musical activities. Even in the place of his birth, Greater Boston, he received next to no performances. However, in 1991, Walter Simmons interviewed David Amos, who was directing a new recording series for Harmonia Mundi, known as "Modern Masters." The aim was to record neglected but accessible works of the twentieth century. Amos told Simmons: "This has seemed to work very well, because the music I recorded has elicited tremendous enthusiasm from listeners. I was just speaking with the music director of New York City's public radio station . . . and he happened to mention that Hovhaness's Concerto No. 8 for Orchestra and some of the Rosner pieces have prompted an unbelievable number of phone calls."[44] The interest was there, if only someone would cultivate it.

Another instance of the defeat of accessible music is provided by Del Tredici's *Final Alice*. After its Chicago premier, in October 1976, Thomas Willis wrote in the *Chicago Tribune* about the audience's response as "the most enthusiastic reception of a new work that I have ever heard at a symphony concert." A recording by Georg Solti and the Chicago Symphony was at the top of the list of best-selling artworks in 1981. Del Tredici won the Pulitzer Prize and much national acclaim. Unfortunately, he found the musical modernists, still in power, to be completely hostile. Influential critics, indifferent to the public's reaction and convinced that originality had to come first, gleefully picked apart the composition. Conductors in other cities were reluctant to take up Solti's leavings. As John Rockwell explained it, Del Tredici was denied "the frequency of performances that a similarly honored accessible composer a century ago would have expected automatically."[45]

There were major stumbling blocks to establishing contemporary music on a healthier basis. First came the refusal of extant modernists and their apologists to modify their stance. Second was the flawed national distribution system for new works, which tended to make most performances local ones mostly. Third was the lack of a mechanism to hold accessible works in public view over a period of years. Fourth and most conducive to keeping contemporary music isolated, the music public's judgment remained of little account in deciding the merits of a work and in insuring future performances.

Notes to Chapter 9

[1] Ned Rorem, *The New York Diary* (New York: Braziller, 1967), 142.

[2] William Phillips, "Artistic Truth and Warped Vision," originally appearing in the *Partisan Review* of 1957, as reprinted in *The Idea of the Modern*, ed. Irving Howe (New York: Horizon, 1967), 105.

[3] See the conclusions reached by Richard Poirier, in *The Renewal of Literature* (New York: Random House, 1987), 98, 112.

[4] Gunther Schuller, *Musings* (New York: Oxford University Press, 1986), 179.

[5] W. Jackson Bates, *The Burden of the Past* (Cambridge: Belknap, 1970), 107.

[6] Sven Birkerts, *American Energies* (New York: Morrow, 1992), 41.

[7] David Ewen, *American Composers* (New York: Putnam's Sons, 1982), s.v. "Kubik, Gail Thompson." Stephen Albert said much the same thing; see Ewen, *American Composers*, s.v. "Albert, Stephen."

[8] John Rockwell, *All American Music* (New York: Knopf, 1983), 83.

[9] Andrew DeRhen, "Morton Feldman Retrospective," *Musical America* (in *High Fidelity/Musical America*) (June 1971): 23.

[10] Aaron Copland and Vivian Perlis, *Copland Since 1943* (New York: St. Martin's, 1989), 395.

[11] Witness Gunther Schuller's advocacy of John Knowles Paine and his music.

[12] Michael Kammen, *Mystic Chords of Memory, The Tranformation of Tradition in American Culture* (New York: Knopf, 1991), 534.

[13] Gunther Schuller, *Musings*, 174-75.

[14] Shirley Fleming, "Jacob Druckman," *Musical America* (in *High Fidelity/Musical America*) (August 1972): 5.

[15] The luncheon took place in a cafeteria on Commonwealth Avenue in Boston. Actually, what the young man, whose name I do not know, said took place during the post-luncheon walk along Commonwealth Avenue.

[16] On this subject, see Michael Polanyi and Harry Prosch, *Meaning* (Chicago: University of Chicago Press, 1975), 202-03.

[17] For further discussion of this point, see Polanyi and Prosch, *Meaning*, 103.

[18] David Keane, "A Composer's Approach to Music, Cognition and Emotion," *Musical Quarterly* 68 (1982): 335.

[19] George Rochberg, *The Aesthetics of Survival*, ed. and with an Introduction by William Bolcom (Ann Arbor: University of Michigan, 1984), 52, 236.

[20] Albert was one of the composers present at the luncheon with Siegmeister, mentioned earlier.

[21] Ed Siegel, "The Sudden Stilling of a Melodic Voice," *Boston Globe* (29 December 1992): 31.

[22] Robert Starer, *Continuo, A Life in Music* (New York: Random House, 1987), 145.

[23] Barbara Jepson, "A Composer Spreads a Little Sunshine (Very Little)," *New York Times* (3 January 1993): Section II, 25.

[24] William Kraft, "Appreciating Siegel," *Boston Globe* (14 February 1993): B38.

[25] William Bolcolm, "Introduction" to Rochberg, *The Aesthetics of Survival*, vii.

[26] "The Composer and Performer and Other Matters: A Panel Discussion with Virgil Thomson and Philip Glass, Moderated by Gregory Sandow," transcribed and edited by J. Bunker Clark, *American Music* 7 (1989): 196.

[27] Mary Lou Humphrey, "Michael Colgrass: Music's Pulitzer Prize-Winning Pitcher," *Music Journal* (December 1978): 25.

[28] Jacket notes to Opus One 77: *Jon Deak: Musical Tales*.

[29] Robert McColley, "Blackwood at Sixty: Easley Does It All," *Fanfare* (May-June 1993): 38, 42, 44, 46.

[30] Cole Gagne and Tracy Caras, *Soundpieces: Interviews with American Composers* (Metuchen, NJ: Scarecrow, 1982), 341-45.

[31] Allan Kozinn, "Barber, Copland and other Moderns," *New York Times* (9 January 1991): C9.

[32] Donal Henahan, "'Highbrow/Lowbrow' And the Area Between," *New York Times* (24 January 1991): C16.

[33] Conrad L. Osborne, "It's Time for Opera to Get Real," *New York Times* (5 December 1993): Section 2, 1, 35.

[34] Ibid, 35.

[35] Edward Strickland, "Downtown: An Interview with Steve Reich," *Fanfare* (March/April 1987): 46.

[36] Gagne and Caras, *Soundpieces*, 226, 315-16.

[37] Richard Dyer, " 'Voyage': This Glass Is Empty," *Boston Globe* (14 October 1992): 75, 80.

[38] Aaron M. Shatzman, "The Sound of Minimalism: Philip Glass in Concert and on Record," *Fanfare* (May/June 1987): 294-95.

[39] Ibid., 298.

[40] Edward Rothstein, "Philip Glass Shows Another Side," *New York Times* (16 November 1992): Section C, 11.

[41] See Howard Kornblum, "Second Time Around," in *Fanfare* (September/October 1987): 64.

[42] Osborne, "It's Time for Opera to Get Real," 35.

[43] Edward Rothstein, "Cities March to Different Drummers," *New York Times* (15 November 1992): Section 2, 27.

[44] Walter Simmons, "David Amos Conducts Modern Masters," *Fanfare* (July/August 1991): 82, 86.

[45] Rockwell, *All American Music*, 72.

Chapter 10

Denouement

The moment has come to summarize and form conclusions about the state of art music at the close of the twentieth century and what this study has brought to light about twentieth-century composers, especially modernist ones, their music, and the relation of both to the American public. As I do this, I must ask that we keep in mind what was already said in previous chapters about the need for balance and mutual concession in our democracy. Also to be kept in mind is the idea that in any society that is based on the principle of equality of rights and privileges, the deciding authority is supposed to be vested in a common citizenry which makes decisions and choices without intermediary or through the option of representatives. In the first instance, the citizenry exercises authority by deciding to listen or not to listen to art music. In the second instance, its representatives, meaning those who vote funds for cultural pursuits and, in more circumscribed ways, those who plan concert programs and perform the music, exercise this authority. It is also understood that there are no inherited class distinctions or entitlements contingent solely upon one person's or one group's discretion. This includes composers. As Wendell Willkie wrote, in *An American Programme* (1940): "The Constitution does not provide for first and second class citizens."

Admittedly, the actualities of our democracy does not correspond at all points to the ideal. But we must always aspire to achieve it. Artists must do the same, even as they consider the curbs on what is achievable in, or germane to, the American democracy. The more vociferous critics among them should ponder the probable outcome of their continual censure of the music public. Their words could promote the entrance of a contemporary philistinism, the likes of which they could not have anticipated. It is all very well to denounce American listeners as comprising a mishmash of tastes, mostly low or mediocre. Indeed, mishmash is at times too kind a word for what exists. However, a considerable music public does exist with excellent taste and understanding, despite the fact that it may not respond to contemporary works. Also, when the criticism falls upon the insecure understructure of cultural democracy, it encourages antagonists to counterattack. Energies thus released can quash artists in unlooked-for ways.

What must further be understood is that no one in a democracy is under obligation to accept the artist's assertion of value for his music. If the artist's music meets with total unacceptance, then his audience is himself alone and his rage at society amounts to a self-centered tantrum. If his audience numbers fifty or so, he should not express surprise when a symphonic work or opera gets no performance or, if it does, elicits a lukewarm response. He, in effect, is expected to write for the performance forces that make feasible the presentation of his music to a tiny audience. If he does not know what comprises his audience, or if he writes with no audience in mind, he must take his chances. Democracy has granted him liberty. He is free to write as he pleases. However, each individual listener must be granted the same liberty. In a democracy, he also is free to listen as he pleases.

In this regard, a remark made by Jacques Barzun, in July 1980, is helpful. He agreed with an interviewer, David Owens, that the artistic experience is like a contract, where composers created whatever music they wanted but later had to "take the brickbats or the praise once they've done it." No longer, as in previous centuries, does someone commission the artist, watch over him as he creates a work, and require a justification for what has accomplished. "I can neither direct him [the composer] nor any of his confrères to give me something. I have only the right of rejection."[1]

As for worry that the tendency in the United States is to debase art by insisting it entertain and achieve popularity, the worry indicates a propensity to paint things either entirely black or white. The serious composer does not have to lower his standards and corrupt his art by attempting to win over huge numbers of people. Principle is compatible with popularity and entertainment, when these criteria are applied in special and delimited fashion. Popularity means music has won the affection of that portion of the American society that is honestly devoted to the cultivation of the finest music. Entertainment means more than mere amusement. It also means to provide for listeners' needs and to occupy listeners' attention in ways pleasing to mind and feeling. Coercion by the majority is not the intent of the Federal Constitution. This document attempts a careful balancing of contending forces that might corrupt the meaning of American democracy—the balancing of the rights and responsibilities of the individual with those of the majority. The allowance for the play of serious and creative thought in writing a work is there, along with the allowance for the public's appraisal of that seriousness and creativity.

The first difficulty the musical citizenry and its representatives encounter in exercising their authority is deciding who is a bona fide composer and what is a truly artistic work. In previous centuries, accepted processes obtained for an aspirant to join the fraternity of master composers. The novice was taken on by an erudite pedagogue or successful older composer. He proceeded from the beginning to the end of a required sequence of phased activities toward mastery of his profession. At the conclusion of these, he presented his own finished pieces for evaluation by musicians and the public. Finally, after he completed these steps competently, he was recognized as a credentialed artist. Such ways of identifying a composer have nearly disappeared. Owing to the lack of this sort of identification, the criteria for deciding who is a composer are altogether too vague and changeable. There is no guide for either the student composer or the music world. Both find that almost anyone can define himself as a composer, an artist, and there is always someone from the communication media who will take his claim seriously. They also find that an upsetting number of today's serious musical artists refuse to have any judgments from the public, older composers, theoreticians, or analysts of aesthetics and music history act upon them. They claim independence from all of these people.

Nevertheless, in less direct but highly significant ways, the American composers could not avoid outside verdicts and influences. Whether they realized it or not, the favorable occasions and obstructions, the enticements and menaces of the outer world did act upon them. Whatever they wished to accomplish had to take into consideration their interaction with American society and its democratic base. There could be no other way in a "government by the people." Furthermore, if they permitted the processes of government, society, and the larger music world to take place without them, making believe they were outside their orbit, it only served to belittle the democratic forces that made up the virtues of America and that allowed artists to subsist and create.

The "good old days" so admired by some contemporary composers, when a Haydn and a Prince Esterházy were supposedly in complete synchronization with each other, have never existed. Unlike America today, two hundred and fifty years ago, a musically gifted person might not have become a composer but instead have remained a peasant and tilled the soil as did his father.[2] If a composer, he would have had the status of servant, not free, as he is today, to do as he wished but as he was told. More often than not, the composer would have been modestly, if not poorly, housed, fed, and clothed. The rich and powerful (unlike the private patrons, academic institutions, and foundations of today) would not have courted him. The self-expression, so prized by artists today, would have had to give way to expression allowed within certain dictated parameters. Writing for the future would have seemed silly then; the composer wrote for immediate consumption and to give undelayed satisfaction. We therefore must challenge the view that the twentieth century is the most unattractive century for creativity and the United States is in every way possible the most hostile country for "high" culture.

Modernists insisted that alternatives did exist for them, that they could select to live apart, and thus preserve their integrity, or live with the rest of the nation, and fatally compromise their principles. Yet, when they opted for the former, they abandoned the possibly valuable exchange of ideas that could come through interaction with their audiences. Musically talented as many of them were, these musicians fell short of grasping that the personal liberation, which they valued so highly, had to be accompanied by further qualities, among them willingness to accept at least partial blame for their failures and to show a concern for and obligation to others. It was not enough for them to state that their obligation lay solely in creating music of excellence for their society, if society would only educate itself to view excellence as they did. Naïveté, arrogance, and ignorance of how cultural consensus takes place are implicit in such statements.

Their difficulties, which arose in large part through the substitution of incessant atonality and experimental innovation for common tonal practices, were not the result of some unavoidable mandate grounded in history. They were the consequence of concrete decisions that composers reached, oblivious of or indifferent to what would happen when the public made their own preferences known. Few accepted the idea that to hope to thrive, they had to accept the responsibility of citizenship in a democracy. As Robert Bellah and his colleagues said, in *The Good Society*, "The question for the responsible citizen today is, Are we responsible only for our own good or also for the common good? Even a benevolent tyranny can permit us the former; only a genuine democracy can make possible the latter." In addition to this, "We are not isolated individuals picking fruit or making money; we are all profoundly dependent on the work of others."[3] For example, other men and women supply the composer's need for shelter, food, clothing, various other living expenses, musical performances, recordings, etc.

Despite all that I have said, there were cultural dilemmas peculiar to the end of the twentieth century for which the past offered few precedents and the present, few solutions.

The Condition of Musical Culture

The historical interconnections between music and the public had gone through remarkable alterations since the year 1900. At the close of the century, art musicians continued to find themselves uneasy about the general population and were more than ever apprehensive about what it might do to their art. Moreover, there were altogether too many particulars about which to feel disturbed. The population had burgeoned and with the burgeoning had occurred possibly a lessening devotion to artistic matters. Amateur musicians, from whose ranks had come the most devoted and knowledgeable concert-goers, had decreased considerably in number. Indicative of this decrease, the National Association of Music Merchants reported a downward curve in the sale of musical instruments. In 1992, only 102,082 pianos were sold, which were only one-third of those sold in 1978.[4] One hundred years ago, almost every household in comfortable circumstances saw to it that children took up an instrument, mainly the piano. Through this means, a number of them had emerged as adults with some knowledge and love for music. Americans then considered music to have a civilizing effect and to be helpful in promoting worthwhile human feeling. Especially for young women, the ability to perform was an attainment that conferred social standing. With the availability of recorded music at reasonable price, of entertainment supplied through radio, television, and video cassettes, amateurism has decreased. If it exists at all, it is in the form of playing the guitar or percussion with popular music-making in mind. Not many amateurs aspire to command a sonata through their fingers.

Music education was less and less to be found in public schools and what education there was took the form of music therapy, the singing of songs already well-known to students, a superficial once-over of "music of the world's people," and training to perform in a marching band. It rarely displayed an awareness of art music. As a percentage of the total population, music lovers were indeed fewer than they were fifty years before. At the same time, the immense American public wielded great cultural influence. Regrettably, this influence was not tempered by taking greater notice of any music of artistic pretensions. As they had never done before, American adults opted not to listen, in any case not to listen to art music. An all-consuming question asked by directors of concert and operatic establishments was: Where are the new audiences to come from that are essential to survival? It was a question that composers also had confronted and tried to address during the Roosevelt era and during the last quarter of the century.

In the nineties, Americans, if they wished, could hear every conceivable manner of music-making originating from almost every world community. Flexibility verging on instability ruled. The programming of music went in any and every direction imaginable. Lack of a ruling mode of expression also characterized art music. How correct Malcolm Bradbury was to call the end of the century "the age of pluristyle . . . the era of culture as world fair!"[5]

A music lover did not know what to expect to be hearing when he attended a concert of contemporary music—would it be conservative, nationalistic, neoclassic, neoromantic, serialist, experimental, minimalist, crossover, oriented toward a non-Western culture? He frequently found himself part of an audience made up of attendees not all of whom had a strong belief that any art music, old or new, played a significant role in American civilization. Indeed, this was but a reflection of the attitude held by the great mass of Americans since the nation's inception. Regarding the last, I read, with sympathy for our art composers, John Baur's statement about the split that has separated the American artist from the populace over the last two hundred years. He cautions us not to accuse the modern artist of overlooking people's needs and being solely responsible for a rift that has existed for decades. He says we should especially not "overlook the fact that popular indifference to the fine arts has at all times forced certain American artists to work at their own salvation outside the narrow field of public taste."[6]

The charge that art music is irrelevant to human life had strengthened with the dismissal of all past music-making by the serialists. It grew even stronger during the upheavals surrounding the Vietnam War, when the indictments from the iconoclastic composers embraced every form of artistic expression that showed any vestige of orthodoxy. In so many ways, the contemporary art composers themselves had aided and abetted the Philistines about whom they were so upset. Numerous members of the audience did not try to have a thorough knowledge of a piece, old or new, that they had come to hear, nor did they have the means for acquiring such knowledge. Furthermore, the iconoclastic composers confirmed them in their ignorance. After all, had not serious writers on music claimed that the non-performance in Cage's *4' 33"* had profounder implications than the melodious introspection in Barber's *Knoxville, Summer of 1915*, that the study of conventional music theory was a waste of time, that knowledge of the cultural past corrupted the mind?

Some prominent observers of the contemporary cultural scene claimed that an upsetting number of attendees at concerts and operatic presentations were willing to settle for music that was agreeable, effortlessly absorbed, and having little else to offer. Although this had been true for audiences from all past eras, it appeared to them to be at its highest peak in the nineties. To this, these observers added the great harm done to art music by the advocates of dogmatic multi-culturalism, who claimed that the survival of symphonies, string quartets, and the like owed more to their support by people in high places than to their inherent merits. People really did not need or want art forced down their throats (a match to what John Cage had said). The advocates confirmed the belief of unlettered people that listening to a Beethoven symphony or watching a video-rock production were of equal significance, that the momentous percussive sounds from the second movement of the Ninth Symphony were of no moment compared to an African drum beat.[7] Here was an example of the pluralism that had entered American thinking and that had eliminated the recognition of only a limited number of significant cultural alternatives as determined by communal tradition. American music no longer had focal points of this nature. A condition existed in which minorities differing in race, religion or ethnic background could belong in the larger society. Nevertheless, they could also keep alive their cultural dissimilarities. The standard was to have no standard whatsoever. Relativism was in style. The door was opened for arbitrary opinions to take the place of a considered evaluation of artistic artifacts. Thus, it seemed that there was no bonds to hold American musical culture together, no longer any group of considerable size conjointly involved with various aspects of art music. Each circle, preoccupied with one or another modern style, seemed completely segregated from each other and from those who listened to the diverse manifestations of traditional art music. The serialists agonized over the want of discipline in contemporary music other than their own and in the way people listened to music. The experimentalists were distressed by the formal and structural proclivities evident in all works not theirs and in all people, who were not blessed with a craving for the absence of control. Music lovers were unhappy because so little in contemporary music-making met their criteria of beauty. And then there was that other world of sundry and separate collections of people who subscribed to anything but Western art music. Each set had interests contrary to those of all others. It was difficult for American society to remain on an even cultural keel with such disunity.

In regard to what was said above, Daniel Boorstin, in an interview published in July 1993, observed: "The menace to America today is in the emphasis on what separates us rather than on what brings us together—the separations of race, of religious dogma, of religious practice, of origins, of language [and of culture]." Later in the interview, he commented: "There has been so much emphasis recently on the diversity of our peoples. I think it's time that we reaffirmed the fact that what has built our country is community and that community is . . . dependent on the willingness of people to build together."[8]

Cities, even those as huge as New York, no longer guaranteed the sustenance essential to the survival of art music, let alone its aberrant contemporary counterpart. Members of the educated middle class from whom came the audiences had moved away to suburbia. The separation of distance, the cost of tickets and parking, and the worry over physical safety kept them there. A representative letter sets forth this viewpoint. Philip Brantingham, of Chicago, wrote to the magazine *Fanfare* explaining the drawbacks to attending musical performances in the city. They included all of the above deterrents, plus annoyance at the "crush of the crowds," the "interminable intermissions," and the "fawning applause of the audience for the performance, be it good or bad." He ends: "It is this latter that disgusts me."[9]

Replacing the middle class in the cities were usually the indigent and poorly educated, more often than not belonging to a third-world ethnic culture. None of these was about to cultivate the arts. Sundry composers had taken shelter at universities and conservatories of music, but even these havens were decreasing in number. Besides, they provided exposure only within narrow academic circles. Seldom was the music disseminated beyond the institution's walls.

In the nineties, too, academic leftists and social-welfare activists were speaking up in support of the newer urban residents and in support of multi-culturalism. They often found a virtue in ghetto culture that they would not vouchsafe to what they called an elitist but bankrupt Western civilization. They placed all art music within the bankruptcy, especially the most modern examples of it. There was no cultural "best that has been thought and done," to use Matthew Arnold's phrase. According to John Patrick Diggins, this set identified with "every color but white" and attacked "racism, sexism" and anything that did not "enhance" the urbanite's "self-esteem and cultural identity." He quotes Randolph Bourne, who wrote: "To have learned to appreciate . . . Dante and Debussy, and not to have learned nausea at Main Street, means an art education which is not merely worthless but destructive."[10]

At the beginning of 1994, I had dinner with a half-dozen academics and social activists of the type just described. The subject of the arts came up over the dinner table. For a reason I have now forgotten, Philip Glass's music was being discussed, when one guest, whose graduate degree had come from Harvard University, began without apology to declaim against the evils of Western culture. She was an activist intent on advancing the cause of minority communities. Although white and of North-European ancestry, she held up Haiti, its paintings and music, as the equal in quality and the superior in meaningfulness to anything by "Beethoven or Bach or that guy Glass."

I have thought at odd moments after that dinner that one of the finest achievements of American civilized life would constitute the ability to keep cultural clashes within bounds, not the elimination of cultural clashes. Conflict now no longer takes place according to unvoiced but generally approved ways of basic conduct in any situation. With the sweeping away of boundaries by modern living, the entry of those who hate art music, for one reason or another, has been facilitated. They, with the acquiescence of a vast bulk of the population, could now assault at will the very foundations upon which all serious Western music, old and new, rested.

Harm was also done to art music by our capitalistic system, which measured merit in terms of profit and the number of paying customers attracted to one or another type of music. So long as American society maintained other values, this propensity was held in check. The check was absent more often than not at the end of the century. An instance of this sort of thinking was provided at the end of 1993, when suddenly WNCN, New York's "classical-music" FM radio station, shocked its listeners by switching to "that horrible rock-and-roll" (the comment of one loyalist). The conversion took place in a city that its spokespeople for the arts described as the cultural center of the United States. The move left this city of millions with only one art-music station, WQXR. The manager of the station claimed the New York market for serious music was too limited and financially unrewarding. More profit was to be gained from a popular-music format. In contrast, Bruce Adolphe, composer and administrator for the Chamber Music Society of Lincoln Center, reacted with horror to "the fast-food, mall mentality of this country," which condoned such a move. He added: "It's a kind of death for New York, and for the education of young people in the city. Those of us who have higher standards and values other than big bucks are increasingly struggling against a kind of wave of people in high places giving up, selling out to sheer commercial interests." Faithful listeners reacted with laments like: "I'm in shock, sick to my stomach. I'd rather walk on broken glass than listen to that stuff [rock music]," and "We're walking around the house saying 'What are we going to do?' "[11]

The above certainly lent weight to several commentaries about how popular music was outdoing art music more and more triumphantly in the marketplace. For example, a music lover in Illinois complained to *Fanfare*, in 1993, that he lived distant from any large city and that the local record stores had eliminated most of their "classical offerings," in order to devote themselves more profitably "to the teen market." He had gone to stores maintained in universities, hoping to fare better, owing to the support of the faculty. These stores had an even skimpier supply of recorded art music. Apparently, the popular arts were winning public interest from people high and low and taking cash and consideration away from the other kind of art. This being so, what was to be said about modern specimens of art music, which had the least popularity of all? Note what this same music lover says about entering local record stores where all of the art music was "specially segregated" into a "'weird' section." Because there was no longer an opportunity to hear a selection before purchase, as had once been the case before the advent of compact disks, he and others were reluctant to take a chance on what was for them " 'new' and unknown."[12]

Because maximizing profits was the supreme value of our economic system, it had a tendency to transform music into a commodity and appeared antagonistic to any art that reached beyond the here and now. The composer was a type of laborer, who was less important for enhancing civilization, and more important for filling the pockets of the performing group, the music publisher, and the record company. In this regard, the contemporary composer was the most menial of workers in the arts.

Seen from every perspective, modern art music was of least merit when the numbers were counted up. Several contemporary composers had instituted some intriguing and drastic musical changes and effectively extended art's meaning. However, they had won over no audiences at all, nor had they touched people's lives. They found that their absorption in reformation, if not in the uncovering of higher truths, had convinced no one but possibly themselves. The configuration of the musical world—its associations, standards, and concepts of what was worthwhile—withstood quick upturning by innovators.

These composers had to realize the importance of taking into consideration the music public's inclination toward intelligible sounds. It expected these sounds to be contained within a unified structure in accord with its understanding, and sensitive to its feeling of discomfort without such structure and intelligibility. The music public also needed the mental and visceral guidance of redundancy and of anticipating in general what might come next. From this came security in and satisfaction from the listening experience. The guidance was either nonexistent or overstated to the point of revulsion in so much contemporary music.

When Gisele Ben-Dor, director of Boston's Pro Arte Orchestra was interviewed as saying that modern art is so highly complex that "today's audiences haven't really had time to get accustomed to it," an immediate response came in a letter to the *Boston Globe Magazine*, in July 1992. The correspondent, Murray Green, of Vineyard Haven, Massachusetts, wrote of how "most so-called modernists have little to say . . . musically" to the public. Whatever gifted melodic composers there were, they gravitated to Broadway and its monetary rewards. Modern art music was:

> . . . left mostly to musical academiciana. Their commissioned efforts, after a few mandatory performances to honor, say, a gift from the National Endowment for the Arts, end up gathering dust—except when a conductor inflicts such an opus on an unsuspecting audience. Invariably, that half-hour or more of painful boredom is programmed between a Verdi overture and (after intermission) a Beethoven symphony. That keeps the audience in place 'till the end. And why do conductors risk the ire of their audiences? To please the professional critics who need to meet a deadline. What can they possibly write about Beethoven's *Eroica* that hasn't been said a thousand times before? So everyone's happy . . . except the concertgoer.[13]

From all that has just been said, we must suppose that the condition of musical culture at the end of the century left much to be desired. Not surprisingly, almost none of the music composed since the end of World War II has entered the stock of instrumental and vocal works that musicians are prepared to perform and some fairly large public is prepared to admire.

The More Immediate Residue of Modernism

Earlier, I mentioned the possible shrinkage of the general public for all art music. Also referred to was a corresponding, if not greater relative, shrinkage in the already tiny audience that affected to like contemporary music. This phenomenon was a substantial residue of the persistent modernism that had alienated more and more people, an estrangement that the works of the conciliatory composers had not reduced. The public persisted in agreeing with Peter Ustinov's quip, when asked about modern music: "First of all, it must be deezagreeable!"[14]

In particular, those performing groups specializing in the most advanced music felt the lessening of listeners' interest. Early in 1991, Allan Kozinn was reporting in the *New York Times* that along with and because of the decrease in attendance, government and private funding was also going down. The result was fewer opportunities to put on the works of the least conventional composers. They had always depended on subsidies for the performance of their music, since at best few people came to hear them and ticket sales did not cover even a fraction of the expenses. Kozinn cites Anthony Korf, of the Parnassus ensemble, as saying that the New York State Council on the Arts had already cut their grant from $11,000 to $9,000 because the ensemble's audiences had fallen away. Then in the fall of 1990, the Council trimmed the grant to $7,000. Korf admitted: "On a percapita basis, the funding for new music has always been absurdly high." He and the ensemble, however, would not settle their differences with the music public but continue to do serial and atonal composers like Babbitt, Wuorinen, Gideon, and Davidovsky. In the face of this and other evidence, Kozinn states: "Whether they specialize in the rigorous atonal Uptown styles, or in the freewheeling experimentalism of the Downtown schools, the musicians . . . insist that they will not abandon their chosen repertoires in the hope of attracting larger audiences to please potential contributors."[15] Despite the fact that they paid some lip service to broadening their programming, they also displayed the mentality of self-destructing lemmings.

Denouement 277

Critics who spoke up for innovative sounds also contributed to the self-destruction. What were the readers of record-review magazines to think about the praise for Cage's *Prelude for Meditation*: it is "boring" but, as Cage says, "very interesting" and "utterly spellbinding in its emptiness"; and the praise for Feldman's Piano Quartet: it is entirely an "apparition" and without "punch"; a variety of "wallpaper music with an enormous moral conscience."[16] Apparently nothing, since most of the letters to the editor rarely mention modern music or its reviewers. By 1993, music lovers were not even bothering to respond to such fatuous and meaningless language.

In 1993, Morley Safer, on the television program *60 Minutes*, which had millions of viewers, was calling modern art, "worthless junk." He found a shift in the standing of innovative art in American life. Michael Kimmelman, who was unhappily reporting Safer's words, admitted that extreme idioms were no longer assured the shield of the once prevalent institutional respect for artists. Very few people could be found who accepted the credo that formerly helped guarantee modernism's continuation—that the new and original were good for their own sake, that incomprehensibility was inherently valuable, that the invention of novel conceptual or chaotic expressions were valid activities in which to engage.[17] Here was a straw in the wind indicating that worse was to come.

The division between modernists and the rest of the cultural world was coming to a head. Into the breach were stepping right-wingers declaiming about a waste of money, multi-culturalists demanding an end of elitism, advocates for the poor and sick saying the helpless deserved aid more than self-centered artists, and capitalistic populists finding merit in the huge numbers of young people who paid for admission to rock events and snapped up rock recordings as soon as they were issued. At the same time, the estranged contemporary composers were so given over to complaining that they were unable to organize and launch an adequate justification for their actions. They had themselves cut off all contact with the larger music world, and would not recognize, in their periods of excessive self-pity, that the criticisms of sincerely concerned music lovers were worthy of notice.

There is no question in my mind but that art music will live on and will not perish. With the usual exaggeration, pessimists proclaim the coming death of all serious culture. There is a cause for concern, but assuredly not one for complete pessimism and despondency. However, it remains difficult to deal with the obvious dissensions over art music of the past century that are still with us. The public has heard years of insults from contemporary musicians, so that they no longer insult. When present-time composers express their grievances, fewer Americans pay them any attention. The public believes it has gotten nothing from these musicians, nor does it expect anything. Saddest of all, and basically mistaken, the traditional music world defines them more and more as wastrels, living off the fat of academia, their taxes, and the largess of benighted private money dispensers. The conciliatory composers and those other composers who have kept faith with traditional procedures for all of their lives have failed to dislodge this idea so embedded in American thinking.

At the same time, there still exists today a large number of composers who emphasize individual experimentation and aesthetic judgment and whose attempts at reconciliation are nil, half-hearted, or unsuccessful. The creative lives they have had to lead denote a distinct testing of their beliefs. Several of them have had a notoriety thrust upon their activities that they can neither manage nor disavow. On the one hand, they mistrust and disdain the society from which acceptance and acclaim must come; on the other, they crave acceptance and acclaim. Some of them are not always certain of the authenticity of their chosen mode of expression. They cannot help but regard themselves as outcasts and appear resentful and dispossessed. Not surprisingly, when interviewed, these musicians prove to have thin skins when asked questions. They may become insulted, show profound hopelessness, or turn belligerent.

Like the sword of Damocles, hanging over their heads is the notion of wasted creative lives, of very limited performances for their works over a year or two and then nothingness. The utmost that their music can count on for the future is that it will have a sufficient effect in the short run so as to be sized up later as having once been shrewdly informed, or suitable for its time, or even valuable but having now grown démodé. Extraordinary works, like Babbitt's *Philomel* and Cage's *Sonatas and Interludes for Prepared* would later exist briefly in the thoughts of some persons, perhaps in respectful or petulant allusions to their style, perhaps as having contributed to one era's forward-looking expression. Nothing else.

Composers could no longer blame the music public entirely for the impasse. This assertion had become a trite accusation in many quarters by the 1990s. Instead they needed to inquire specifically concerning who brought the predicament about and why. They had to understand that listeners were not easily sloughed off as part of a mass society, as cogs in a technomechanical nation. Every music lover was, as Daniel Bell said of people in general, not a "thing" within a bureaucratized society, but a "subject who can remake life in accordance with his own desires." Members of the public "are not tabulae rasae. They bring varying . . . [aesthetic] conceptions to the same experience and go away with dissimilar responses. They may be silent, separate, detached, and anonymous while . . . [attending a performance], but afterward they talk about it with friends and exchange opinions and judgments." [18]

There was a tremendous judgmental attempt to blame Americans in most cases, and this included the more informed, because they did not realize the worth of twentieth-century compositions. Yet, the reality was that the basic attraction of the modern movement was to the composer or to others who make it a common practice to defend him. Nor did Europeans generally like posttriadic compositions more than did Americans. It was scarcely only an American phenomenon. Heed should have been taken of warnings like those that Geoffrey Parsons, chief editorial writer of the *New York Herald Tribune*, gave Virgil Thomson in a memorandum, dated 14 October 1940. The composer was then the music critic for the newspaper. Parsons advised Thomson to rethink his criticism of audiences, since they numbered the music lovers he wanted to have listen to him. Demeaning them, Parsons said, only made them abandon him and his music. Another mistake about which he warned Thomson was the composer speaking as if he were looking down on listeners. When Thompson cited the opinion of musically educated people who, Thomson claimed, could not abide Sibelius, although the public did, he made every ordinary listener who disagreed "snort and quit. 'What the hell, the experts have always been wrong in estimating the importance of creative work. Here's another cocksure wise-guy. Provincial is Sibelius? Well, then, that's what I like.' And so on."[19]

Thomson had engaged in a pretentiousness that was effective only as long as those injured assented to its assumptions. Americans would not do so any longer.

The composer Robert Starer takes an opposite view when he writes about his Third Piano Concerto, performed in January 1980. After the first chord, an extremely harsh one, sounded, he saw a member of the audience get up and dash for the exit. Starer felt the fault was his for not trying to understand the listener. Modern composers, he said, had a deservedly bad reputation. They had served up a great deal of unrelieved hideousness in sound and given neither enjoyment nor intellectual stimulation to music lovers. The easy way out was to blame the audience: "Some years ago Milton Babbitt wrote a much-quoted article called 'Who Cares If You Listen?' Clearly he does not care, and very few indeed do listen."[20]

Dashing for the exit was no longer a characteristic of only the musically ignorant. The contemporary composer had to accept that it was also the tendency of seasoned music lovers. He could not have the luxury of unilaterally intellectualizing or of waxing philosophical about the nature of art, allowing his conclusions to dominate the music he produced, and then demanding that his works and the thinking behind them be accepted. Audiences would not subscribe to the idea that the twentieth century was all ugliness, alienation, and gloom, and should be so depicted in art. Nor were they ready to give up older music with depths of meaning for them that were lacking in new works. To them, sentiment, imagination, the giving of pleasure had been replaced by mathematical rules, lifeless computer noises, and sounds that were purposely unpredictable and uncontrollable. More than one or two listeners had decided that those left in the modern movement were an anomaly, a sterile group without a past to delight in or a future that would be populated by its offspring.

From everything that has just been said, it should be obvious that the residue of modernism has been non-acceptance. As a last case in point, in 1992 Ralph Shapey's *Concerto Fantastique* was denied the Pulitzer Prize, although the jury made up of modern composers had recommended it. The board composed of non-musicians had taken into account the audience's point of view. The composers on the jury and their friends immediately denounced the decision of the lay board, saying that its ignorance had taken precedence over the jury's expertise. Music critics then entered the controversy on the side of the jury, and spoke in praise of the music's brutal power and staggering complexity.[21] However, they should have taken seriously a comment by Max Raimi, a violist in the Chicago Symphony that played the work. In a letter to the *New York Times*, he said that he wished the critics could have joined him on stage at the premier of the Shapey piece and seen the faces of the audience: "It was a scene of suffering out of Dante. After each movement there was an exodus from the hall unprecedented in my experience. The listeners were not provoked or challenged—this was no 'Sacre de Printemps.' They were merely enduring a prison sentence (or choosing not to)." When novelists, playwrights, and filmmakers failed to win over a following, they admitted to failure. Why, under similar circumstances did composers and their sympathizers claim a success? Mr. Raimi criticizes Mr. Rothstein, critic of the *New York Times*, for saying that the Pulitzer Prize in music should not be based on popularity, because it is "a professional award certifying a high level of achievement." Here is another indication of how dead art has become. "How moribund must our art become before arbiters of achievement require composers to write for the vast public rather than just one another?"[22]

It is not my purpose to go into the merits of Shapey's composition. What I do wish to note is this present age's close to total disenchantment with the music that has most diverged from the tonal practices of a hundred years ago, and with the institutions and writers that support the divergence. The disenchantment is far-reaching to a magnitude not envisioned in the 1920s. Once, it may have been the attitude of a turned-off but potentially convincible group. At the close of the century disenchantment had seeped into the thinking and feelings of vast multitudes of Americans. Keep in mind, the revulsion is not to a composer here and another there, but to very nearly all contemporary music with a preponderantly posttriadic sound. At one time, if a composer failed to please, audiences anticipated other composers who would. At one time, too, if a style proved unsatisfactory to people, the unceasing denial of endorsement could successfully modify musical procedures. This had not been so now for most of the century. As the controversy over the Pulitzer Prize in 1992 proves, the disenchantment with modern composers and with the institutions and writers that uphold them are closely associated.

The Music Public: Its State of Mind

The recognition of the worthiness of art music is an event not directly connected with everyday living in the United States. Only few pieces serve a vital function that is attached to some ceremony, in which the entire community participates. Among these exceptions are Copland's *Fanfare to Common Man* and Barber's *Adagio for Strings*. Otherwise, one allocates leisure time and a sequestered place (a living room, a concert hall) for the purpose for music listening. Historically, art music has commonly had the attribute of a nonessential indulgence in American thinking. Nevertheless, there continue to be listeners, and not a few, whose love of art music is intense.[23] Music occupies a significant place in their minds. For them to be denied music is an affliction. Each of them, musically trained or not, does "understand" in his own fashion, and takes delight in, the compositions he holds dear. The justifications of music start for them with minds managing and adapting musical sound in order to obtain meaning from it, and the special ability of the lover of music to derive expressive meaning from the sounds which composers offer him.

An individual understanding and delight invests a statement made by one woman who speaks of "growing [so] tired of my generation's rock and roll" that "I started some four or five years ago listening to classical music. It didn't take me long to get 'hooked,' and I don't think I will ever reach a day when this music sounds tiresome or boring to me." Because she had previously known nothing about art music, she wishes that knowledgeable writers would take people like her into consideration when they write. She and others like her "are interested, very interested" in artworks. Another member of the music public states that she and her husband were part of "the baby boom generation" and "raised on rock and roll. Our parents listened to 'junk,' and we were never exposed to classical music." Hearing art music over the radio got them interested, despite their lack of musical knowledge, and they began purchasing records. "This inauspicious start led to friends enjoying our records and purchasing their own in record stores. Several of our friends, all in their early 30s, have since become totally addicted to classical music. None of us had ever been exposed to it while at early ages." A third listener speaks of his growing interest in art music, including that of the twentieth century. He cites the music of Hovhaness, Thomson, Barber, "and many others." A deterrent to appreciation, he says, is the poor sound fidelity of "a lot of 'modern' serious music."[24] Beginning in 1979, music lovers from all walks of life started to send "best" lists of memorable recorded music to *Fanfare* magazine. The number of composers and the variety of titles were surprising. Even more surprising were the number of American composers on the lists—among them, Piston, Creston, Barber, Harrison, Kirchner, Persichetti, Schuman, Copland, and Thomson.

Understanding for all of these people meant, first of all, that the listener's mind had detected or applied a structural gestalt to what was heard. This included melody whose series of tones sounded as if they belonged together, and dissonances whose eventual resolution into consonances gave a satisfactory sense of completion. The listener could perceive harmonies that moved along in logical progression and hear repetition or recognizable variation in the material so that the various sections were knitted together. In short, some sort of systemization in the arrangement of sounds facilitated a personal interpretation of what they heard.

When a twentieth-century work prevented the listener from gaining this understanding, then repudiation of composer and composition was assured. The wonder was that knowing incomprehensibility will probably result, some members of the general public still attended concerts of new music. In other words, not all minds of the music public were closed to everything new. This is an argument I advance based on my observation of and discussions with music lovers over the past four decades. Note the tolerance revealed in a letter sent by a reader who objected to a reviewer's severe criticism of Elliott Carter's advanced music: "The truly nasty references to the music of Elliott Carter was disturbingly gratuitous. Carter's music, not to my taste either, may well be eclipsed in its turn. But his music is not contemptible; it can be appreciated highly, and some people in fact do so appreciate it. Why insult it and them? Do musical politics really require this?"[25]

Boston's Musica Viva is an ensemble that specializes in atonal and experimental pieces, which it performs at the Longy School of Music. During one intermission in early 1994, I recognized a married couple who regularly attended the fairly traditional chamber concerts given at a local museum and the mostly standard presentations of the Boston Symphony Orchestra. I expressed surprise at seeing them present at a concert of "way-out" music. The wife replied that they did go to new-music performances, not regularly, but certainly not just once or twice a year. Yes, they considered much of what they heard to be inane, boring, gimmicked, and without a glimmer of talent. Yet, they felt strongly that "someone should encourage the avant-garde or else music would stagnate." A tiny handful of works that Musica Viva performed did prove understandable to them, in a special sense. Regrettably, even in these pieces, delight did not usually accompany understanding.

Without question, the music public is not made up entirely of bigots. Rephrasing Ambrose Bierce's definition of a bigot in *The Devil's Dictionary* (1906), artists wield the word "bigot" as a weapon against anyone "who is obstinately and zealously attached to an opinion that" they "do not entertain." Why the contrary opinion? What did this man and woman and others like them find missing? First, the music had not stirred them on a visceral level. There was no disarming melody, catching rhythm, evocative turn of harmony, colorful orchestration, or rousing dramatic contrasts to win them over whether they would or not. At this level, music was expected to "grab" them and to allow a release of those stored-up emotions that accompany physiological stimulation. None of this had happened.

Second, the music had denoted nothing beyond itself. Music listeners desired most to discover meanings of transcendental value, which included an acknowledgment of the dignity of humankind and of the vivifying and resilient aspects of life. They had seen enough of ugliness, tension, and unreason in everyday existence not to want them also in the arts. Their spirit demanded not just the earthbound exploration of the afflictions of evil on humanity, but also the arousal of wonder—a participation in something beyond and nobler than their mundane selves. To their way of thinking, art had to be perceived as human, as serving people and not as dehumanizing them.[26] It was not enough for the contemporary composer to say that his music did this; he had to convince his listeners through his music that it was actually so. George Rochberg put it well, when he wrote of the larger music public that "through the direct experience of the artwork they intuit that they may be put in touch with that larger realm, the desire for which haunts them all their lives as an indefinable yet palpable hunger." He speaks of art as a mediator between what they desire, hunger after, and desire to experience. People are not satisfied "by the daily round of existence." They long to transcend themselves by sharing in an "artist's vision." They dream of the "possibility of leaving behind the crushing literalness of the world of modern society, which presses on them from all sides daily, and of opening themselves to the reality which art mysteriously channels into their lives."[27]

Music that strikes the ear as anarchic, consistently disagreeable, schizophrenic, or displaying hostility to the listener acts against the human grain. The diseases of the world and the artist's distortive psyche become the diseases of art. The composer cannot simply reflect the state of utter confusion and fragmentation in civilization's present situation. Listeners expect him to respond to the submerged wants of every person who confronts that utter disorder and division.

Afterword

From everything that I can see, American culture at the turn of the century occupies a position where much of the rubbish about the exclusive rights of the artist and the extensive ignorance of the Philistines is being swept away, one hopes, to make room for renewal and rediscovery of art's wider meaning. The tiredness of contemporary styles of art music that dismiss customary modes of musical expression and dwell on individual procedures and aesthetic judgment is obvious. History has made plain the apparent sterility in the creative endeavors of many modern artists and the unpromising rut occupied by intemperate egos. After the passage of decades, there still exists an absence of recognizable content in much of the music and of promising dialogue in the unyielding diatribes against the public, which are still unleashed by several unreconstructed modernists. The evidence suggests that a unique cultural period is now ending. The present musical world searches uncertainly for a different musical lexicon.

Nevertheless, I have confidence that a new beginning has started, no matter what the perceived circumstances of contemporary life. Furthermore, major contemporary composers have dedicated themselves to expansion of this beginning. What ultimate shapes the renewal and rediscovery will take cannot be foreseen. They may or many not articulate the innermost perceptions of the music public. That the shapes themselves will continually alter is a certainty. That some aspects of style and expression will endure from one decade to the next is probable. Those art forms capable of prolonged life, however, must be ones firmly threaded into the essence of American civilization.

We have lived long enough with the era of collapse in traditional convictions and disunification in culture. As concerned observers, we worry about narrow advocacies that try to promote their limited breadth of view into universals. The number of men and woman grows, and composers as well, who attempt to hold onto those artifacts of humanity that they believe have significance for every human being. They want a reexamination of the past in order to retrieve its virtues and to pick up again the thread of continuity.[28]

For almost a century now, composers with esoteric predispositions have received nourishment and forbearance from society as a whole. Their peccadilloes have been overlooked, their more outrageous utterances treated benignly. The tyranny of the majority and punitive actions against artistic nonconformists have been held in abeyance.

No matter what the decade, Americans are found who willingly listen to and show a readiness to accept new music if given half a chance. A good many of them long for an approachable music other than popular music, a music of rich and varied meanings. They may now be about to overcome the views cultivated by so-called musical authorities that have deterred them from vital musical experiences, among them that appreciation comes only through musical training and intellectual comprehension. Concert attendance as a sort of cultural worship service occupies fewer thoughts. The tenet that serious music must always remain serious weakens. The dour declaration that art does not encompass the enjoyment of catchy tunes and kinetic rhythms falls by the wayside.

When trust improves between composer and public, then musical education will also improve. First, we must change the extant American mass judgments of contemporary music. Our music culture can no longer afford the luxury of the vast multitude fleeing any contact with new music because at best they believe it dull, at worst, excruciatingly disagreeable to hear. Needed are composers of more constructive outlook, whose words can encourage people to listen, and new music of less forbidding mien, whose sound emboldens people to explore contemporary musical offerings. We have started along this road and should keep on traveling it. More composer-public dialogue and personal contact must mitigate the tendency to aloofness of artists with hideaways in academia and disconnected Greenwich Village localities. Spokespeople for the new music should underscore positive expectancies from the listening experience, not that it is not too painful or difficult to listen, nor that immediate satisfaction will never ensue and appreciation will come only after protracted effort. Charles Ives gave ill-considered advice when he told a listener to face unpleasant music and "take it like a man."

Music is not medicine that, however distasteful, must be swallowed because it is beneficial to one's health. Give audiences the idea that they can understand and are counted on to enjoy what they hear, provided, of course, that the work offered is potentially understandable and enjoyable. Everyone engaged with art music, past and present, whether composers, writers on music, or music teachers, should endeavor to make the concert hall a place where all can feel at ease and open their senses to a performance.

A musical "outreach" effort is needed. For the mass of Americans, all art music, let alone the new, occupies an alien space that never abuts on their own cultural environment. Altogether too many educators know little of the music's contents and accept the widespread misconceptions that art music is attempting to live down. A great many of the programs reaching out to a wider section of the public, although conscientiously elaborated on by various musical experts, are founded on erroneous beliefs about what the public could understand and would like. Who thinks to take the pulse of the public and monitor its progress into the territory of art music? This is the nitty-gritty essential to any enriching process.

Educators ultimately take their cue from the public they serve. They will follow their community if it perceives that presenting students with the already popular and familiar, rather than the worthy and unfamiliar, is no education at all. I hope that as the student goes from grade level to grade level, education will go from simpler to more complex music, American traditional music to American art music, world and ethnic musical practices to world and ethnic art music, if any. The study of mathematics, chemistry, history, etc. are not contingent on uninformed students' tastes. That would be the road to disaster. Yet, today this is precisely what is usually described as music education.

People by themselves do not cheapen music. Music is cheapened by those who in the music world condescend to the public or who dismiss it as of no consequence. Giving it pabulum for monetary profit or giving it nothing because by definition the artist does not entertain produces the same result. The lowering of public esteem for contemporary art music has come with denigration of listeners' viewpoints, with works that disregard audiences' capabilities for listening, and with musicians who insist that they, as authorities, and their peremptory opinions of what constitutes art, come first. These are the ways that art music is cheapened.

An imperative of democracy is the understanding that the audience, who will be considerably affected by decisions made by any composer, must and does have a say in the final outcome. Nevertheless, there are composers who refuse to recognize this truism. As Gunther Schuller once said: "We composers should remember that after all the artistic, aesthetic battles have been fought and all injustices to misunderstood composers rectified, the audience—the large over-all audience, in short, the culture—is the final arbiter of that which survives." Robert Starer agrees and adds: "No performer will persist in playing what his listeners truly hate, even if the press adores it." Though at first shocking, Stravinsky's *Rite of Spring* has found acceptance, while Schoenberg's *Pierrot Lunaire* is still considered abnormal, depends on ensembles specializing in modern music for performance, and is permanently confined to the "artistic ghetto" of modernism.[29]

Composers are advised to take pride in the United States and its democracy even as they labor to improve both. Yes, inequities abound. The native composer is not always given a fair shake. Yet, for all America's faults, our country has been kinder to contemporary artists than they care to admit. The process of discovery of our own authentic voices (not voice) will continue strongly if we have a respect for what Americans have already accomplished in the arts and do not work continuously to overthrow the past. Starting with the works of Louis Moreau Gottschalk, John Knowles Paine, and George Chadwick, a tradition of artistic excellence is already in place to which we must reawaken. They were then not timid about exploring a wide gamut of emotions and expressions from comic to tragic, whimsical to stern, clownish to heroic, satirical to worshipful, earthy to divine. They took pleasure in their craftsmanship. Nothing of the precious, decadent, abusive, or exclusive was evident in the music. Their aim (they called it their "duty") was to communicate something worth communicating in sounds that did effectively transmit their ideas. Those bugaboos of modernism, originality at all costs and experiment as a way of creative life, came second.

At the end of the twentieth century, that aim continues among composers who have never deviated from it and is being reinstated by others who once thought that some version of modernism was the be-all and end-all of music. Not everything they do will meet with success. But the cultural pump needs continuous priming. Eventually, if discouragement does not set in, viable works will flow out to a public that become, once more, expectant and enthusiastic.

Notes to Chapter 10

[1] Jacques Barzun, *Critical Questions*, ed. Bea Friedland (Chicago: University of Chicago Press, 1982), 226.

[2] I also shudder to think of what I might have become if my parents had not emigrated to the United States!

[3] Robert Bellah, Richard Madsen, William M. Sullivan, Ann Swidler, and Steven M. Tipton, *The Good Society* (New York: Knopf, 1991), 81, 104.

[4] Carol Stoker, "A Room with a Piano," *Boston Globe* (23 December 1993): A3. During the same year, 46,004 electronic pianos were sold. Higher prices, cuts in school budgets, video amusements are mentioned as contributing to the drop.

[5] Malcolm Bradbury, *Doctor Criminale* (New York: Viking Penguin, 1992), 90.

[6] John I. H. Baur, *Revolution and Tradition in Modern American Art* (Cambridge, MA: Harvard University Press, 1966), 121-22.

[7] For a detailed study of the state of music in the postwar years, see Nicholas E. Tawa, *Art Music in the American Society* (Metuchen, NJ: Scarecrow, 1987).

⁸ Tad Szuk, "The Greatest Danger We Face," *Parade* (25 July 1993): 4.

⁹ Philip Brantingham, letter, in *Fanfare* (March/April 1980): 7-8.

¹⁰ John Patrick Diggins, *The Rise and Fall of the American Left* (New York: Norton, 1992), 292-93, 297.

¹¹ Dennis Hevesi, "The Day the Music Died: Mourning Classical WNCN," *New York Times* (19 December 1993): 48.

¹² Nicholas F. O'Riordan, letter, in *Fanfare* (January/February 1993): 4. See also, Jacques Barzun, *The Culture We Deserve*, ed. Arthur Krystal (Middletown, CT: Wesleyan University Press, 1989), 35.

¹³ Murray Green, letter to the *Boston Globe Magazine* (5 July 1992): 5.

¹⁴ Jack Hiemenz, "Leon Kirchner," *Musical America* (in *High Fidelity/Musical America* (January 1971): 5. Hiemenz was quoting Kirchner, who said Ustinov was right when he made this jab at modern music.

¹⁵ Allan Kozinn, "For Contemporary Music, Times Are Hard," *New York Times* (8 January 1991): C11.

¹⁶ Reviews of Damon Krukowski and Mard Weidenbaum, respectively, in *Classical Pulse* (December 1993): 44-45.

¹⁷ Michael Kimmelman, "A Few Artless Minutes on '60 Minutes'," *New York Times* (17 October 1993): Section 2, 39.

¹⁸ Daniel Bell, *The End of Ideology* (Glencoe, IL: Free Press, 1960), 23-24.

¹⁹ John Vinton, *Essays After a Dictionary* (Lewisburg, PA: Bucknell University Press, 1977), 35-36.

²⁰ Robert Starer, *Continuo: A Life in Music* (New York: Random House, 1987), 142, 144-45.

[21] Edward Rothstein, who weighs in on the side of the jury, discusses the controversy in "In the Fracas Over a Prize, No One Won," *New York Times* (19 April 1992): Section 2, 25.

[22] Max Raimi, letter to the *New York Times* (10 May 1992): Section 2, 6.

[23] For a detailed discussion of the late-twentieth-century audience for art music, see Tawa, *Art Music in the American Society*.

[24] Respectively, Janine Beckert, of Reading, Massachusetts, in a letter to *Fanfare* (November/December 1980): 2; Ann de Vries, of Manitouwadge, Ontario, in a letter to *Fanfare* (September/October 1981): 2; Paul A. Elias, of Greenwich, Connecticut, in a letter to *Fanfare* (March/April 1981): 14, 16.

[25] R. James Tobin, of Sheboygan, Wisconsin, in a letter to *Fanfare* (July/August 1989): 22.

[26] The last sentence rephrases a comment made by Hans Küng, in *Art and the Question of Meaning* trans. Edward Quinn (New York: Crossroads, 1981), 50-51. Many twentieth-century writers have spoken about what listeners ask of music: See, Howard Mumford Jones, *One Great Society* (New York: Harcourt, Brace, 1959), 9-10; Josef Paul Hodin, *The Dilemma of Being Modern* (New York: Noonday Press, 1959), 172; Robert Baska, "Man as Music Listener," *Music Journal* (February 1975): 38; Samuel Lipman, *Arguing for Music, Arguing for Culture* (Boston: Godine, 1990), 55.

[27] George Rochberg, *The Aesthetics of Survival*, ed. William Bolcom (Ann Arbor, MI: University of Michigan Press, 1984), 205.

[28] On this point, see the interview with Stephen Albert, in Ed Siegel, "A Critic's Lament," *Boston Globe Magazine* (23 August 1992): 12-13, 23-24, 27-29.

[29] Gunther Schuller, *Musings* (New York: Oxford University Press, 1986), 174. See also, Starer, *Continuo*, 146-47.

Bibliography

Aaron, Daniel, and Robert Bendiner, eds. *The Strenuous Decade, A Social and Intellectual Record of the 1930s*. Garden City, NY: Anchor, 1970.

Amram, David. *Vibrations*. New York: Macmillan, 1968.

Antheil, George. *Bad Boy of Music*. 1945. Reprint. New York: Da Capo, 1981.

Armitage, Merle. *George Gershwin, Man and Legend*. New York: Duell, Sloan & Pearce, 1958.

Arvey, Verna. *In One Lifetime*. Fayetteville, AR: University of Arkansas Press, 1984.

Babbitt, Milton. "Who Cares If You Listen?" *High Fidelity* (February 1958): 38-40, 126-27. Also reprinted in Schwartz, Elliott, and Barney Childs, eds. *Contemporary Composers on Contemporary Music*. New York: Holt, Rinehart & Winston, 1967.

Ballantine, Christopher. *Music and Its Social Meanings*. New York: Gordon & Breach Science Publishers, 1984.

Barrett, William. *The Truants, Adventures Among the Intellectuals*. Garden City, NY: Anchor/Doubleday, 1982.

Barzun, Jacques. *Critical Questions*. Edited by Bea Friedland. Chicago: University of Chicago Press, 1982.

―――――. *The Culture We Deserve*. Edited by Arthur Krystal. Middletown, CT: Wesleyan University Press, 1989.

―――――. *Music in American Life*. Bloomington: University of Indiana Press, 1965.

―――――. *The Use and Abuse of Art*. Princeton, NJ: Princeton University Press, 1974.

Bate, W. Jackson. *The Burden of the Past and the English Poet*. Cambridge, MA: Belknap, 1970.

Baur, John I. H. *Revolution and Tradition in Modern American Art*. Cambridge, MA: Harvard University Press, 1966.

Bell, Daniel. *The Cultural Contradictions of Capitalism*. New York: Basic Books, 1976.

——————. *The End of Ideology*. Glencoe, IL: Free Press, 1960.

——————. *The Winding Passage: Essays and Sociological Journeys, 1960-1980*. Cambridge, MA: ABT Books, 1980.

Bellah, Robert, Richard Madsen, William M. Sullivan, Ann Swidler, and Steven M. Tipton. *The Good Society*. New York: Knopf, 1991.

Benser, Caroline Cepin, and David Francis Urrows. *Randall Thompson, A Bio-Bibliography*. Westport, CT: Greenwood, 1991.

Berger, Arthur. *Aaron Copland*. New York: Oxford University Press, 1953.

Bergonzi, Bernard. *The Myth of Modernism and Twentieth Century Literature*. New York: St. Martin's, 1986.

Berman, Marshall. *All That Is Solid Melts Into the Air*. New York: Simon & Schuster, 1982.

Berman, Phillip L. *The Search for Meaning, Americans Talk About What They Believe and Why*. New York: Ballantine Books, 1990.

Bernstein, Leonard. *Findings*. New York: Simon & Schuster, 1982.

——————. *The Infinite Variety of Music*. New York: Simon & Schuster, 1966.

——————. *The Unanswered Question*. Cambridge, MA: Harvard University Press, 1976.

Birkerts, Sven. *American Energies.* New York: Morrow, 1992.

Bloom, Allan David. *The Closing of the American Mind.* New York: Simon & Schuster, 1987.

Boretz, Benjamin, and Edward T. Cone, eds. *Perspectives on American Composers.* New York: Norton, 1971.

Broder, Nathan. "The Evolution of the American Composer." In Lang, Paul Henry, ed. *One Hundred Years of Music in America.* New York: Schirmer, 1961.

———. *Samuel Barber.* New York: Schirmer, 1954.

Brooks, Van Wyck. *An Autobiography.* New York: Dutton, 1965.

———. *The Early Years.* Edited by Claire Sprague. New York: Harper & Row, 1968.

———. *From a Writer's Notebook.* New York: Dutton, 1958.

Brunswick, Mark. "After Munich." *Modern Music* 16 (November-December 1938): 3-9.

Buchanan, Charles L. "Ornstein and Modern Music." *Musical Quarterly* 4 (1918): 174-83.

Bürger, Peter. *The Decline of Modernism.* Translated by Nicholas Walker. University Park, PA: Pennsylvania State University Press, 1992.

Burk, John N. "The Democratic Ideal in Music." *Musical Quarterly* 5 (1919): 316-28.

Butler, Christopher. *After the Wake.* New York: Oxford University Press, 1980.

Cage, John. *Silence.* Middletown, CT: Wesleyan University Press, 1961.

Carter, Elliott. "Shop Talk by an American Composer." In Lang, Paul Henry, ed. *Problems of Modern Music*. New York: Schirmer, 1960.

───────. *The Writings of Elliott Carter*. Edited and annotated by Else Stone and Kurt Stone. Bloomington: Indiana University Press, 1977.

Cavalieri, Walter. "Lee Hoiby, A Summer of Success." *Music Journal* (November-December 1980): 10-12.

Chase, Gilbert. *The American Composer Speaks*. Baton Rouge: Louisiana State University Press, 1966.

Chasins, Abrams. *Music at the Crossroads*. New York: Macmillan, 1972.

"The Composer and Performer and Other Matters: A Panel Discussion with Virgil Thomson and Philip Glass, Moderated by Gregory Sandow." Transcribed and edited by J. Bunker Clark. *American Music* 7 (1989): 181-204.

Cone, Edward T. "Conversations with Aaron Copland." In Boretz, Benjamin, and Edward T. Cone, eds. *Perspectives on American Composers*. New York: Norton, 1971.

───────. "Conversations with Roger Sessions." In Boretz, Benjamin, and Edward T. Cone, eds. *Perspectives on American Composers*. New York: Norton, 1971.

Copland, Aaron. "The Composer in America, 1923-1933." *Modern Music* 10 (January-February 1933): 87-92.

───────. *Copland on Music*. Garden City, NY: Doubleday, 1960.

───────. *Music and Imagination*. New York: Mentor, 1959.

───────. "Music Since 1920." *Modern Music* (March-April 1928): 16-20. Volume 5, paginated by issue.

───────. *The New Music, 1900-1960*. Revised and enlarged edition. New York: Norton, 1968.

———. "One Hundred and Fourteen Songs." *Modern Music* 11 (January-February 1934): 59-64.

———. *Our New Music*. New York: Whittlesey House, 1941.

Copland, Aaron, and Vivian Perlis. *Copland, 1900 Through 1942*. New York: St. Martin's/Marek, 1984.

———. *Copland Since 1943*. New York: St. Martin's, 1989.

Cowell, Henry, ed. *American Composers on American Music*. New York: Ungar, 1962.

Cowley, Malcolm. *And I Worked at the Writer's Trade*. New York: Viking, 1978.

———. *Exile's Return*. New York: Viking, 1951.

Dickstein, Morris. *Gates of Eden: American Culture in the Sixties*. New York: Basic Books, 1977.

Diggins, John Patrick. *The Rise and Fall of the American Left*. New York: Norton, 1992.

Edelstein, Arthur, ed. *Images and Ideas in American Culture*. Waltham, MA: Brandeis University Press, 1979.

Einstein, Alfred. "Art and Technology." *Modern Music* 2 (January-February 1935): 55-61.

Engel, Carl. "The Miraculous Appeal of Mediocrity." *Musical Quarterly* 5 (1919): 453-62.

Engel, Lehman. *This Bright Day: An Autobiography*. New York: Macmillan, 1974.

Ewen, David, ed. *The New Book of Modern Composers*. Third edition, revised. New York: Knopf, 1961.

———. *The World of Twentieth-Century Music*. Englewood Cliffs, New Jersey: Prentice-Hall, 1968.

Farwell, Arthur. "Roy Harris." *Musical Quarterly* 18 (1932): 18-32.

Fawcett, Edmund, and Tony Thomas. *The American Condition*. New York: Harper & Row, 1982.

Friedman, Gus. "Metamorphosis of a 20th Century Composer." *Music Journal* (March 1976): 12-13, 38.

Gablik, Suzi. *Has Modernism Failed?* New York: Thames & Hudson, 1984.

Gagne, Cole, and Tracy Caras. *Soundpieces: Interviews with American Composers*. Metuchen, NJ: Scarecrow, 1982.

Gilbert, Henry F. "Notes on a Trip to Frankfurt in the Summer of 1927." *Musical Quarterly* 16 (1930): 21-37.

―――――. "Originality." *Musical Quarterly* 5 (1919): 1-9.

Gleason, Harold, and Warren Becker. *20th-Century American Composers*. Second edition. Bloomington, IN: Frangipani, 1980.

Goldberg, Isaac. *George Gershwin*. Supplemented by Edith Garson. New York: Ungar, 1958.

Goldman, Richard Franko. *Selected Essays and Reviews 1948-1968*. Edited by Dorothy Klotzman. I.S.A.M. Monograph Number 13. New York: Brooklyn College, 1980.

Goosens, Eugene. "The Public—Has It Changed?" *Modern Music* 20 (January-February 1943): 71-77.

Goss, Madeleine. *Modern Music-Makers: Contemporary American Composers*. New York: Dutton, 1952.

Gray, Cecil. *Predicaments, or Music and the Future*. London: Oxford University Press, 1936.

Gruen, John. *Close-up*. New York: Viking, 1968.

―――――. *Menotti*. New York: Macmillan, 1978.

———————. *The Party's Over Now.* New York: Viking, 1972.

Haas, Robert Bartlett, ed. *William Grant Still and the Fusion of Cultures in American Music.* Los Angeles, CA: Black Sparrow, 1972.

Haggin, Bernard. *Music in the Nation.* Freeport, NY: Books for Libraries, 1971.

Hanson, Howard. "American Procession at Rochester." *Modern Music* (March-April 1936): 22-28. Volume 13, paginated by issue.

Harrison, Lou. *About Carl Ruggles.* Yonkers, NY: Oscar Baradinsky at the Alicat Bookshop, 1946.

Hart, Philip. *Orpheus in the New World.* New York: Norton, 1973.

Heinsheimer, Hans. "Challenge of the New Audience." *Modern Music* 16 (November-December 1938): 28-32.

Henderson, W. J. "The Function of Musical Criticism." *Musical Quarterly* 1 (1915): 69-82.

Hennessee, Don A. *Samuel Barber: A Bio-Bibliography.* Westport, CT: Greenwood, 1985.

Heyman, Barbara B. *Samuel Barber.* New York: Oxford University Press, 1992.

Hodin, Josef Paul. *The Dilemma of Being Modern.* New York: Noonday, 1959.

Hoffman, Frederick J. *The Twenties.* Revised edition. New York: Free Press, 1965.

Hoover, Kathleen, and John Cage. *Virgil Thomson: His Life and Music.* New York: Yoseloff, 1959.

Houseman, John. *Run-through: A Memoir.* New York: Simon & Schuster, 1972.

Howard, John Tasker. *Our American Music.* Fourth edition. New York: Crowell, 1965.

Howe, Irving. *The American Newness.* Cambridge, MA: Harvard University Press, 1986.

———. *The Decline of the New.* New York: Harcourt, Brace & World, 1970.

———. *A Margin of Hope.* New York: Harcourt Brace Jovanovich, 1982.

———. *Selected Writings, 1950-1990.* New York: Harcourt Brace Jovanovich, 1990.

———, ed. *The Idea of the Modern.* New York: Horizon, 1967.

Hughes, Robert. *Culture of Complaint.* New York: New York Public Library and Oxford University Press, 1993.

Jablonski, Edward. *Gershwin.* Boston, MA: Northeastern University Press, 1990.

Jacoby, Russell. *The Last Intellectuals: American Culture in the Age of Academe.* New York: Basic Books, 1987.

Jepson, Barbara. "A Composer Spreads a Little Sunshine (Very Little)." *New York Times* (3 January 1993): Section 2, 25, 33.

"John Cage and Roger Reynolds: A Conversation." *Musical Quarterly* 65 (1979): 573-94.

Kammen, Michael. *Mystic Chords of Memory, the Transformation of Tradition in American Culture.* New York: Knopf, 1991.

Kermode, Frank. *Modern Essays.* London: Collins Sons, 1971.

Kostelanetz, Richard, ed. *John Cage.* London: Alan Lane, Penguin Press, 1971.

Kozinn, Allan. "For Contemporary Music, Times Are Hard." *New York Times* (8 January 1991): C11, 15.

Kramer, A. Walter. "American Composers, III: Louis Gruenberg." *Modern Music* (November-December 1928): 3-9. Volume 8, paginated by issue.

Küng, Hans. *Arts and the Question of Meaning*. Translated by Edward Quinn. New York: Crossroad, 1981.

Lang, Paul Henry, ed. *Problems of Modern Music*. New York: Schirmer, 1960. Published as the *Musical Quarterly* 46, No. 2 (April 1960).

Lasch, Christopher. *The Culture of Narcissism*. New York: Warner, 1979.

Lears, T. J. *No Place of Grace: Antimodernism and the Transformation of American Culture, 1880-1920*. New York: Pantheon, 1981.

Lederman, Minna. *The Life and Death of a Small Magazine (Modern Music, 1924-1946)*. I.S.A.M. Monograph Number 18. New York: Brooklyn College, 1983.

Lenneberg, Hans. "The Myth of the Unappreciated (Musical) Genius." *Musical Quarterly* 66 (1980): 219-31.

Leuchtenburg, William E. *The Perils of Prosperity, 1914-32*. Chicago: University of Chicago Press, 1958.

Levine, Lawrence W. *Highbrow/Lowbrow: The Emergence of Cultural Hierarchy in America*. Cambridge, MA: Harvard University Press, 1988.

Lipman, Samuel. *Arguing for Music, Arguing for Culture*. Boston: Godine, 1990.

——————. *Music After Modernism*. New York: Basic Books, 1979.

Lippard, Lucy R. *Overlay*. New York: Pantheon, 1983.

Luening, Otto. *The Odyssey of an American Composer*. New York: Scribner's Sons, 1980.

Luhan, Mabel Dodge. *Movers and Shakers*. New York: Harcourt, Brace, 1936.

Lukacs, John. *The Passing of the Modern Age*. New York: Harper & Row, 1970.

McColley, Robert. "Blackwood at Sixty: Easley Does It All." *Fanfare* (March-April 1993): 38, 40, 42, 44, 46, 50.

Manion, Martha L. *Writings About Henry Cowell*. I.S.A.M. Monograph Number 16. New York: Brooklyn College, 1982.

Mann, Alfred, ed. *Randall Thompson: A Choral Legacy*. Boston, MA: E. C. Schirmer, 1983.

May, Henry, ed. *The Discontent of the Intellectual: A Problem of the Twenties*. Chicago: Rand McNally, 1963.

Mead, Rita. *Henry Cowell's New Music, 1925-1936*. Ann Arbor, MI: UMI Research Press, 1981.

Mellquist, Jerome, and Lucie Wiese, eds. *Paul Rosenfeld, Voyager in the Arts*. New York: Creative Age, 1948.

Mendel, Arthur. "First Fruits of the Season." *Modern Music* 6 (January-February 1929): 30-32.

Mertens, Wim. *American Minimal Music*. Translated by J. Hautekiet. New York: Broude, 1983.

Meyer, Leonard B. *Emotion and Meaning in Music*. Chicago: University of Chicago Press, 1956.

―――. *Explaining Music*. Berkeley, CA: University of California Press, 1973.

―――. *Music, the Arts, and Ideas*. Chicago: University of Chicago Press, 1967.

Midgley, Mary. *Can't We Make Moral Judgments?* New York: St. Martin's, 1991.

Montague, Stephen. "John Cage at Seventy: An Interview." *American Music* 3 (1985): 205-16.

Moore, Douglas. *From Madrigal to Modern Music.* New York: Norton, 1942.

——————. "Our Lyric Theatre." *Modern Music* 18 (November-December 1940): 3-7.

Mussulman, Joseph A. *Dear People . . . Robert Shaw.* Bloomington, IN: Indiana University Press, 1979.

O'Grady, Terence J. "Aesthetic Value in Indeterminate Music." *Musical Quarterly* 67 (1981): 366-81.

Olmstead, Andrea. *Conversations with Roger Sessions.* Boston, MA: Northeastern University Press, 1987.

Osborne, Conrad L. "It's Time for Opera to Get Real." *New York Times* (5 December 1993): Section 2, 1, 35.

Ouellette, Fernand. *Edgard Varèse.* Translated from the French by Derek Coltman. New York: Orion, 1968.

Peacock, Kenneth. "Ross Lee Finney at Eighty-Five: Weep Torn Land." *American Music* 9 (1991): 1-19.

Peyser, Joan. *Bernstein.* New York: Morrow, 1987.

——————. *Boulez.* New York: Schirmer, 1976.

Phelps, Robert, ed. *Twentieth-Century Culture: The Breaking Up.* New York: Braziller, 1965.

Poirier, Richard. *The Renewal of Literature.* New York: Random House, 1987.

Polanyi, Michael, and Harry Prosch. *Meaning.* Chicago: University of Chicago Press, 1975.

Pound, Ezra. *Antheil, and the Treatise on Harmony.* 1927. Reprint. New York: Da Capo, 1968.

Reis, Claire R. *Composers, Conductors, and Critics*. New York: Oxford University Press, 1955.

Revill, David. *The Roaring Silence, John Cage: A Life*. New York: Arcade, 1992.

Robinson, Paul. *Bernstein*. London: Macdonald, 1982.

Rochberg, George. *The Aesthetics of Survival*. Edited and with an Introduction by William Bolcom. Ann Arbor, MI: University of Michigan Press, 1984.

Rockwell, John. *All American Music*. New York: Knopf, 1983.

—————. "Experimental Music." In *The New Grove Dictionary of American Music* 2. Edited by H. Wiley Hitchcock and Stanley Sadie. London: Macmillan, 1986.

Rorem, Ned. *An Absolute Gift*. New York: Simon & Schuster, 1978.

—————. *Critical Affairs*. New York: Braziller, 1970.

—————. *The New York Diary*. New York: Braziller, 1967.

—————. *Pure Contraption*. New York: Holt, Rinehart & Winston, 1974.

—————. *Settling the Score*. New York: Harcourt Brace Jovanovich, 1988.

Rosenberg, Bernard, and David Manning White. *Mass Culture Revisited*. New York: Van Nostrand Reinhold, 1971.

Rosenberg, Deena. *Fascinating Rhythm*. New York: Dutton, 1991.

Rosenberg, Harold. *The Anxious Object*. New York: Horizon, 1964.

—————. *Art on the Edge*. New York: Macmillan, 1975.

———. *The Tradition of the New.* New York: McGraw-Hill, 1965.

Rosenfeld, Paul. "The Destiny of Exile." *Modern Music* (January-February 1931): 3-8. Volume 8, paginated by issue.

———. *Discoveries of a Music Critic.* New York: Harcourt, Brace, 1936.

———. *An Hour with American Music.* Philadelphia, PA: Lippincott, 1929.

———. *Musical Chronicle (1917-1923).* New York: Harcourt, Brace, 1923.

———. *Musical Impressions.* Edited by Herbert A. Leibowitz. London: Allen & Unwin, 1970.

Rosenthal, Erwin. *Contemporary Art in the Light of History.* New York: Wittenborn, 1971.

Rothstein, Edward. "Cities March to Different Drummers." *New York Times* (15 November 1992): Section 2, 27.

———. "In the Fracas Over a Prize, No One Won." *New York Times* (19 April 1992): Section 2, 25.

———. "The State of the Union in the Kingdom of Pan." *New York Times* (3 January 1993): Section 2, 25, 32.

Salzar, Adolfo. *Music in Our Time.* Translated by Isabel Pope. New York: Norton, 1946.

Salzman, Eric. *Twentieth-Century Music: An Introduction.* Englewood Cliffs, NJ: Prentice-Hall, 1967.

Sayre, Henry M. *The Object of Performance, The American Avant-Garde Since 1970.* Chicago: University of Chicago Press, 1989.

Schonberg, Harold. *Facing the Music.* New York: Summit Books, 1981.

Schuller, Gunther. *Musings.* New York: Oxford University Press.

Schwartz, Charles. *Gershwin, His Life and Music.* Indianapolis, IN: Bobbs-Merrill, 1973.

Schwartz, Elliott, and Barney Childs, eds. *Contemporary Composers on Contemporary Music.* New York: Holt, Rinehart & Winston, 1967.

Schwartz, Elliott, and Daniel Godfrey. *Music Since 1945.* New York: Schirmer, 1993.

Seeger, Charles. "Carl Ruggles." *Musical Quarterly* 18 (1932): 578-92.

Sessions, Roger. *The Correspondence of Roger Sessions.* Edited by Andrea Olmstead. Boston, MA: Northeastern University Press, 1992.

——. "Music in Crisis." *Modern Music* 10 (January-February 1932): 63-78.

——. *The Musical Experience of Composer, Performer, Listener.* Princeton, NJ: Princeton University Press, 1950.

——. *Questions About Music.* New York: Norton, 1971.

——. *Roger Sessions on Music: Collected Essays.* Edited by Edward T. Cone. Princeton, NJ: Princeton University Press, 1979.

Shepherd, John, and Phil Virden, Graham Vulliamy, Trevor Wishart. *Whose Music?* New Brunswick, NJ: Transaction, 1977.

Shils, Edward. *Tradition.* Chicago: University of Chicago Press, 1981.

Siegel, Ed. "A Critic's Lament." *Boston Globe Magazine* (23 August 1992): 12-13, 23-24, 27-29.

Siegmeister, Elie. "Three Points of View." *Musical Quarterly* 65 (1979): 281-86.

Simmons, Walter. "David Amos Conducts Modern Masters." *Fanfare* (July-August 1991): 82-89.

Slater, Philip. *The Pursuit of Loneliness*. Revised edition. Boston, MA: Beacon, 1976.

Slonimsky, Nicolas. "Composers of New England." *Modern Music* (February-March 1930): 24-27. Volume 7, paginated by issue.

Sonneck, Oscar G. "Modernists, Classics and Immortality in Music." *Musical Quarterly* 11 (1925): 572-90.

Speckman, Stephen. *Wallingford Riegger: Two Essays in Musical Biography*. I.S.A.M. Monograph Number 17. New York: Brooklyn College, 1982.

Starer, Robert. *Continuo: A Life in Music*. New York: Random House, 1987.

Stearns, Harold E. *Civilization in the United States: An Inquiry by Thirty Americans*. New York: Harcourt, Brace, 1922.

Stehman, Dan. *Roy Harris: An American Musical Pioneer*. Boston, MA: Twayne, 1984.

Strickland, Edward. "Downtown: An Interview with Steve Reich." *Fanfare* (March-April 1987): 43-51.

—————. "The Well-Tuned Piano: An Interview with La Monte Young." *Fanfare* (September-October 1987): 80-92.

Taylor, Deems. *Of Men and Music*. New York: Simon & Schuster, 1943.

Thompson, Randall. "American Composer, V: George Antheil." *Modern Music* (May-June 1931): 17-27. Volume 8, paginated by issue.

—————. "The Contemporary Scene in American Music." *Musical Quarterly* 18 (1932): 9-17.

Thomson, Virgil. "Aaron Copland." *Modern Music* 9 (January-February 1932): 67-73.

———. *Music Reviewed, 1940-1954*. New York: Vintage, 1967.

———. *Selected Letters of Virgil Thomson*. Edited by Tim Page and Vanessa Weeks Page. New York: Summit, 1988.

———. *The State of Music*. New York: Morrow, 1939.

———. *Virgil Thomson*. New York: Knopf, 1966.

Tingsten, Herbert. *The Problem of Democracy*. Translation arranged by the Swedish Institute. Totowa, NJ: Bedminster, 1965.

Toffler, Alvin. *The Culture Consumers*. New York: Random House, 1964.

Trilling, Diana. *Reviewing the Forties*. New York: Harcourt brace Jovanovich, 1978.

Van Vechten, Carl. *Interpreters and Interpretations*. New York: Knopf, 1917.

———. *Music After the Great War, and Other Studies*. New York: Schirmer, 1915.

———. *Music and Bad Manners*. New York: Knopf, 1916.

Varèse, Edgard. "The Liberation of Sound." In Boretz, Benjamin, and Edward T. Cone, eds. *Perspectives on American Composers*. New York: Norton, 1971.

Varèse, Louise. *Varèse, A Looking-Glass Diary*. London: Davis-Paynter, 1973.

Vinton, John, ed. *Dictionary of Contemporary Music*. New York: Dutton, 1974.

———. *Essays After a Dictionary*. Lewisburg, PA: Bucknell University Press, 1977.

Weil, Irving. "The American Scene Changes. *Modern Music* (May-June 1929): 3-9. Volume 6, pagination by issue.

Whitesitt, Linda. *The Life and Music of George Antheil, 1900-1959.* Ann Arbor, MI: UMI Research Press, 1983.

Wians, William. "The Complete Musician: A Conversation with Gunther Schuller." *Fanfare* (January-February 1993): 74, 76, 78, 80, 82.

Wilder, Alec. *Letters I Never Mailed.* Boston, MA: Little, Brown 1975.

Index

— A —

Adams, John, 256
Albert, Stephen, 243-244, 248
American Society of University Composers, 178
Americanist music, 9, 18, 25, 73, 91, 99, 251
Anarchy, 237
Antheil, George, 7, 18, 34-35, 37, 54-56, 66-67, 119-121, 191
Anti-art, 205, 269-270
Argento, Domenick, 247-248
Armory Show, 3
"Artist," 2, 28, 31-35, 38, 152, 154-155, 185
Ashley, Robert, 209, 216, 219, 226
Asian music influences, 7, 206-207, 221-222
Atonality, 6-7, 52, 108, 155, 163, 172, 188, 218, 267
Autonomy, 185-189
Avant-garde, 8, 12, 23, 146-148, 236, 243

— B —

Babbitt, Milton, 7, 12, 140, 148, 174, 176-177, 181, 190, 197

Balance, 242, 263
Barber, Samuel, 9, 14, 109, 128-29, 131-139, 164-165, 183, 238, 245
Becker, John, 23
Beeson, Jack, 164, 246
Berger, Arthur, 23, 106
Berio, Luciano, 148
Bernstein, Leonard, 246
Blackwood, Easley, 184, 249
Blitzstein, Marc, 5, 97, 124, 127, 139, 251
Bolcolm, William, 245-246
Boredom, 238, 277
Boulanger, Nadia, 5, 22, 26
Boulangerie, 23, 64
Boulez, Pierre, 148, 176, 192-193
Bowles, Paul, 23
Brant, Henry, 148, 224
Brown, Earl, 148, 209, 220

— C —

Cadman, Charles Wakefield, 101
Cage, John, 7, 11-12, 35, 148, 151-152, 209-219, 228-229, 238, 241, 277
Capitalism and culture, 273-274
Carpenter, John Alden, 4, 26

Index

Carter, Elliott, 5, 7, 11, 97, 109, 148, 177, 179, 187, 190, 197
Centralists, 98-101
Chance music, 212, 214
Chaos, 214-215
Charlatanism, 29, 156, 228
Charm, 165
Citkowitz, Israel, 23
Colgrass, Michael, 164, 247
Columbia-Princeton Electronic Music Center, 149, 176
Communication, 92-93, 96, 98, 102-103, 117, 133, 157, 208-209, 217, 236-237, 247
Conservatism, 9-10, 137
Converse, Frederick Shepherd, 101
Copland, Aaron, 5, 7, 14, 17-18, 21-23, 25, 31, 36-37, 39-41, 59-61, 66, 91, 95, 98, 102-103, 105-106, 110, 121-123, 133, 139, 179-180, 183-184, 238-239
Copland-Sessions concerts, 23
Corigliano, John, 248
Cowell, Henry, 7, 18-19, 22-23, 35-37, 52-53, 102, 121, 139, 221
Creston, Paul, 129-130
Crossover audience, 254-255
Crumb, George, 7, 224-226

— D —

Dada, 62, 206, 210
Davidovsky, Mario, 187, 193
Deak, Jon, 247
Debussy, Claude, 5
Del Tredici, David, 226, 238, 247, 249, 258-259
Democracy and music, 11-12, 33, 158, 263-267, 289
Dett, Robert Nathaniel, 126
Directional music, 224-225
"Downtown" composers, 162, 252-253
Druckman, Jacob, 240-241, 248-249
Duchamp, Marcel, 206, 210

— E —

Eclecticism, 245, 250
Electronic music, 149, 223-224, 252
Emotion, 117, 137, 242
Engel, Lehman, 23, 25
Entertainment and music, 27, 109, 125, 182, 264-265
Europe, 3
Expatriates, 6, 23, 94-95
Experimentation, 7, 35-36, 52, 57, 93, 108, 163, 243, 267

— F —

Farwell, Arthur, 4, 8
Feldman, Morton, 148, 207-209, 219-220, 227, 238, 277
Fine, Vivian, 23
Finney, Ross Lee, 173
Flagello, Nicolas, 165-166
Flanagan, William, 189
Floyd, Carlisle, 164, 251

Foss, Lucas, 177, 220, 227
Fragmentation of culture, 160-161, 218, 269-270
Freedom from restraint, 27-28, 152, 158, 185, 242, 245
French influence, 4
Functional music, 100-101, 122, 282
Futurism, 37-38, 147

— G —

Gaburo, Kenneth, 226-227
German influence, 3-4
Gershwin, George, 9, 66, 68-71, 124, 138, 238, 251
Giannini, Vittorio, 164, 167
Gilbert, Henry, 4, 8
Glass, Philip, 246, 253-256
Goeb, Roger, 164
Gould, Morton, 9, 119
Gradualism, 8
Great Depression, 92-95, 116, 133
Griffes, Charles, 4, 25, 206
Gruenberg, Louis, 18, 23, 66-68

— H —

Hadley, Henry, 26
Hanson, Howard, 9, 19, 71-73, 129, 138
Harbison, John, 247-248
Harris, Roy, 5, 23, 34, 73-74, 98, 100, 109, 126-127
Harrison, Lou, 7, 209, 221
Hermann, Bernard, 23

Hill, Edward Burlingame, 8, 18
Hiller, Lejaren, 209
Hoiby, Lee, 164, 184, 246
Honegger, Arthur, 38
Hovhaness, Alan, 164, 221, 227, 258

— I —

I Ching, 210, 213
Iconoclasts, 204-206, 223, 238, 269-270
Ideal listener, 189
Imbrie, Andrew, 177
Incomprehensibility, 188
Indeterminacy, 210-212
Integrity, 184, 189, 266
International Composers' Guild, 17, 23, 56, 77
International Society for Contemporary Music, 76, 177
Intolerance, 150
Inventors, 35-36
Isolation, 177-185, 235, 266
Ives, Charles, 18, 22, 36, 166, 189, 210, 238

— J —

Jazz Age, 65
Jazz and blues, 36-37, 59-61, 65-71
Johnston, Ben, 209
Joplin, Scott, 60

— K —

Kirchner, Leon, 177, 197, 208

Index

Krenek, Ernst, 107
Kubik, Gail, 237

— L —

La Montaine, John, 164, 246
League of Composers, 17, 23, 76-77, 177
Lees, Benjamin, 164, 246
Lost generation, 50-52
Lucier, Alvin, 209, 223
Luening, Otto, 149, 183
Luhan, Mabel Dodge, 24, 42
Luke, Ray, 164

— M —

Machine music, 37-38, 69, 108
Martirano, Salvatore, 226
Marxism, 96-98
Mason, Daniel Gregory, 18, 102
Masterpiece syndrome, 21-22, 93, 188-189
Maxfield, Richard, 223-224
McPhee, Colin, 7, 206
Meaning in music, 30, 240, 285
Melody, 118, 283
Mencken, H. L., 32-33, 40
Mennin, Peter, 164, 193, 246
Menotti, Gian Carlo, 109, 131-132, 164, 168, 183
Messiaen, Olivier, 176
Milhaud, Darius, 36
Minimalism, 252-257

Modernism, 2-4, 7-10, 12, 34, 105, 148-151, 162, 205, 246, 281
Mollicone, Henry, 252
Moore, Douglas, 9, 18, 73, 99, 106, 124-125, 128, 164, 251
Moross, Jerome, 23
Mossolov, Alexander, 38
Mumma, Gordon, 209, 225
Music of today, 37

— N —

National Endowment for the Arts, 257
Nationalists, 18, 25, 59-60, 73, 99, 107, 119-127
Neoclassicism, 7, 22, 58-65, 128
New Music Edition, 106
New Music Society, 23
New Romanticism, 241
New School for Social Research, 76, 221
Newspapers and periodicals, 139

— O —

Oliveros, Pauline, 225-227
Originality, 28-29, 99-100, 131-132, 189, 236-237
Ornstein, Leo, 17-18, 20, 27, 29-30, 37, 52

— P —

Paik, Nam June, 209
Pan-American Association of
 Composers, 23
Paris, 5, 10, 22
Partch, Harry, 7, 207
Patrons and sponsors, 77-80, 276
Perle, George, 173
Persichetti, Vincent, 164
Perspectives of New Music, 174-175, 185
Picker, Tobias, 197
Piston, Walter, 5, 23, 26, 37, 64, 128-129, 174-175
Pluralistic society, 160-161, 270-272
Popular music, 157-161, 182, 253
Popularity, 41, 131, 183, 187, 238-239, 264-265
Post-Civil War composers, 4, 26, 101, 239
Pound, Ezra, 32, 35, 152
Powell, John, 18
Powell, Melvin, 177
Pro Musica, 23
Progressive composers, 4-5, 26, 101-102
Prokofiev, Serge, 38, 95
Psychiatric ideas, 23-25
Public for music, 2, 8, 10, 12-14, 17, 51, 69-70, 77, 81-84, 94, 160, 189-198, 229-230, 244, 257-258, 263, 264, 274-275
Pulitzer Prize (1992), 281-282
Puritanism and New England, 39

— R —

Radicals, 52-57
Radio, 137-138, 159
Rationalism, 172-189, 218
Ravel, Maurice, 5
Reich, Steve, 190, 252-253
Reinventing the past, 20-21, 151, 186, 266
Reis, Claire, 23
Riegger, Wallingford, 7, 23, 27, 57-58, 173, 188-189
Riley, Terry, 227, 252
Rochberg, George, 175, 177, 242-243, 250
Romanticism, 9, 26, 71-73, 131, 133, 139, 147, 218, 239, 245
Rorem, Ned, 164-165, 246
Rosenfeld, Paul, 6, 8, 106-107
Rouse, Christopher, 244
Rug Concerts, 194
Ruggles, Carl, 7, 12, 18, 23, 26, 30, 33-34, 36, 56-57, 107, 173
Rzewski, Frederic, 247

— S —

Salzedo, Carlos, 17
Saminsky, Lazare, 23
Satie, Erik, 38, 62, 210, 252
Schoenberg, Arnold, 5-8, 27, 51, 77, 96, 107, 172-173
Schuller, Gunther, 236, 240
Schuman, William, 107, 164
Schwantner, Joseph, 247, 249
Science and music, 35-36, 108
Self-expression, 23-27

Index

Serialism, 146-148, 155, 172-177, 188, 191-192, 207-208
Sessions, Roger, 7, 10-12, 17, 22-23, 32-33, 64-65, 108-109, 173, 179, 181
Shapey, Ralph, 194, 197
Shepherd, Arthur, 101-102
Shifrin, Seymour, 177
Shostakovich, Dmitri, 95
Siegmeister, Elie, 23, 97-98, 241, 164
Sincerity, 34-35, 180, 236-237
Starer, Roger, 243-244
Stein, Gertrude, 50, 62-63
Still, William Grant, 66, 68, 109, 125, 182
Stockhausen, Karlheinz, 148, 176
Stravinsky, Igor, 5, 33, 36, 58, 96, 107
Street, Tilson, 248
Sublimity, 34
Subotnick, Morton, 224

— T —

Taylor, Deems, 19, 25
Thompson, Randall, 9, 18, 73, 96, 110, 126
Thomson, Virgil, 5, 7, 18, 22-24, 36, 38-39, 61-64, 76, 78-79, 95, 98-99, 103-104, 124
Tradition, 28, 91, 98, 218, 239, 244, 251
Traditionalists, 91-92, 109, 163-168, 239, 244, 246
Truth in music, 34
Tudor, David, 209

— U —

Universities, 178-181
"Uptown" composers, 162, 253
Ussachevsky, Vladamir, 149

— V —

Values of modernists, 19-30
Values revised in the 1930s, 92-95, 100
Vanguard audiences, 74-81, 104-105, 159, 257, 276
Varèse, Edgard, 7, 12, 17-18, 23, 33, 35, 37, 39-40, 51, 53-54, 107-108, 138, 146, 191

— W —

Ward, Robert, 164, 251
Weber, Ben, 173, 177
Webern, Anton, 172, 174
Weiss, Adolph, 173
Westergaard, Peter, 197
Wilder, Alec, 182
Wolff, Christian, 209
Wolpe, Stefan, 208
Women and genteelness, 42-43
World War II, 123, 144
WPA Arts Projects, 93-95, 108, 137, 144
Wuorinen, Charles, 7, 12, 177, 181-182, 193, 196, 208

— X, Y, Z —

Yaddo Festivals, 23, 37, 96
Young Composers' Group, 23
Young, La Monte, 223, 227, 229, 252
Zen Buddhism, 210, 227-228
Zwilich, Ellen Taaffe, 247-248

About the Author

NICHOLAS E. TAWA (B.A., Harvard College; M.A., Boston University; Ph.D., Harvard University) is Professor Emeritus of the University of Massachusetts at Boston, where he has taught seminars in music research and courses in music history. He has published ten books and numerous articles on American music and music life in America. A cofounder of the Sonneck Society, an association devoted to furthering knowledge about American music and music in America, he was its first vice-president and editor of its newsletter. Among the awards he has received are the Arthur P. Knight Chamber Music Award, 1951, for the Quartet for Strings No. 2; the Bohemian Club Award, 1951, for the Sonata for Clarinet and Piano; the National Music Teachers' Association Award, 1953, for the *Concerto Grosso for Symphonic Band*; and the Distinguished Scholar Award, University of Massachusetts, 1990. His *Art Music in the American Society* (Scarecrow, 1987) is a companion piece to the present publication.